DÉTENTE
AND
DOLLARS

DÉTENTE AND DOLLARS

DOING BUSINESS WITH THE SOVIETS

Marshall I. Goldman

BASIC BOOKS, INC., PUBLISHERS

NEW YORK

Library of Congress Cataloging in Publication Data

Goldman, Marshall I.
  Détente and dollars.

  Includes bibliographical references.
    1. United States—Commerce—Russia.   2. Russia
—Commerce—United States.   I.   Title.
HF3105.G58   382'.0973'047   75-6671
ISBN: 0-465-01612-x

DESIGNED BY VINCENT TORRE
75 76 77 78 79   10 9 8 7 6 5 4 3 2 1

To Bella and Sam

Contents

PART IV

APPENDICES

Preface

A S in any study of this sort, it is always pleasant to acknowledge the cooperation of numerous individuals and institutions.

I appreciate the willingness of the *Harvard Business Review* to let me republish portions of my article "Who Profits More From U.S.–Soviet Trade?" which appeared in their November–December 1973 issue and of *Foreign Policy* to let me use portions of my article "Red Black Gold," which appeared in their Fall 1972 issue. I am also grateful for the financial and logistical support of Wellesley College and the Russian Research Center of Harvard University. In particular, Helen Blatt, Ruth Halpern, Mary Towle, Rose Di Benedetto, Betsy Mead, Chris Porto, and Helen Constantine deserve my thanks. Only they know how many drafts and redrafts were typed and under what nagging. Susan Gardos and Elena Vorobey in the Russian Research Center Library have also been cooperative and understanding as have numerous executives of the Pullman, Singer, Raytheon, PepsiCo, and Holcroft corporations.

Although it is against the rules I also want to express my thanks to my editor, Martin Kessler, with whom I have worked since 1962. He is stubborn but perceptive and although I do not always show it, I value his counsel. Finally, my wife Merle deserves someone's sympathy for having to go over everything I write. That she still is willing to suffer this agony after all these years is as important to me as seeing the manuscript finally turned into a book.

DÉTENTE
AND
DOLLARS

CHAPTER

1

Introduction

W H O says there is nothing new under the sun? After all, it was only in 1959 that Nikita Sergevich Khrushchev, Secretary General of the Communist Party, came to the United States to rant, rave, and bang his shoe. Emboldened by impressive agricultural and industrial success at home, Khrushchev boasted that by 1970 or by 1980 at the latest, Soviet economic output would overtake and surpass ours. While Khrushchev did dangle some trade opportunities before American businessmen, the lasting impression of Khrushchev's visit was that he had come not to praise American industry, but to bury it. Given Khrushchev's performance, who could have predicted that his successor, Leonid Ilich Brezhnev, would return in 1973 to cavort, clown, and spill champagne? More unusual, he wooed American congressmen, businessmen, bankers, and farmers with visions of large-scale exports; in a word, profits and contracts for all. This time, chastened by serious industrial and agricultural problems at home, Brezhnev stressed that he had come not to bury, but to buy.

For that matter, who would have dreamed back in 1959 that one day the Chase Manhattan Bank would open an office at 1 Karl Marx Square, or that the chairman of the New York Stock Exchange and the national commander of the American Legion

3

would go to Moscow as honored guests? Who would have imagined that Pepsi Cola, that erstwhile symbol of capitalist imperialism, would be produced and sold in the Soviet Union? Is nothing sacred?

The unprecedented flourishing of American-Soviet détente in the 1970s has been accompanied if not provoked by an equally impressive growth in American-Soviet trade. Until 1971, American exports to the Soviet Union seldom totaled more than $100 million a year, Suddenly, in 1971, American exports jumped to $162 million, and then in 1972 they totaled $550 million, a threefold increase between 1971 and 1972. Within a few months the United States had become the second largest exporter to the Soviet Union of the noncommunist developed countries. Only Germany, with exports of $712 million, exceeded the United States. We even exported more to the Soviet Union than the Japanese, who have outsold us in so many other places. (See Table 2–4.) By 1973, with exports totaling $1.19 billion, the United States had become the largest noncommunist exporter to the Soviet Union.

As exciting as this is, it should be remembered that in terms of our total exports of $50 billion for 1972, our sales to the Soviet Union even at the 1973 level constitute not much more than 2 percent of our total. In contrast with the $1.19 billion we exported to the Soviet Union in 1973, during the same year we exported $400 million more to small Belgium and three times more to the United Kingdom and Germany, over seven times more to Japan, and twelve times more to Canada. We even exported twice as much to Mexico. Moreover, in 1974, once the wheat deal had been completed, the volume of exports from the United States to the U.S.S.R. fell off sharply to one-half the 1973 level. Considered against the perspective of our dealings with the major noncommunist countries of the world, American exports to the Soviet Union are not that large. Moreover, they tend to be erratic. In many ways, American exports to the Soviet Union seem to be more important for them than they are for us.

4

Much of the American business community, however, has no patience with efforts to put American-Soviet trade in perspective. Consequently, many firms devote a disproportionate amount of their efforts to East-West trade. The temptation of large and heretofore forbidden markets is irresistible to them. Reports of single contracts totaling $500 million or more tempt the most conservative skeptics. The prospect is all the more attractive if business is adversely affected by a recession. For many the current fad is American-Soviet trade. Otherwise cautious executives all but trample over one another in their efforts to establish a foothold on this new frontier. Senior executive time expended on Soviet trade would never be wasted over similar negotiations with traditional customers in Western Europe, Latin America, or Asia, where the contracts are often as large or larger but the atmosphere considerably more prosaic.

Great expectations about the prospects for American-Soviet trade are nothing new. Similar expectations and enthusiasm have been aroused periodically throughout the course of our 60-year relationship with the U.S.S.R. Americans have usually had highly charged emotional attitudes whenever the Soviet Union is involved. For the most part our attitude can best be described as manic-depressive. Either we are euphoric, assuming that an era of harmony and happiness has finally come, or we are depressed, fearful that the world will soon be torn apart by strife and distrust. In the same way, it often appears that we either love the Russians or we hate them. When we love them, they can do no wrong; when we hate them, they can do no right. Seldom do we take a neutral or balanced attitude toward anything having to do with the Soviet Union.

Our psychological reactions inevitably have had a significant effect on America's trade policy with the Soviet Union. In our antagonistic stage we seek to restrict trade with the Russians as much as possible. Anti-Soviet groups insist on boycotting or banning the sale of Soviet goods within the United States and embargoing the shipment of American goods to the U.S.S.R. Usually

5

there is considerable pressure on other noncommunist governments to adopt policies similar to ours. In this climate of hostility, the easiest and safest course for most businessmen to follow is one of no trade or credit.

When American-Soviet relations begin to improve, businessmen's attitudes also begin to change, in some cases dramatically. Many of those who formerly were naysayers to all talk of trade now rush to outbid each other with attractive offers and struggle to see who can come up with the most elaborate and far-reaching arrangement. Once a few such negotiations are announced, the desire for more trade and friendship develops a momentum of its own. Some businessmen fear being left out of all the action and finding themselves behind their competitors in prestige and profit. Thus there is an intensive race to win favor in the Soviet Union and Eastern Europe. The best way for many American firms to do this is to offer "loss leaders." Businessmen seem to be willing to offer unusually favorable terms on their initial dealings with the Russians on the assumption that the first contract is the most difficult to arrange. They rationalize that the low profit margin they are prepared to accept on the first contract will be more than compensated for by the very substantial contracts which the Russians hint lie just ahead.

This willingness to compromise more than halfway and to concede most of what the Russians want is compounded by the fact that when our relations are good, we tend to be very paternal toward the Soviet Union. Many Americans have always felt that if the Russians would only take our advice, they could easily solve most of their economic problems. Now that the Russians have indeed started to ask us for help, we feel we have an obligation to lean over backward to do our best. If anything, we feel complimented that after all these years they have finally had the wisdom to turn to us for guidance. Consequently we tend to be more forthcoming with them than we often are with our more traditional allies or potential competitors. This paternalism helps to explain why we generally do not think of the Russians as competitors, at least in economic terms, but instead as wayward wanderers waiting to be shown the way toward more rational economic and technological development. Therefore the give and take between the two countries occasionally turns out to be one-sided, at least during our euphoric moments.

To some extent the intense desire of the American business community to increase trade and commercial relations may derive from a sense of guilt at having previously restricted trade and other normal relations. Conversely, the effort to restrict trade is often prompted by embarrassment at the realization that we were too soft in our previous trade and political dealings with the U.S.S.R., particularly when it appears that the Russians have taken advantage of us.

But as attractive as it may appear at the time, switching from one extreme to another is hardly conducive to the long-run normalization of trade relations between the Soviet Union and the United States. Given the difference in philosophy and makeup of the two societies, it may well be that a stabilized trading relationship between them will not in itself assure international harmony. Despite recurrent talk of convergence, the fact remains that the political systems of both countries are radically different. There is much about the Soviet Union that distresses most thoughtful Americans. Certainly no one can take seriously the argument that we should only trade with those of whose economic and political systems we approve. If that were so, there would be times when we would even be precluded from trading with ourselves. Nonetheless, the differences between the Soviet Union and the United States are so great and the antagonisms and rivalries so deep as to cause some hesitation over the wisdom of promoting trade and technology transfer to the Soviet Union. Moreover, there are many who question the effectiveness of increased trade in generating a more favorable political climate within the Soviet Union. Military, diplomatic, political, and even psychological consideration probably play as much or more of a role in determining the temperature of East-West relations. The question that those con-

7

templating trade must answer for themselves, therefore, is whether the chance for amelioration of the antidemocratic conditions in the Soviet Union is greater with or without détente and an increased flow of trade.

The purpose of this book is not only to explore the nature of, and possibilities for, increased American-Soviet trade for the general reader, but to provide a perspective on such trade—a perspective which American businessmen and policy makers sometimes lack. Having been involved with the practical as well as the theoretical aspects of this problem for many years, I have been struck by the lack of information and the prevalence of misconceptions. My hope is that this book will help provide the necessary information and at the same time clear up some of the confusion.

In the course of writing this book, I have interviewed and consulted numerous businessmen already engaged in or contemplating trade with the U.S.S.R., who have shared with me their insights and experiences. In turn, while testifying before both House and Senate committees of the U.S. Congress and while meeting with senior officials in the Departments of Commerce and State, I have had the chance to hear and absorb opposing viewpoints. This exposure to differing perspectives is typified by the fact that at times I have worked with the staff of Senator Henry Jackson, who has been cautious about extending most favored nation status to the U.S.S.R., and also worked as a member of the American Committee on U.S.-Soviet Relations, which is an advocate of détente and increased trade between the Soviet Union and the United States and the extension of most favored nation status.

For those wishing to obtain the same variety of perspectives and to learn more about both the opportunities and the pitfalls, it is necessary to examine not only the current trading situation, but the past as well. Part I (Chapters 2 and 3) takes up the history of American-Soviet relations and the current enthusiasm for such trade, from the perspective first of the Soviet Union and then of the United States. The peaks and troughs of the relationship are considered, as well as the peculiarities and legal complications governing that trade. Part II addresses itself to the question of whether or not the Russians can pay for what they want to buy from the United States. In Chapter 4 we describe the Soviet Union's gradual evolution as a major force in world petroleum and natural gas markets, and how the Soviets have tried to take advantage of this situation. Then in Chapter 5 we examine the strengths and weaknesses of the other export potential of the Soviet Union, and discuss whether or not the U.S.S.R. is a good credit risk. Part III is the "how" portion: how—and how not—to deal with the Russians. The mechanisms, procedures, techniques, and institutions for trading with the Soviet Union are the focus of Chapter 6. This could be subtitled "A primer on buying and selling in the U.S.S.R." The remaining chapters offer three case studies and the conclusions to be drawn from them. The grain deal in Chapter 7 is an example of what to avoid in American-Soviet trade. Chapter 8 is an analysis of the Raytheon Corporation's efforts to sell the Soviet Union an air traffic control system. Chapter 9 focuses on the experiences of Armand Hammer and the Pullman Corporation. Finally, in Chapter 10, an effort is made to distill the meaningful findings from the experience thus far and to suggest steps which might be taken to insure that both sides profit from such trade so that it strengthens rather than weakens détente.

Throughout the book, the manic-depressive flavor of the American attitude toward the Soviet Union will show itself affecting many of our past and present trading relationships. An effort will be made to suggest a more balanced approach and to anticipate to what extent continued trade is dependent on mutually advantageous contractual arrangements rather than unilateral political and economic considerations.

Just as mutually advantageous trade can facilitate détente, so one-sided contracts can damage it. Thus Americans contemplating trade with the Russians must be aware of the pitfalls. If American firms end up losing money or becoming hostage to the U.S.S.R., or if the American public comes to feel it has been taken by the sharp Soviet "commissars," détente will suffer. The effect will be the same if the Russians feel the Yankee traders are discriminating against their products or selling them second-rate material at first-rate prices. Mutually advantageous trade arrangements require that neither side lean over so far as to end up making a fool of itself.

PART I

LESSONS FROM THE PAST AND PROSPECTS FOR THE FUTURE

CHAPTER

2

The Soviet Perspective

W H I L E American dealings with the U.S.S.R. have been marked by manic-depressive tendencies, we are not alone in our schizophrenia. Soviet attitudes toward American-Soviet trade are affected by similar if not more extreme reactions. In many ways they are even more obsessed with the United States than we are obsessed by the Soviet Union. We see them alternately as a threat or as a sometime reluctant friend. Though they experience the same polarity of feeling toward us, in addition they have almost always held out the United States as the model to which they aspire in terms of economic wealth and productive efficiency. This attitude is reflected in the story of a Soviet teacher who asked her pupils to characterize American capitalism. One replied, "The United States is a country suffering from debilitating unemployment, the wasteful production of 10 million automobiles a year, industrial pollution, and agricultural surpluses." To the teacher's further query, "What is the goal of the Soviet Union?" the class responded, "To overtake and surpass the United States!" This anecdote reflects the hate-love feelings most Russians have for the United States. Such disparate sentiments also help explain how the Russians can be in the midst of a ferocious political attack on the United States and at the same time express open admiration for American products and processes.

DÉJÀ VU AND UNITED STATES-SOVIET UNION TRADE RELATIONS

In our fascination with the current state of American-Soviet relations, we often tend to forget that this is not the first time that the United States has been the major noncommunist exporter to the Soviet Union. In fact, Soviet purchases from the United States often have been larger than from any other country in the world.

Although Soviet foreign trade in the aftermath of the Russian Revolution was generally in a state of disruption, Soviet imports from the United States rose rapidly once some semblance of domestic control had been restored and the boycott by the capitalist countries had been lifted. Beginning in the fiscal year 1923/24, the Soviet Union frequently imported more from the United States than from anyone else. (See Table 2–1.) Thereafter, except in fiscal year 1925/26 and the calendar years 1932 to 1934, Soviet purchases from the United States consistently exceeded those from Great Britain. The Germans exported more than the British, but even so, American exports exceeded those from Germany in 1923/24, 1924/25, 1930, 1935, 1937, 1938, and even after the signing of the Nazi-Soviet pact in 1939 and 1940. At their highest, Soviet imports from the United States totaled 207 million rubles in 1930 or about $230 million, a significant sum at the time.[1]

The turn in Soviet trade preferences from the West European countries, their traditional prerevolutionary suppliers, to the United States is not hard to explain. The first order of priority after World War I was to survive. In the wake of the war, the Americans rather than the British and Germans were in the best position to supply the food and raw materials the Russians desperately needed. Furthermore, many British and French businessmen and bankers, having invested large sums in prerevolutionary Russia that the new Bolshevik government refused to honor, did all they could to discourage their countrymen from providing further

TABLE 2-1

Trade in the Early Years: The U.S.S.R. Trade Balance and Imports, 1918–1950
(in millions of 1969 rubles)

	OVERALL TRADE BALANCE (EXPORTS MINUS IMPORTS)	IMPORTS FROM		
		UNITED STATES	GERMANY	UNITED KINGDOM
1918	−76	11		9
1920	−21	1	5	5
1921	−151	32	43	48
1921/22 [a]	−163	35	66	42
1922/23	−12	4	48	29
1923/24	110	40	36	38
1924/25	−114	158	81	87
1925/26	−42	96	138	102
1926/27	73	114	127	79
1927/28	−121	147	195	37
1929	34	139	153	43
1930	−18	207	197	63
1931	−230	180	322	58
1932	−101	25	257	72
1933	116	13	116	24
1934	146	14	23	25
1935	99	23	17	18
1936	1	37	55	17
1937	74	42	34	11
1938	−16	69	11	30
1939	−64	52	10	19
1940	−6	76	72	2
1946	−104	213	[b]	8
1947	23	99		32
1948	76	47		24
1949	−38	23		33
1950	305	7		36

Source: Ministerstvo Vneshnei Torgovli SSSR (hereafter MVT SSSR), *Vneshniaia Torgovlia SSSR,*
1918–1966 (Moscow: Mezhdurnarodnye Otnosheniia, 1967), pp. 8–13, 64–68. (Hereafter statistical
handbooks of the MVT SSSR will be referred to as *VT SSSR.*)

[a] Fiscal years.

[b] Germany not included because of division into two Germanys.

exports and credits to the U.S.S.R. Thus it was only natural that during the early 1920s a higher percentage of Soviet imports should come from the United States, where there were more of the kinds of goods needed by the Soviet Union and fewer unsatisfied creditors.

The Soviet Union's purchases from the U.S. during the early years reflected the nation's postwar and postrevolutionary needs. The Soviets bought food or basic items like shoes, which constituted 80 percent of American exports in 1921.[2] But in addition to food and shoes, they also began to import large quantities of raw materials. One would have thought that the Soviet government would have used its scarce foreign exchange to buy machinery. Yet its purchase of raw materials was not as unsound as it may have appeared at first. After victory in the Civil War had been more or less assured, the main priority in the NEP (New Economic Policy) period that followed was the revival of industrial production. To do this it was necessary first of all to replenish industrial inventories, largely exhausted during the war and the chaos that followed, so that existing Soviet machinery would have something to process. Without these industrial raw materials it was impossible for factories to produce and for the proletariat to work. For instance, one of the main Soviet industrial activities at the time was the production of textiles, but it was only in the late 1920s that the cotton harvest in Central Asia returned to its prerevolutionary levels. Accordingly, cotton accounted for as much as 76 percent of Soviet imports from the United States in 1923 and remained close to or over 50 percent until 1928.

The Russians were extremely hard-pressed for foreign currency throughout most of the decade and, except in the fiscal years 1923/24 and 1926/27, their balance of trade was consistently negative. Yet because their economy would have ground to a halt without infusions of American raw materials, they found it necessary to spend their money on raw materials rather than on the machinery they would have preferred to buy. Significantly, the Russians reacted somewhat similarly in 1964 and again in 1972 when they found it expedient to divert their foreign currency from imports of machinery to grain. Such emergency purchasing shifts are to be expected at least on a short-time basis whenever there are domestic shortfalls in the supply of raw materials, and until such time as domestic sources of materials (such as cotton in the late 1920s and wheat in the 1960s and 1970s) can be substituted.

When crop failures occur, it is to be expected that the Soviet Union will have a serious balance of trade deficit in its dealings with the United States. But it turns out that even when crops are good, the Soviets usually find more to buy from the United States than they can sell. For example, just as in 1971, which was a good crop year, Soviet imports from the United States in the 1920s exceeded Soviet exports to the United States by a ratio of over three to one, and sometimes, as in 1926/27 and 1972 and 1973, by as much as six to one. Finding something to sell to the U.S. is not a new dilemma for the Russians.

But while they may have trouble finding something to sell the United States, Soviet officials usually know what they want to buy from us. Unless sidetracked by a raw materials crisis, the Soviets will normally concentrate their foreign exchange and credit on the purchase of American machinery. With the inauguration of the First Five-Year Plan in October 1928 and the improvement in the procurement of cotton from Soviet farms, U.S. machinery became a much more important proportion of total Soviet imports.[3] The increased purchase of machinery coincided with the beginning of the concerted drive toward industrialization. Whereas prior to 1929 Soviet purchases of machinery from the United States were never more than 25 percent of the total, in 1929 machinery constituted 40 percent of Soviet purchases from the United States. In 1930, when American sales to the Soviet Union reached their pre–World War II peak and exceeded those of all other countries, 75 percent of what the U.S.S.R. purchased was machinery. In 1931 machinery purchases rose to 94 percent, and in the years before World War II, machinery purchases were never less than 40 percent of total imports from America.

The U.S.S.R. was interested not only in American machinery but also in American technicians. Along with many West Europeans, scores of American technicians and engineers were either sent by their American companies or recruited directly by the Soviet Union to help install and operate new machinery as well as existing industrial operations. The 2,000 or so German engineers and technicians who came to the U.S.S.R. after the signing of the 1922 Rapallo Treaty had returned home by the late 1920s and were largely replaced by Americans.[4] In particular the Albert Kahn Co., Inc. of Detroit played a key role in designing Soviet factory construction in the early days of the First Five-Year Plan. Having designed the River Rouge works for Ford as well as major plants for General Motors, Chrysler, and Burroughs, the Kahn Co. (which still exists) was ideally suited to provide guidance on the large-scale plants so basic to Soviet industrial strategy.[5] Kahn engineers helped to organize Gosproektstroi (State Project Construction Trust), the major Soviet design and construction organization at the time.[6] In all, a dozen Soviet factories were designed in Kahn's Detroit offices. Reportedly the Kahn Co. was asked to prepare over $2 billion worth of possible plant construction, although Soviet funds ran out before all the projects could be undertaken.

While the United States was important for the Soviet Union, the Soviet Union was also important for the United States. Initially the depression had relatively little impact on the state-owned and autarchic industry of the U.S.S.R., and so it kept on buying foreign goods. Thus while the depression virtually eliminated business opportunities elsewhere, exports to the U.S.S.R. continued unabated, with the result that by 1931 sales to the Soviet Union constituted two-thirds of all U.S. exports of agricultural equipment and power-driven metal-working machinery.[7] Among the major companies supplying equipment, technological assistance, and employees during the 1920s and 1930s were International Harvester for the Stalingrad Tractor Works, General Electric for the KHEMZ Turbine plant in Kharkov, Du Pont for the

Kalinin and Shostka nitric acid plants, and Ford for the Gorky and Moscow automobile and truck plants.[8]

The Soviet appetite for Western equipment quickly depleted its ability to pay. By 1931 the peak of machinery and technology imports from the United States and Germany had been reached. No matter how autarchic it wanted to be, the Soviet Union had to export something in order to pay for its imports; unfortunately, the volume of its exports did not keep up with its imports. Because of the world-wide depression, hardly anyone was interested in or able to buy Soviet goods regardless of how much the Russians tried to cut prices. As Table 2–1 shows, the Soviet Union found itself encumbered with major deficits in its trade balance. After a slight surplus of 34 million rubles ($38 million) before the crash in 1929, the Soviet annual trade deficit rose rapidly until it peaked at 230 million rubles ($255 million) in 1931. This precipitated a serious foreign exchange emergency in which the Russians found themselves without valuta.[9]

To cope with the new emergency, the Russians began to cut back sharply on their foreign purchase commitments for equipment and personnel. Many contracts were unilaterally broken. Several American firms found their operating and export plans disrupted and their bills rejected,[10] and many Western engineers were stranded inside the Soviet Union without funds to pay their way home. Though such drastic measures reduced the 1932 deficit somewhat, the Russians found their total imbalance still totaled about 100 million rubles. Subsequently, hard currency expenditures and commitments were cut back even further in 1933 and thereafter. Such tactics ultimately paid off; and from 1933 to 1937 the U.S.S.R. was able to earn a foreign trade surplus.

Now it is not unusual for businessmen to break their contracts in time of trouble such as a depression, and it would hardly be fair to expect Soviet officials to behave differently from businessmen in capitalist countries. Yet some of the more vocal supporters of the Soviet Union sometimes lose sight of the fact that the Soviet Union may do such things. Thus projected sales to the Soviet

Union have often been subjected to cancellation just like sales to other countries. There is no such thing as a guaranteed or assured market in the Soviet Union.[11] American businessmen discovered this for themselves in 1932 and conceivably the lesson could be repeated if the recession becomes serious enough in the mid 1970s. After having sold about $200 million (180 million rubles) worth of goods to the U.S.S.R. in 1931, American exports to the Soviet Union fell by 85 percent the following year. Note, however, that when Soviet officials decide to cut back on their imports, they do not necessarily cut their orders equally with all suppliers. While purchases from the United States were being cut back by 27 million rubles ($30 million) in 1931, purchases from Germany were simultaneously being increased by 125 million rubles. Similarly in 1932, while Soviet imports from the United States were slashed 85 percent, Soviet imports from Germany were reduced by only 20 percent. Further, imports from the United Kingdom in 1932 actually increased by 14 million rubles over what they had been in 1931, the foreign exchange crisis notwithstanding. (We shall see that in 1946 and 1964 the Soviet Union also found it necessary to cut back drastically on its expenditures of foreign currency in selected countries.)

But while purchases from the United States may have been cut back more than those from some other countries, the fact remains that total imports of all foreign goods fell from 867 million rubles in 1931 to 273 million rubles in 1933, to 182 million rubles in 1934. While the worldwide depression benefited the Soviet Union in its capacity as an importer, it also adversely affected it as an exporter. It was only sometime in 1936 that Soviet purchases of foreign goods began to rise again.

It may be that history in this instance is not necessarily any indicator of the future. Certainly we hope the depression of the 1930s and the rise of Hitler in Germany are events that will not be repeated. But whatever the reason, it is important to recognize that in the past the development of a large foreign trade relationship between the U.S. and the Soviet Union has not in itself been enough to prevent an abrupt cessation of that relationship.

POST-WORLD WAR II

Large-scale delivery of American goods to the U.S.S.R. resumed during, and continued until immediately after, World War II. Soviet imports from the United States in 1946 totaled 213 million rubles or about $236 million, surpassing even the level set in 1930. Indeed, in 1946 Soviet imports from the U.S. exceeded those from every other country. Considering that almost all the other large industrial countries of the world had been devastated by the war and that in 1946 the United States was financing its Soviet exports with Lend-Lease credits, the large role of the U.S. in the trade of the Soviet Union is not surprising. Nevertheless, the 1946 dollar level of sales was not to be reached again until 1972. Even in 1947, Soviet imports from the U.S., though reduced by half, still exceeded those from all other countries except Poland, which by then was more or less forced to follow Stalin's dictates. And imports from the United States continued to surpass Soviet purchases from all the other noncommunist countries until 1949.[12] With the onset of the cold war, however, American sales of goods to the Soviet Union fell in 1950 to less than $10 million a year.

When analyzing historical occurrences like the cold war, it is always difficult to ascertain who provoked whom. Yet even those who feel the cold war was largely due to the provocative actions of the United States concede that the decline in East-West trade fitted in nicely with Stalin's prewar determination to attain national self-sufficiency for the U.S.S.R.[13] After World War II, Stalin broadened his economic horizons to include the countries of Eastern Europe and China in his economic bloc. From all appearances, therefore, the formation of virtually isolated East and West blocs in the late 1940s did not upset Stalin unduly.

Yet while the insistence on autarchy within the bloc was largely Stalin's, no one can argue that East-West trade fell off solely because Stalin wanted it that way. Even if Stalin had opened up his borders to salesmen from the West, most likely some Western governments would have cut off the export flow not only of industrial equipment, but of consumer goods as well. In any case, the issue is academic. It takes two to trade and the Russians were clearly having very little of it.

If the Soviet Union could opt for autarchy in the 1930s when it had virtually no other allies as trading partners and still survive, its isolation from the West was much easier to implement in the post-World War II years, when the autarchic circle could be expanded to include the newly communist governments in Albania, Bulgaria, Czechoslovakia, East Germany, Hungary, Poland, Rumania, and Yugoslavia, as well as China in 1949. Indeed, Soviet trade relations with Eastern Europe were institutionalized in January 1949 with the creation of the Council for Mutual Economic Assistance (CMEA), or Comecon. All the countries of Eastern Europe except for Yugoslavia, which was then feuding with Stalin, became charter members. After a short time, Mongolia was also included.

In itself the existence of CMEA did little to affect Soviet foreign trade policy. Even before the establishment of CMEA and the subsequent formation of the European Common Market, the trade flow of countries within Eastern Europe had already been sharply reoriented inward. The extent to which historic trade patterns were rearranged by the Soviet government can be sensed by comparing Soviet trade flows with the eight countries in Eastern Europe and China before and after World War II.[14] Because the figures are not entirely consistent, certain assumptions have to be made. Assume that as much as one-half of the German exports and imports to and from Russia in 1913 and in 1930 originated in what subsequently became the German Democratic Republic or East Germany. That would mean that total Russian exports in 1913 and 1930 to what was to become the CMEA bloc plus China amounted to 20 percent of total Russian exports. Given the same assumption, Russian imports from these areas totaled about 20 to 30 percent.

Even if such heroic assumptions are made, there was still a radical shift in trade patterns as soon as the Communist governments came to power in Eastern Europe and China. By 1947 Soviet exports to and imports from Eastern Europe already exceeded 50 percent of the Soviet Union's total world exports and imports. By 1950 over 80 percent of total Soviet exports and imports were confined to Eastern Europe and China. The figure fell slightly in the years following but still constituted 60 to 70 percent in 1960. (See Table 2–2.)

This highly inbred trading pattern within Eastern Europe has not necessarily been regarded with enthusiasm by the parties most involved.[15] Throughout the late 1940s and 1950s, there were numerous reports of unhappiness among the non-Soviet members of CMEA over the restraints imposed on them by the Soviet Union. They were particularly upset by what they regarded as the unduly low prices the Soviet Union was paying for their goods.[16] In addition, many of the East Europeans also resented being cut off from cheaper sources of supply outside the CMEA bloc, and they resisted Soviet pressure to make their economies even more dependent on Russian raw materials. But when they protested too much, some trade officials were brought to trial. In Bulgaria in December 1949 and in Czechoslovakia in November 1952, for instance, senior officials of the Ministry of Trade were arrested and accused of being nationalistic and anti-Soviet; several of them were subsequently executed. Their crime, based on the charges against them, was that they sought to obtain better economic terms for their countries in their dealings with the Soviet Union.

The effect of the forced redirection of foreign trade flows became the subject of considerable debate among Western economists such as Franklyn Holzman, Horst Mendershausen, and Frederic Pryor.[17] Ultimately it was concluded that artificial "custom unions" of this sort inevitably cause mutual trade and pricing distortions which may help as much as they hurt any given participant, for while these countries are forced to pay high prices for their imports, they also collect high prices for their exports. Yet this was little consolation for many of the East European countries

TABLE 2–2

Share of Soviet Foreign Trade by Category [a] *of Country*
(in percentage)

| | SOCIALIST COUNTRIES | | NONSOCIALIST COUNTRIES | |
	TOTAL	CMEA [b]	TOTAL	INDUSTRIALLY DEVELOPED CAPITALIST COUNTRIES (OFFICIAL SOVIET LIST [c])
1946	54%	41%	46%	38%
1947	61	39	39	34
1948	60	43	40	30
1949	72	52	28	21
1950	81	57	19	15
1951	81	58	19	15
1952	81	59	19	15
1953	79	55	21	17
1954	79	53	21	15
1955	79	53	21	15
1956	76	50	24	17
1957	74	54	26	17
1958	74	52	26	16
1959	75	52	25	16
1960	73	53	27	19
1961	72	55	28	19
1962	70	57	30	18
1963	70	59	30	19
1964	70	59	30	20
1965	69	58	31	19
1966	66	56	33	21
1967	68	57	32	21
1968	67	58	33	21
1969	65	57	35	22
1970	65	56	35	21
1971	65	56	35	21
1972	65	56	35	23
1973	59	50	41	27

Sources: Various issues of *VT SSSR*.
[a] Category as defined by Soviet statistical handbook. Includes imports and exports.
[b] Bulgaria, Czechoslovakia, East Germany, Hungary, Mongolia, Poland, Rumania.
[c] Includes Austria, Belgium, Canada, Finland, France, West Germany, Great Britain, Italy, Japan, The Netherlands, Sweden, United States.

who continued to complain that their export prices were not high enough. Other countries, like Poland with its coal and Rumania with its oil, were upset because they felt their products could have been traded more profitably in international markets, where they could have obtained hard currency and technologically more sophisticated Western machinery.

Since the distortions caused by such "custom unions" are not unilateral, it is not surprising that soon even some Soviet economists began to complain that the U.S.S.R. was also suffering because too much of its trade was being diverted to CMEA and other communist countries.[18] Ironic as it might have appeared to the East Europeans, the Soviet economists began to protest that Soviet economic obligations under CMEA laid the U.S.S.R. open to exploitation by the smaller East European countries. The Soviet Union saw itself becoming little more than a supplier of raw materials for its Eastern European allies, who were at the same time using the Soviet Union as a dumping ground for their manufacturing industries. Certainly such a result was never anticipated when CMEA was first formed.

By the mid-1960s, Soviet officials had come to realize that while making Eastern Europe dependent on Soviet raw materials may have brought them short-run benefits, in the long run it was harmful. Because it seemed sensible to supply Eastern Europe from Soviet mines and oil wells in the Western part of the U.S.S.R., Soviet industry found itself forced to fulfill its own needs for raw materials by reaching into Siberia—which, in turn, increased its investment, transportation, and labor costs. Thus there was some truth to the assertion that the Soviet Union was supplying to its Eastern European allies raw materials that cost less in real economic terms than the raw material that Soviet industry was forced to use as a substitute. Of course, the Soviet government neglected to balance this off with the real economic savings it derived from the machinery that it obtained from Eastern Europe in exchange for the raw material.

As the Soviet Union began to trade more with noncommunist

countries, moreover, it soon discovered that its most salable products were raw materials. To the extent that such items were already committed to Eastern Europe or other communist countries, there was that much less available for the hard currency countries. The Soviet Union sought to reverse or at least check this trend. In the mid-1960s Soviet officials publicly warned their allies, particularly in Eastern Europe, not to become too dependent on the U.S.S.R. for their raw materials. It would be wise for the East European countries, the Russians advised, to structure their foreign aid programs so that future aid would generate repayment in raw materials, particularly oil and ferrous and nonferrous metals.[19] Such pressure became more pointed as world-wide raw materials shortages developed and the Russians began to realize they had goods the hard currency countries were most eager to buy.

THE TURN TO THE
NONCOMMUNIST WORLD

The decision to engage in economic intercourse with countries outside of the communist block was slow in coming. Like many decisions of this sort, there were many teasing invitations and false starts before the actual fulfillment. For a long time the promise turned out to be more exciting than the act itself.

The first hint of any change in policy came in 1951, when Stalin announced the convening of an international economic conference and invited foreign businessmen to attend. While the April 1952 gathering turned out to be one of the first breeches in the "Iron Curtain," it did not lead to much trade with the U.S.S.R. True, trade with the developing countries in the noncommunist world expanded, but for the industrialized nations there was only an insignificant increase in the immediately succeeding years. (See Table 2–2.) Overall the basic trade patterns varied only slightly and Soviet trade (exports and imports) with the socialist countries continued at levels of 74 percent or more until 1959.

It was only in 1960, seven years after Stalin's death, that the Russians under Khrushchev began to expand trade (particularly purchases) with the industrialized countries of the noncommunist world. At first Khrushchev apparently felt the Soviet economy was deficient in only one major area—chemicals. After all, Soviet industry and agriculture were posting ever-larger production records, while the United States was stumbling through the recession of the late 1950s. At the same time, Soviet science had managed to orbit the first Sputnik months ahead of the United States. Given such success, Khrushchev felt little need for any major expansion program except in a few limited areas where he felt the Soviet economy lagged. But having announced his decision to develop a strong chemical industry in 1958, Khrushchev soon discovered that the U.S.S.R. lacked the wherewithal to build its own chemical machinery and that his Eastern European allies were only slightly better equipped. Of necessity a good portion of the machinery would have to come from the noncommunist world. In March 1959 he announced that the Soviet Union would commence buying whole factories from the West.[20] From 1959 to 1961 the Soviet Union ordered approximately 50 complete chemical plants from foreign suppliers.[21] The immediate surge in exports from Western Europe and even Japan to the Soviet Union in 1959 and the next few years is reflected in Tables 2–3 and 2–4. In the four-year period 1960 to 1963, chemical machinery sales to the Soviet Union totaled $132 million from the United Kingdom, $93 million from West Germany, $72 million from Italy, and $61 million from France.[22] A few of these orders found their way to American manufacturers of synthetic textile equipment or export intermediaries like Intertex of New York, but for the most part American export restrictions precluded the sale of more sophisticated machinery.

A crop failure in 1963 cut short this surge in machinery buy-

TABLE 2-3

Imports and Exports of Machinery by Selected Countries in Trade with the U.S.S.R.
(in millions of dollars [a])

	UNITED KINGDOM		FRANCE		GERMANY		ITALY		JAPAN		UNITED STATES	
	IMPORTS	EXPORTS	IMPORTS	EXPORTS	IMPORTS	EXPORTS	IMPORTS	EXPORTS	IMPORTS	EXPORTS	IMPORTS	EXPORTS
1958	—	18	—	13	—	41	—	7	—	3	—	1
1959	—	44	—	39	—	39	1	11	—	11	—	7
1960	—	58	1	63	1	96	1	30	—	19	—	28
1961	—	77	1	69	1	91	1	43	1	29	—	16
1962	—	62	1	88	—	59	1	33	2	77	—	20
1963	1	64	1	33	1	73	1	80	2	86	—	1
1964	1	47	2	42	2	134	1	52	3	133	—	4
1965	1	70	2	28	2	71	1	39	2	73	—	6
1966	2	102	3	55	2	98	1	38	1	106	—	7
1967	3	93	5	101	5	60	4	83	2	66	—	8
1968	7	134	5	193	9	103	6	110	2	65	—	9
1969	2	125	5	183	5	172	4	200	4	75	—	38
1970	5	110	7	174	28	136	5	196	3	122	—	24
1971	5	95	7	173	15	182	3	151	6	140	—	29
1972	10	108	10	160	20	367	6	146	6	241	1	58
1973	17	121	18	189	17	513	12	197	5	214	1	226

Source: From annual issues of *VT SSSR*.

[a] Converted from the ruble at the rate of 1 to $1.11 prior to 1972; 1 to $1.21 in 1972; and 1 to $1.34 in 1973.

TABLE 2–4

Imports and Exports by Selected Countries with the Soviet Union

(in millions of dollars)

	UNITED KINGDOM		FRANCE		GERMANY		ITALY		JAPAN		UNITED STATES	
	IMPORTS	EXPORTS	IMPORTS	EXPORTS	IMPORTS	EXPORTS	IMPORTS	EXPORTS	IMPORTS	EXPORTS	IMPORTS	EXPORTS
1958	167	146	95	76	92	72	40	31	22	18	18	3
1959	177	98	101	90	105	91	78	44	40	23	28	7
1960	210	149	95	116	160	185	126	79	87	60	23	38
1961	238	194	97	110	198	204	150	90	145	65	23	46
1962	236	161	111	138	215	207	166	102	147	149	16	20
1963	271	179	141	64	209	154	176	114	162	158	21	23
1964	272	111	141	64	234	194	147	91	227	182	21	146
1965	333	129	146	72	275	146	181	98	240	168	43	45
1966	352	141	172	76	286	135	190	90	300	215	50	42
1967	337	179	187	155	274	198	274	132	454	158	41	60
1968	379	250	183	257	294	273	285	179	464	179	58.4	57.5
1969	473	233	205	265	335	406	247	285	462	268	52	106
1970	528	245	203	273	342	422	281	307	481	341	72	118
1971	512	216	256	260	367	460	297	295	496	378	58	162
1972	612	227	296	342	430	712	325	268	593	505	96	550
1973	880	238	434	577	762	1184	442	352	1078	487	215	1190

Source: From country-by-country data in various editions of International Monetary Fund, Direction of Trade.

ing. (See Table 2–5.) Large sums of foreign currency had to be diverted to purchase foreign grain. This must have been an agonizing decision for Khrushchev. It slowed down his whole program of modernization. Had he wanted to, Khrushchev could have ignored the crop failure and proceeded with his purchase of industrial machinery instead. Prior to 1964, such callousness was part of the Russian tradition. No matter how poor the harvest may have been, the Russian government had seldom felt it necessary to have any net importation of grain. Despite occasional famines, the Russian government could almost always be counted upon to find some grain to export. This was true before the revolution under Witte and after the revolution under Stalin. If a shortage of grain precipitated some starvation, as it did in the 1930s or 1947, that was

TABLE 2–5

Soviet Grain Harvest and Livestock Herds

	GRAIN HARVEST (MILLION METRIC TONS)	ALL CATTLE (MILLION HEAD)	PIGS (MILLION HEAD)
1950	81	58.1	22
1955	104	56.7	31
1958	134	66.8	44
1960	126	74.2	53
1961	131	75.8	59
1962	140	82.1	67
1963	108	87	70
1964	152	85.4	41
1965	121	87	53
1966	171	93.4	60
1967	148	97.1	58
1968	170	97.2	51
1969	162	95.7	49
1970	187	95.2	56
1971	181	99.2	68
1972	168	102.4	71
1973	223	104	67
1974	196	106.2	70

Source: From various editions of Tsenral'noe Statisticheskoe Upravlenie, *Narodnoe Khoziaistvo.* No attempt has been made here to readjust Soviet figures to allow for widely acknowledged shortcomings, often of 25 percent or more, in grain harvest reports.

unfortunate. Khrushchev, however, like Lenin in the 1920s, decided that he would import grain rather than risk the economic, moral, and political consequences of starving his people.[23] Consequently after the 1963 crop failure, Khrushchev imported 10 million tons of grain from Canada and the United States at a cost of several hundred million dollars.

The agricultural crisis had deep ramifications. It not only prevented further purchases of machinery from the West but also reduced the total flow of raw materials to Soviet industry, causing a slowdown in the industrial growth rate. Ultimately the economic setbacks, together with what was sometimes described as adventurism in both domestic and foreign policy, led to Khrushchev's ouster in 1964. His past successes were not enough to compensate for his present difficulties.

Nevertheless, the retrenchment in the foreign import program was continued under Khrushchev's successors. As Tables 2–3 and 2–4 indicate, the period from 1963 to 1967 saw precipitous reductions in imports from the United Kingdom, France, Germany, and Italy. Even Japan, which at first appeared to escape this sharp cutback, ultimately saw its exports to the U.S.S.R. fall in 1965.

The situation again changed significantly in 1966. By then the agricultural situation had improved and Premier Kosygin and Secretary General Brezhnev had been in office for almost two years, long enough to conclude that past Soviet planning and foreign trade policies were in need of change. The planning system was not generating the kind of innovations and economic growth that seemed appropriate for the 1960s. The shortcomings appeared particularly acute when compared with the growth in the American, West European, and Japanese economies. The prevailing policy of autarchy and isolation was only viable on the assumption that Russian industry could keep pace with (or surpass) the technology being developed in the rest of the world. This it had seemed to be doing, at least until the 1960s. But while Soviet technology had proven itself in basic metallurgy, atomic energy, astronautics, and defense, there were embarrassing deficiencies in electronics, computers, sophisticated forms of assembly line production, and, as before, chemicals. And it was these latter areas which were important in the 1960s. Ironically, just as the Russians were about to declare themselves the winner in their race to overtake and surpass industrial production in the United States, they discovered that while they had indeed won the industrial race of the 1950s—for more steel and coal production—the race of the 1960s had shifted to newer, more exotic fields of technology. Here the Russians were as far behind as ever.

Why did the Soviet Union, which performed so well in heavy industry and indeed outproduced the United States in steel, coal, and certain machine tools, have such difficulty in these more technologically advanced areas? Some of the blame must be shouldered by the rather inflexible Soviet planning system, with its traditional emphasis on increasing the *quantity* of output. In this, as indicated by the record of the last five and a half decades, the U.S.S.R. did very well. Such a system, however, provides planners and managers with little incentive to innovate or experiment with technology. Any interruption of the production line in order to experiment with new products or production methods risks underfulfillment of the all-important quantitative production goals. Although long-run production may benefit from such innovation, under the Soviet system, pay and recognition for the manager depend primarily on short-run performance.

The inability of the U.S.S.R. to keep up in technologically innovative fields has stood in sharp contrast to its enormous emphasis on the importance of science. Thus the U.S.S.R. claims to have more than twice as many people working on research and development as the United States, and each year since 1951 has been adding to research and development personnel at a rate of 9 percent or more a year, compared to only a little over 6 percent for the U.S. But Soviet scientists have very little contact with industry; those who do usually devote themselves to increasing output in the traditional way. Whereas about 75 percent of research and development personnel in the United States are employed in industry, only about 12 percent are so employed in the Soviet Union.[24]

The links between research institutions and industrial enterprises in the Soviet Union have always been unsatisfactory. The reason for this is that industrial research, like everything else in the Soviet Union, is administered under the central plan. Such work is concentrated in separate institutes, and the institutes tend to develop a dynamic of their own, seldom related to the day-to-day needs of the factory. All of this helps to explain the paradox of highly sophisticated and advanced Soviet laboratories and backward and unresponsive factory production technology.

The lack of innovation became particularly serious in the 1960s and 1970s when, like the rest of the world, the Soviet Union decided to shift emphasis from staple goods and basic metals to computers, chemicals, and electronics. Such a shift called for speedy adaptation and rapid decision making. The Soviet planning mechanism was simply too ponderous and clumsy. Instead of catching up with international technology, the Russians found themselves falling further and further behind.

As a result, Soviet leaders began to question the efficacy of the way they had traditionally sought to introduce Western technology into the Soviet economy. Their preferred technique (except during the early 1930s, the Lend Lease years, and 1959–1963, when they undertook to buy whole factories) was to buy one or two prototypes of a finished product and then reproduce both the product and the factory process. In this way the Russians reproduced an array of products ranging from coal-mining equipment and scotch tape to trucks and Polaroid cameras. However, as technological change became more rapid, it was almost certain that the copy and the process would be obsolete by the time the Russians had managed to duplicate the production stage. Because of the difficulty involved in trying to reproduce someone else's work, moreover, such products also tended to be outdated, more expensive and qualitatively inferior to the original. Consequently the decision was made to go back to the practice of buying whole factories and licenses rather than prototypes.

The change in approach was first signaled privately by the reorganization and upgrading of the State Committee for the Coordination of Scientific Research, which in September 1965 was transformed into the State Committee on Science and Technology and charged with promoting and modernizing Soviet industry and technology.[25] The importance of this new group was further underlined by the appointment of V. A. Kirillin (who was ultimately to become a deputy chairman of the Soviet Council of Ministers) as chairman of the committee, and of the son-in-law of Premier Kosygin, Gherman Gvishiani, as its vice chairman. The public signal came from Premier Kosygin himself when a few months later, in one of his speeches to the Twenty-third Congress of the Communist Party in April 1966, he officially conceded that the U.S.S.R. had been wasting time and effort reinventing processes and commodities that had previously been developed in other advanced countries. Kosygin sought to halt this wasteful practice. As he put it, "It is more profitable for us in many cases to buy foreign licenses than to try to work out this or that problem ourselves." [26]

Then in May, only a few weeks after Kosygin's speech, the Russians began to negotiate with Fiat. In August 1966 they announced the signing of an agreement with Fiat to build a $1.5 billion automobile plant. Ultimately $600 million worth of machinery, including $300 million worth from Italy, was purchased in the West for use in the plant.

But the Fiat plant was only the beginning. Officials from the Ministry of Foreign Trade began to swarm all over Europe and Japan with order books in hand. True, there was almost always an inordinate delay between first inquiries and final orders. Still, if we compare imports in 1965 and 1968, the about-face in Soviet attitudes shows up clearly. (See Tables 2–3 and 2–4.) In an extreme case, French sales of machinery to the Soviet Union, which were $88 million in 1962, fell to a low of $28 million in 1965 and then soared to $193 million in 1968.

THE TURN TO THE UNITED STATES

For the most part, only a few American firms participated in these developments, and when they did it was generally a foreign American subsidiary, not the domestic parent, that was involved. Thus, until 1971 American exports to the Soviet Union seldom exceeded $100 million, less than one-quarter of what the Germans and Japanese were selling and one-half of the levels reached by Britain and France. It was not until the early 1970s that American industry became involved in substantial East-West trade.

Why did it take so long for American-Soviet trade to develop? In the 1950s most of the blame belonged to the Soviet Union and its policy of autarchy. But while Soviet political antagonism continued into the 1960s, after the mid-1950s it was the United States which was primarily responsible for the lack of trade. Until the early 1970s, official U.S. government policy sought to discourage machinery exports to the U.S.S.R. It was all but impossible for American exporters of sophisticated equipment to obtain export licenses if the ultimate purchaser was the Soviet government. But as we shall see in Chapter 3, attitudes in Congress and among the American business community began to change in the late 1960s. Anticipating that this would happen, the Soviet Union periodically tested the American market to see if any new interest had developed. With time Soviet expressions of interest in American products became more than just political maneuvering. Ultimately their economic needs, particularly in agriculture, became so pronounced that at one point in 1972 the Soviet leaders apparently concluded that Soviet international political principles and the sensitivities of its communist allies would not be allowed to stand in the way of buying American products, and they began to mount an extremely ambitious campaign for the American market.

It may well be that with the war in Indochina nearing an end, with China increasing its hostile noises toward the North, and with the cost of military technology mounting at unreasonable rates, the Russians would have decided on a more friendly policy toward the United States and a more active and earnest interest in American products in any event. Yet the speed of their turnabout was breathtaking. Nowhere was this better demonstrated than in May 1972 when, despite Nixon's sudden decision to blockade Haiphong and resume the bombing of North Vietnam, the Russians decided to go ahead with their invitation to President Nixon to visit Moscow. Reportedly after listening to President Nixon announce his decision on television, the Soviet minister of foreign trade, Nikolai Patolichev, remarked to the then Secretary of Commerce Peterson, "Well, let's get back to business." [27]

Given what we know now, there is reason to believe that the Russians had almost no alternative. In 1972 the United States was apparently the only country in the world with the grain reserves necessary to satisfy Soviet needs. Within a few weeks after President Nixon's return from Moscow, Russian purchasing agents had secretly placed the bulk of their $1.1 billion of orders for American grain. Before they were finished, they were to buy up one-quarter of our 1972 wheat crop plus a substantial amount of our corn and other animal feeds, mostly, as we shall see in Chapter 7, at needlessly low and subsidized prices.

Soviet interest in American industrial goods is a little harder to explain. In retrospect, it is amazing just how determined they were to buy American equipment. At a time when cheaper substitutes and even originals were becoming available outside of the United States, and other buyers all over the world were beginning to turn their backs on American products, the Russians kept trying to convince American manufacturers that they should sell to, or build for, the U.S.S.R. In one instance, officials of Warner and Swasey Co. reported that the Russians told them they were determined to buy American-made goods, even though one of Warner and Swasey's subsidiaries in the United Kingdom produced the same product at prices almost 30 percent cheaper.[28] After the devaluations of the dollar in 1971 and 1973, when American goods had become more competitive, such obvious favoritism toward American industrial goods made more sense, but earlier it did not appear to be entirely rational from an economic point of view.

Soviet persistence was all the more remarkable in light of the consistent rebuffs that greeted Soviet offers. The Russians just kept trying. Thus the Ford Motor Company turned down a Soviet offer to build what was later to become the Fiat plant at Togliatti. Subsequently Ford was sounded out on building the Kama River truck plant. This time Ford was interested, but the American government said "no," so Mack Truck was approached. A deal was almost completed when suddenly Mack backed out for what seem to have been financial and administrative reasons.

Given their lack of success, why were they so persistent? The Russians simply felt that American equipment and engineering were the best available and they wanted only the best for their industry, regardless of the cost. Many Russians pointed to the way that some years earlier Japan had relied on American technology and equipment to initiate and sustain its industrial transformation. As these Russians saw it, what worked for the Japanese should work for them.

Of all the developed countries, moreover, only the United States came close to matching the size of the Soviet market. Discussions with Soviet officials always leave one impressed with how preoccupied the Russians are with the importance of size. In their minds, there are only two countries that matter in the world, the United States and the U.S.S.R. No one else but the United States has factories and production needs of a magnitude comparable to those in the U.S.S.R. This is important not only because of the scale of the equipment used, but the system of administration and management as well. The Russians always want the biggest of whatever it is they are buying.

For example, the Russians were determined that the Kama River truck plant had to be at least double the size of anything comparable in the United States. Indeed, when the Kama River plant reaches its scheduled output of 150,000 diesel trucks a year, it will produce more diesel trucks than were produced by all the firms in the United States put together in any one year until 1973. To undertake an operation of this magnitude requires experience not only with large productive capacity but also with large-scale systems analysis and management—and that is more likely to be found in the United States than anywhere else. Apparently even the Fiat managers found themselves unable to coordinate properly all the multifaceted tasks needed to put together an operation on the scale of their Togliatti plant.[29] In sum, products from other countries are considered to lack the cachet, superiority, and prestige that a "Made in the U.S." label confers on a product or process.

But how long will the Soviets be interested in maintaining the present flow of U.S. imports? This depends, among other things, on whether or not the U.S.S.R. will be able to pay for all that it wants to buy. As we have already seen, lack of foreign currency caused the Soviet Union to curtail sharply its import program in 1931 and 1964. It is likely that future Soviet actions will be just as heavily dependent on the Soviet Union's ability to finance its trade with the West. (We shall consider this whole question in Chapter 5.) But even if financing ceases to be a problem, once the Soviet Union is able to generate its own technological innovations on the production floor it may very well decide to curb its foreign import program. Certainly the pattern of Soviet trade practices over the last 55 years suggests that the Soviets tend to revert to autarchy just as soon as circumstances permit or require.

It still remains to be seen, however, whether, like the Japanese, the U.S.S.R. will be able to develop a momentum of its own after the initial purchase of American and West European technology and equipment. Without some substantial change in their managerial and incentive system, it is hard to see how the Soviets will be able to do this. Past attempts at economic reform, such as the so-called Liberman Reform, have not been successful. Until such efforts prove more effective, it is unlikely that the U.S.S.R. will be able to generate much in the way of technological innovation within any but a few high priority sectors. Thus, as long as they have the purchasing capacity, it is likely that the Russians will find it necessary to continue in the market for industrial technology for at least the next several years.

3

The U.S. Perspective

A S we saw in Chapter 2, the Soviet Union's relatively recent decision to increase its imports from the West, particularly from the United States, stems from its desire to increase productivity and solve temporarily pressing commodity needs. But what accounts for the even more sudden surge of American interest in buying and selling to the U.S.S.R.? Just as we tend to forget that at one time Soviet officials were largely uninterested in trading with the United States, so we frequently block out how hostile we used to feel about "trading with the enemy." That was only a few years ago. To illustrate how far and how fast we have come, it is instructive to go back and trace the shift in events which have made us so receptive to East-West trade. It is important to understand how such swings originate, since there can be no guarantee that the cycle will not be repeated.

FROM HOSTILITY TO HOPE
AND BACK AGAIN

The origins of our anti-Soviet policy are a matter of some dispute. While Americans were not particularly saddened by the overthrow of the Czar, neither were most of them pleased when Lenin and his Bolshevik party took over. There was generally a distrust of communism and bolsheviks, who were often equated with bomb-throwing anarchists. Nor did the new communist government's decision to abrogate all debts of the Czarist and provisional governments do much to win support for its cause. Under the circumstances, Americans at best had mixed emotions about the new regime. While one branch of the American government sponsored a major program of famine relief for Russia in 1921–1923, another participated in an Allied invasion of the Soviet Union a few months earlier. True, the Allied force was relatively inefficient and was soon withdrawn. Still, the invasion could hardly have fostered the cause of good relations between the United States and the Soviet Union. Indeed, formal recognition of the Soviet Union was not extended until after President Roosevelt took office in 1933.

Yet whatever our reluctance to extend formal government support or recognition, our general export policy in the late 1920s and 1930s could not be called unreservedly anti-Soviet. As we saw earlier, U.S. corporations sold large quantities of goods to the U.S.S.R. and there were even times when we exported more to the U.S.S.R. than any other country in the world. Skeptics have noted that our eagerness for Soviet trade in the 1930s happened to coincide with a world-wide depression which virtually eliminated our more traditional markets elsewhere. Still, in the latter part of World War II and in the immediate postwar years, the U.S. did come through with Lend Lease exports for the Soviet Union. Thus it seems fair to assert that prior to 1947 there was only limited and not very effective opposition to trading with the U.S.S.R. In fact, although there was to be no financing for several decades to come, the U.S. government created the Export-Import Bank in 1934 primarily to aid in the funding of exports to the U.S.S.R.

World War II precipitated a series of major changes in American attitudes toward the Soviet Union. When Molotov joined with Von Ribbentrop in the Nazi-Soviet Pact in 1939, and later when the Soviet Union attacked Finland in 1940, American attitudes toward the Soviet Union became decidedly hostile. Yet when the Nazis invaded the Soviet Union in June 1941, this coldness turned to sympathy, particularly when the United States also found itself at war with Germany a few months later. Such sudden flip-flops in attitude have become common ever since.

Despite hopes for a new era of harmony predicated on the cooperation of the Soviet Union and the United States during World War II, the two nations soon found themselves at odds again. It is hard to trace who did what first and under what provocation, and in any case efforts to attribute blame in this period immediately enmeshes us in the debate over the origins of the cold war, a topic beyond the scope of this book. Still, there is no denying that a large segment of the American population had and has a fundamental distrust of the U.S.S.R. which makes it reluctant to have much trade with it. This hostility to the Soviet Union is so deep that there is opposition to trade with the Soviets even at a time of détente. This distrust is shared not only by capitalists who fear their property will be confiscated, but by union members who worry that their unions will become vehicles of collective restraint and repression rather than of collective bargaining and pressure. George Meany, head of the AFL-CIO, has been particularly hostile to any improvement in American-Soviet relations.

The fact that the second most powerful country in the world also happens to be the Soviet Union does nothing to allay fears about Soviet intentions. For many, it is often hard to tell whether dislike of the Soviet Union stems from anticommunist ideology or from balance of power considerations. There are also those who seek to isolate the Soviet Union because of specific or localized grievances. This usually has more to do with Russia's traditional forms of totalitarianism and prejudice than with ideology. Thus there are those who feel that the Soviet Union should be denied full international rights as long as the Soviet Union in turn denies various rights to Soviet intellectuals and various minority groups such as the Jews, Ukrainians, and Lithuanians within the U.S.S.R.

Despite this core of antagonism toward the U.S.S.R., the lure of profits has frequently overcome whatever ideological misgivings most American businessmen might have had about trading with the Soviets. It is one of the peculiar aspects of American relations with the Soviet Union that segments of the business community have often been in the vanguard of those seeking an accommodation with the Soviet Union—in spite of the fact that presumably these same businessmen would be the first to suffer in any communist revolution. Indeed, a survey conducted for *Fortune* in 1945 found that the business community was optimistic and desirous of maintaining good relations. The "least friendly" toward the U.S.S.R. were "the poor; the most friendly the businessmen."[1]

Such expectations were adversely affected by the radical redirection of Soviet trade to Eastern Europe and the political and military actions of the Soviet Union in Poland, Czechoslovakia, Iran, Turkey, and Greece. At the least such actions provided those opposed to further trade with powerful arguments about the nature of Soviet intentions and dampened the enthusiasm of most of those who wanted to continue their economic links with the Soviet Union. In a short time there was widespread support for cutting off trade with the U.S.S.R. and imposing an export boycott on almost all goods of significance.

BOYCOTTS

It is entirely possible that there would have been no trade boycott of the U.S.S.R. after World War II if the rest of the world, including the United States, had been engulfed in another depression. In that case the prospect of trade and jobs for Americans could probably have been enough to overcome any political qualms about Soviet purposes. But with a reviving economy and the deterioration of military and political relations between the U.S. and

43

the Soviet Union, economic ties also suffered. On the one hand, Stalin, in his effort to cut himself and the rest of CMEA from the West, shifted the Soviet Union's exports and imports away from the U.S. Thus even if the U.S. had been more forthcoming, it is unlikely that the Russians would have been much more responsive. On the other hand, many Americans felt they had been double-crossed once before after trading with another "enemy" prior to World War II, and there was a strong feeling against falling victim to such short-sightedness again. Right-wing accusations that American machinery or even metals could be used by the Russians to strengthen their military capacity against the U.S., just as Japanese purchases of our scrap iron prior to World War II had gone into the production of munitions, were usually enough to discourage most American businessmen from engaging in further trade with the Soviet Union.

The use of an economic boycott is an old but largely ineffective instrument of foreign policy. Boycotts of one sort or another were applied with questionable results against the French, the British, and even the U.S. in the eighteenth and nineteenth centuries. In more recent times, the League of Nations voted a boycott of Italy after its invasion of Ethiopia, and the Arabs imposed an embargo on the shipment of petroleum to countries like the Netherlands and the United States. In almost all cases the efforts have fallen far short of their stated goals. Still, when another country adopts a hostile stance, an economic boycott usually helps to mollify those who feel something has to be done to vent their anger, but who feel war is too extreme a measure.

But even in a time of overt hostilities, economic warfare has been a weak weapon. For example, during World War II strategic planners sought to cripple German military efficiency. They looked for the one key item or bottleneck that was crucial in the operation of all German industrial and military equipment and which could be destroyed by bombing only one or two sites. After considerable analysis they concluded that *ball bearings* were the bottleneck.[2] Thus German ball bearing factories were subjected to some of the most intensive bombing of World War II. Yet the Germans managed to continue supplying themselves with ball bearings, and the strategy did not work.

Despite such lessons, economic boycott against the communist countries of Eastern Europe attracted many supporters. Since the East Europeans seemed to be dependent on the outside world for all of their natural rubber and much of their copper and titanium, (at least until the late 1950s), these seemed to be natural pressure points.[3] They were also in need of Western technology. Thus an embargo was imposed on the sale of several raw materials and numerous manufactured goods to the U.S.S.R. and its East European allies.

Just how ineffective such boycotts sometimes are can be seen by what happened to Soviet titanium. Although we had banned all shipments of titanium to the U.S.S.R., in 1968 the Soviet Union started shipping large quantities of the same metal to the United States at such low prices that Soviet exporters were charged with dumping! Indeed, while life under a boycott may become more difficult and more costly, there is little evidence so far that a boycott ever brought about the collapse of any government (although Allende's regime in Chile may be a first).

This does not mean, as has sometimes been argued, that economic boycotts have an effect that is exactly the opposite of the one intended. According to such arguments, countries subjected to a boycott are forced to produce the goods themselves since they cannot import what they want.[4] By having to rely on themselves in this way, it is argued that the Russians were pressured into building up imposing aircraft and turbine industries. Thus instead of halting and frustrating growth and innovation, economic boycotts are said by some to promote economic growth and innovation as well as economic independence. Granted that boycotts may have this effect in a few specific areas, but they certainly do not affect every sector of a country's technology in such a manner. To argue the opposite is to deny the concept of division of labor and comparative advantage. No country can produce everything itself and not sacrifice something in the process. In other words, overall growth does suffer when a country either chooses or is forced to be entirely self-sufficient.

Equally questionable is the argument that the best way to keep one country in "a second-class industrial status" is to make available to it the latest technological achievements of other nations so that it will not bother to undertake innovations on its own.[5] If this were so, the best way for a country to develop its technology would be to refuse to import technologically advanced products. Yet this would deny the experience of the Japanese, who availed themselves of the latest foreign technology and *then* used protective tariffs and quotas to build up their own productive competence. While the latest foreign prototype may become outdated, restricting oneself to earlier models or trying to do everything from scratch is likely to make a country's technology even more outdated. Catching up will then be all but impossible. Such arguments are no more convincing than the contrary suggestion that economic boycotts are always effective.

While our boycott did not accomplish all that its advocates had hoped, there is strong evidence that it did retard Soviet growth, particularly over the long run. The inability to buy certain products and processes hurt. As we shall see when we discuss the types of products the Russians are most interested in buying from the West and the Japanese, foreign trade for the Soviet Union is expected to perform only limited, but nonetheless important, functions. For most countries, imports are intended to serve two needs: to supply goods and technology that are otherwise unavailable domestically, and to provide goods that are cheaper than domestically produced items. Soviet importers, on the other hand, are usually little concerned about obtaining foreign goods simply because they are cheaper. For the Russians, imports are primarily a way of compensating for their innovational shortcomings.

Therefore, when the United States withheld a particular item such as titanium, this usually had only a short-run impact, because sooner or later the U.S.S.R. would find substitutes or local supplies, although at a higher price. When, however, the U.S. sought to prevent the sale of technology, this often had a long-run effect on Soviet growth. As long as Soviet innovations could not keep pace with innovations in Japan and the West, the Soviet Union often found itself a generation or more behind in the introduction of different product lines. In the case of chemicals, the whole industry lagged behind. The Soviet Union was thus unable to keep abreast of important areas of the Western world's product mix. Just how much the U.S.S.R. has suffered is suggested by the type of foreign purchases the U.S.S.R. is currently making. (See Appendix II.) A surprising number of orders duplicate almost exactly the types of technology purchased in the 1930s. Thus once export licenses became more readily available in the late 1960s and early 1970s, the Soviet Union ordered a set of heat treating furnaces from the Holcroft Company for the Kama River truck plant in 1973. Similar furnaces were purchased from Holcroft for the Fiat plant in the 1960s and for the Gorky automobile plant in the 1930s. Again, the Soviet Union purchased two ammonia plants from the Chemical Construction Company (Chemico) in 1974. Chemico had sold the Soviet Union similar plants back in 1932 and 1933. The Soviet Union's failure to duplicate such technology in the interim meant that for 40 years the Soviet economy was denied the products that this technology could have provided.

Undoubtedly some of the more crippling effects of the boycott were offset by creative responses devised by Soviet technicians. Yet even if the economic boycott was not 100 percent effective, to American policy makers it was illogical to trade with a potential enemy as if there were no matters of dispute between the two countries. Since the Soviet Union and the United States were engaged in a cold war and the United States had technology that was considerably more advanced than that available in the U.S.S.R., the rational thing for the United States to do was to seek to deny this technology to the U.S.S.R. Unfortunately, even in the context of economic warfare, not all of the laws adopted were rational or even effective.[6]

EXPORT CONTROLS

The effort by Congress to use economic laws to penalize and isolate the Soviet Union and other communist countries began in earnest in 1949.[7] As it happened, there was considerable precedent within our own country for such a strategy in times of war. Thus the United States had passed a Trading With the Enemy Act in 1917 after it entered World War I. A somewhat similar law was passed in 1940, even though it was not until the following year that the United States entered the war. But such legislation was regarded as "temporary" and was in fact abandoned once a peace agreement was signed. In contrast, the Export Control Act of 1949 was essentially a peacetime measure intended to restrict exports to the Soviet Union and its East European allies on a continuing basis. While there was no actual fighting between the Soviet Union and the United States, the 1949 law was not adopted in a vacuum. There seems to be a direct relationship between American and Soviet military confrontation and restrictive trade legislation. The Blockade of Berlin, which began in April 1948, provided an impetus for the restrictive trade legislation of the following year. The Korean War of 1950 stimulated another surge of controls.

The stated objectives of the Export Control Act of 1949 were to: 1) protect the domestic economy from abnormal foreign demand for our products; 2) promote American foreign policy; and 3) see that American security was not jeopardized by the export of strategic goods. (See Appendix I.)

This legislation was not issued solely as an anticommunist measure; one of its most important purposes was also to protect American resources at a time of tremendous international demand following the destruction of World War II. Nevertheless, under this law the president was authorized through the Department of Commerce to establish a licensing system designed to prevent the shipment of any goods that would make a significant contribution to a communist country's military potential.

The law, which continues in effect today, stipulates that licenses have to be obtained for the export of virtually all United States goods. Basically exporters are issued one or two types of licenses. The first is a "general license" which is an open license to export certain specified goods without the need to obtain a special license for each transaction. This kind of license applied primarily to nonstrategic goods—items that were set out in a published General License (GL) list. The second type of license was called a Validated License and was required for more sensitive items. These licenses were issued only after the exporter certified the purpose for which the export was intended and to whom it was to go. For guidance, the Department of Commerce also maintained a "positive list" of goods that were regarded as strategic and for which export licenses to communist countries generally would be denied.

At the peak of the cold war, the Department of Commerce proscribed over 1,000 items. The law was rigidly interpreted, leading Bernard Baruch to comment that the only product he could think of that had no military potential was bubble gum. Presumably even bubble gum could have been banned when in 1962 the Export Control Act was extended to prohibit the export of goods that would have "economic significance" as well.[8] By requiring exporters to obtain licenses for most of the goods they might want to export to the U.S.S.R., the American government sought to deprive the Soviet economy of long lists of strategic items and to hamstring general commercial intercourse with Eastern Europe with red tape. The United States also pressured other major capitalist countries to adopt similar policies by promoting the work of the Consultative Group Coordinating Committee (COCOM), which published control lists of embargoed goods that the major capitalist countries in NATO plus Japan agreed should be denied the communist countries.

Once all the restrictions and controls had been set in place, it was not easy to dismantle them. But just as increased political and military tensions between the United States and the Soviet Union had precipitated increasingly restrictive trade legislation against the Soviet Union, so in somewhat the same way liberalization of trade restrictions had to be preceded by cessation of hostilities. Thus the GL list for the U.S.S.R., which made it easier to sell some goods, was canceled in March 1951 and only reinstituted in the mid-1950s, a few years after Stalin's death and at the end of the Korean War.

But in the late 1960s there was a noticeable change in this "war-restriction, peace-liberalization" pattern. Despite the ever-growing involvement of the United States in Vietnam, strong counterpressures began to develop in Congress for increased trade with the U.S.S.R. and even with China. Much of this pressure came from American corporations which were becoming increasingly envious of the contracts their competitors in Western Europe and Japan were signing with the Russians. COCOM's power had been eroding rapidly as the Soviet Union began to dangle ever more attractive contracts before prospective sellers, and as Japan and the countries of Western Europe became less dependent on the United States. At first the U.S. resisted most attempts to reduce COCOM's list of embargoed goods, but at last even it began to yield. Finally, in 1969, the Congress of the United States, after a valiant struggle of several months, replaced the 1949 Export Control Act. The new Export Administration Act of 1969 carried an entirely different orientation toward East-West trade.

In passing the new law, Congress did not go so far as to abolish all export controls. It did, however, decree that controls be abolished in those instances where it could be shown that the proscribed goods could be purchased by communist buyers from other Western countries or from Japan. Only if it could be demonstrated that the sale of such goods by American firms would threaten American national security were export permits to be denied. The fact that Soviet economic power would benefit was no longer in itself a reason for denial of a license. In other words, instead of restriction, Congress asked for liberalization. The 1969 act was further broadened, after some temporary uncertainty, by the Equal Export Opportunity Act of August 1972. Within a short time over 1,500 goods were put on the list, thus freeing them from most controls, and the Department of Commerce began to facilitate rather than frustrate exports to the U.S.S.R.

FINANCIAL CONTROLS

Export controls were not the only obstacle put in the path of East-West trade; American exporters and importers of Soviet goods also had to contend with restrictive financial controls. Again, as with the Trading With the Enemy Act, the original legislation was not specifically aimed at the Soviet Union, but by the early 1950s the Russians and their East European allies were virtually the only ones adversely affected.

Most of the difficulty stems from the loans extended by the United States during World War I. In the aftermath of the war and the world-wide depression of the 1930s, most countries (except for Finland) began to default on their loans from the U.S. As of 1934, $22 billion of principal and $12.5 billion in interest were in default. It was to stimulate more diligence or at least prevent further default that Congress passed the Johnson Debt Default Act of 1934,[9] under which no private person or corporation can lend money or buy or sell the securities of any foreign government which has defaulted on its debts to the United States government.

At the time, there was no intention of singling out the Soviet Union, for the law applied equally to all countries in default. But if enforced literally, the Johnson Act would have hampered the post–World War II recovery of most of Europe. Not only had most European countries incurred huge new debts as a result of World War II, but most (including the U.S.S.R.) had still not settled their World War I loans. Consequently, to prevent economic collapse in Europe and make it possible to reopen private lines of credit, the Johnson Act was amended to exclude any country that had become a member of the World Bank and the International Monetary Fund. Since the countries of Eastern Europe refused to join either organization or withdrew as did Poland and Czechoslovakia shortly after joining, what started out as a general law quickly became an anticommunist measure. The only East European countries that could obtain loans from the United States were Albania, because it had no loans of significance from the American government to default, and Yugoslavia, which was a charter member of the IMF and World Bank and did not withdraw. Subsequently Rumania, in December 1972, also joined both organizations.

While the credit policies of the United States toward Eastern Europe were affected more by the Johnson Act than anything else, there were also other restraints imposed by international practice. The Berne Union was particularly important, at least for a time. Although the agreement reached in Berne, Switzerland, in 1934 predates World War II and the cold war and was originally intended to bring order to the international credit markets of the 1930s, it too eventually became a weapon to limit credit concessions to Eastern Europe. Members of the Berne Union agreed in 1958 to limit commercial credit to the communist bloc to five years, and to require a 20 percent down payment on all loans. However, Japan was never a signatory to the agreement and was soon tempted to extend credit on more appealing terms. The East Europeans were thus able to play off one potential seller against another until almost all of the Western European countries came to ignore their gentleman's agreement. Today credits are sometimes issued for periods of ten years or more.

Although the Berne Union has not been particularly effective, the Johnson Act has, for it is generally much easier to enforce a law unilaterally than as an international agreement. Even the Johnson Act, however, has never served as an absolute barrier to the financing of Soviet or East European purchases. Thus almost from the beginning the United States government has ruled that the Johnson Act did not exclude private *commercial credits* extended up to 180 days, thereby leaving most commodity trade unaffected. Moreover, when extra funds and longer terms were needed to finance the first large sale of American grain to the U.S.S.R. in October 1963, Robert Kennedy as Attorney General ruled that the Johnson Act applied only to the extension of financial loans, not "supplier credits," that is, loans provided by or arranged by the supplier or manufacturer. Thus loans from manufacturers which were refinanced by their banks were permissible, while direct loans from banks or other financial institutions that did not cover specific products were not. In effect, credit arrangements for the medium term (18 months for wheat) which covered specific goods were legal. Any longer-term credit (five years or more) or any credit issued as an open-ended loan by banks rather than for a specific package of goods would apparently be illegal. But neither the law nor the courts have provided a definite statement on the maximum term that would be allowable.

The Johnson Act clearly puts domestic American manufacturers and banks at a disadvantage with foreign competitors. Samuel Pisar also points out that since the law exempts foreign subsidiaries of American corporations from its provisions if the funds are raised solely outside the United States, another effect has been to divert exports from the U.S. to foreign subsidiaries.[10] Nor does the Johnson Act apply to overseas branches of American banks, which thus can make loans to the U.S.S.R. without having them related to specific exports.[11]

There is no doubt that the Johnson Act, in spite of the many exceptions and its liberal interpretation, has created a significant burden for the U.S.S.R. and for those East European countries judged to be in default. They are seriously limited as to what goods they can buy. This may explain why, despite threats that they would turn elsewhere and protestations that the demanded settlement would be too burdensome, they have made serious efforts to settle their overdue debts. Even so, it still was something of a shock to pick up the *New York Times* of June 29, 1973, and see a most atypical ad from the Polish government. According to the advertisement, the communist government of Poland had reached an agreement with the Foreign Bondholders Protective Council of New York and agreed to pay off the $40 million debt of the precommunist government of Poland. Terms of the settlement were spelled out and bond holders were urged to turn in their securities before June 30, 1975. This belated concern for the sanctity of financial commitments is certainly impressive. As laudable as such a motive may be, it is also likely that the Poles agreed to such an arrangement to enhance their eligibility for long-term financing in the future. In March 1973 Hungary agreed to make restitution of about $19 million for American property it had nationalized. In September 1973, talks contemplating a similar settlement for over $7.5 million of 1929 debt were begun with the Rumanians; an agreement was signed in September 1974. Bulgaria has also entered into similar negotiations.[12] A preliminary agreement was reached with the Czechs in July 1974 to settle an $80 million debt owed the United States. Since such claims are usually settled at about $.40 on the dollar, this means the Czechs will have to pay about $32 million. However, this will be offset by the return of 18.4 million metric tons of Czech gold which has been held by the United States, Great Britain, and France since World War II, and a credit for an American-built steel mill the Czechs had ordered and paid for but never received.

In somewhat the same spirit, the Soviet Union has also made a serious effort to settle the bulk of its debts. Here the main dispute has focused on the old Lend Lease debt of World War II. There has been considerable misunderstanding about this issue. Many critics of the U.S. charged that the United States was being unfair by insisting on repayment of the $11.1 billion extended under the Lend Lease agreement. After all, the Russians sacrificed greatly during the war, with more than 20 million of their people killed. Was it fair, these critics asked, to equate dollars with blood?[13]

What these critics often overlooked was that the United States never sought to collect for the military goods delivered to the

U.S.S.R. during the war, any more than it tried to collect for similar goods delivered to the British. For that matter, by Soviet standards, it is apparently perfectly permissible to expect reimburse-
ment for military equipment as well. Thus the Russians insisted
upon, and ultimately obtained, complete repayment for the military loans they provided the Chinese to fight the Korean War.
Needless to say, the Chinese were less than enthusiastic about having to make such repayments, particularly because they came to
feel that they had involved themselves in fighting a war on behalf
of the Soviet Union in order to prevent a head-on clash between
the United States and the Soviet Union.[14] The Chinese were quick
to note that, in contrast with what the Russians were demanding
from the Chinese, the Americans merely sought to collect for the
nonmilitary goods that were in Soviet hands after the war was over as
well as the "pipeline goods" that were on order before the war
ended but not delivered until later.[15] In 1947 the United States
valued these civilian and pipeline goods at $2.6 billion and asked
for a 50 percent settlement of $1.3 billion. The British ultimately
agreed to the same type of terms.

During initial negotiations in 1947, the Soviets responded by
calling the United States heartless and materialistic. As a coun-
teroffer, they proposed that we reduce our already compromised
$1.3 billion to $170 million. Ultimately the United States did
reduce its claims to a final offer of $800 million, but the Soviet
Union refused to go above $300 million. As a result, the talks fi-
nally collapsed in June 1952. A breakthrough of sorts occurred,
however, in 1954 when the Russians agreed to begin payment for
that portion of the "pipeline" deliveries they had received from the
United States after October 15, 1945. Since 1954 they have paid
off about $200 million and owe only $45 million more on that
specific portion of the debt.[16]

The next series of negotiations over the remaining $1 billion or
so took place briefly in 1960 when the Russians renewed their
offer of $300 million. We again responded with a demand for
$800 million. As before, no one was willing to budge. However,

as the desire of the Russians to purchase heavy equipment from the United States increased, so did their need for long-term financing, and no such financing was possible until the Lend Lease debt was settled. Thus in March 1972 the Russians again proposed a resumption of negotiations on their Lend Lease debt. With time, the issues were becoming more complex because interest on the debt was accumulating and some decision had to be made as to what interest rate to charge after all those years. There was also a dispute over how long the Russians should have to repay. After months of discussion, an agreement was finally reached on October 18, 1972, under which the Soviet Union agreed to pay $722 million over a 28- to 32-year period. (In the end the Russians apparently compromised the most since, if we ignore the interest, the final settlement is much closer to the $800 million asked by the Americans than the $300 million offered by the Russians.) In return for the Soviet agreement to settle its Lend Lease arrears, negotiators for the American side promised to ask Congress to extend most favored nation (MFN) treatment to the U.S.S.R.[17]

As a result of this settlement and the October 18, 1972, trade agreement which was reached simultaneously, the United States declared itself willing to make long-term loans to the Soviet Union through the Export-Import Bank, a privilege it extends to other countries. First, however, President Nixon had to satisfy the terms of the 1965 Foreign Assistance and Related Agencies Appropriation Act which made it illegal to lend Export-Import Bank funds to any communist country unless a specific determination had been made that such a loan would be in the national interest. It was ironic that the Export-Import Bank, which was originally established in February 1934 to finance trade with the U.S.S.R., should be so restricted. But in 1968 an amendment was passed to the Export-Import Act of 1945 which precluded all such financing (the president could not even authorize a waiver) to any country that was found to be aiding a country engaged in an armed conflict with the United States. Fortunately, in 1971 the Export Expansion Finance Act made it possible to extend loans to communist countries with whom the United States was not actively or directly at war. Again the president would have to declare that such credit was in the national interest. President Nixon made such a determination for the Soviet Union on October 18, 1972, as part of the overall trade agreement.

In spite of the Lend Lease settlement, there remained serious legal obstacles to the issuing of credits to the U.S.S.R. Nothing has been done so far about the prerevolutionary debt owed to the United States government, which has grown from less than $200 million to a sum that may now be as large as $700 million, due to the unpaid interest accumulation.[18] This is important, since it may still be illegal under the Johnson Act for American firms to extend *private* long-term loans to the Soviet Union until all the debt arrears (pre-World War I as well as World War II) are settled.[19] Yet because of President Nixon's declaration, loans made directly by the U.S. government's Export-Import Bank or with its participation or under its guarantee *are legal,* as are *private commercial credits.* As of 1975, however, nobody has been able to obtain a precise legal definition of where *private commercial credits* end and *private long-term loans* begin. To say the least, this is a fuzzy area.

But however the Johnson Act is interpreted, the 60 largest private banks in the United States are probably still precluded from lending the Soviet Union more than a combined total of $1.5 billion under existing procedures. United States banking laws impose maximum limits on how much a bank can lend any one customer. And even though the credits intended for the Soviet Union are being extended for a variety of projects, they are all being signed for by one Soviet borrower, the Vnestorgbank (Foreign Trade Bank). If larger credits are to be made available, either the United States or the Soviet Union will have to change its methods of operation, and so far neither country has made any such move.

Finally, it is necessary to remember the fragility of the arrangement to extend Export-Import Bank credit. Continued issuance of Export-Import Bank credit depends on Soviet settlement of the

Lend Lease debt, which in turn is contingent on the U.S. Congress agreeing to extend MFN treatment to the Soviet Union. Thus United States credit export policies toward the U.S.S.R. in turn depend on what we decide to do about our import policy toward it.

IMPORT RESTRICTIONS

When the United States imposed the extremely high 1930 Smoot-Hawley tariffs during the depression, these tariffs applied to all countries of the world. There was no thought of singling out Soviet imports for special discrimination, yet through a combination of both economic and political developments, that is what happened.

Beginning in 1934 with the Trade Agreement Act (later extended by the Trade Expansion Act of 1962), the United States allowed the president to reduce tariffs in exchange for similar concessions by another country. Spurred by the General Agreement on Tariffs and Trade (GATT), most countries (except those belonging to customs unions like the Common Market) agreed that the best tariff concessions they extended to one nation (the most favored nation) would be extended to any other nation which in turn offered similar concessions. All such participating countries then would have MFN status. By providing similar concessions to the United States, such countries, when selling to the United States, are eligible for significantly reduced tariff rates on most of their goods. In contrast, those countries that do not have MFN status with the United States must pay the high Smoot-Hawley tariff rates.

After the signing of the first United States-Soviet Union Trade Agreement on July 13, 1935, the United States extended lower tariffs and then, by 1937, MFN status to the U.S.S.R. This lasted until 1951 when, in the midst of the Korean War, Congress passed the Trade Agreement Extension Act which withdrew MFN treatment from the U.S.S.R. and all of the countries of Eastern Europe except Yugoslavia. (Poland's MFN treatment privileges were restored in 1960.) Denial of this privilege can be very expensive. Thus without MFN the tariff on pig iron imports from the Soviet Union is more than five times higher per ton than it is from MFN countries. In other cases such as cadmium imports, shipments from MFN countries are brought in tariff-free, while there is a $.15 per pound charge on Soviet imports.[20] According to the Soviets, absence of MFN treatment has made it difficult for them to compete in the United States market and is a major reason for their adverse balance of trade with the United States.[21]

A recent study by Anton Malish, has shown, however, that the Russians may not have suffered as much as they claim.[22] First of all, many Soviet goods are of such poor quality and outmoded style that even if they could be sold tariff-free, or at lower tariffs, they would probably not be attractive to American buyers. Second, Malish found that most of the goods that the Soviet Union expects to or already does export to the United States—for example, raw materials—have never been subject to tariffs even under the Smoot-Hawley law. Thus Malish concludes that in 1970, only about 10 to 15 percent of Soviet sales to the United States were subject to substantial discrimination. A similar study made for 1972 shows that 25 percent of Soviet sales to the United States were subject to discrimination, but even this is still fairly low. In contrast, 85 percent in 1970 and 76 percent in 1972 of the goods from East Germany, and 73 percent in 1970 and 87 percent in 1972 of the goods from Czechoslovakia, were affected, since both countries sell more highly fabricated items on which the tariffs are heavier.

Restoration of MFN status would probably induce the Russians to offer a wider variety of goods than it has been profitable for them to export, and they would make more money on what they sell. Yet cost considerations have not often kept the Russians out of hard currency markets in the past, particularly when they are in short supply of such currency. As the Russians see it, there are two separate markets and two separate currencies. The goods they produce are paid for almost entirely in soft domestic Russian rubles. Thus their costs need bear no relationship to hard currency or world dollar prices. When the Russians want dollars, as they have recently, they are usually willing to sell whatever they can for as low a price as it takes to find a customer. If necessary, that may be below the world price and even the domestic Russian ruble price at the stated rate of exchange. But that does not matter. While they would like to charge high prices, all that seems to matter to them is that they earn as much foreign currency as possible.

If that means charging low prices, that is what they will do, for as long as the foreign trade sector is less than 10 percent of the Soviet gross national product (GNP), they can afford to export their domestically produced goods at what appears to be a loss with no major impact on the rest of the economy. Thus they have offered to sell Soviet automobiles in the foreign market at prices equivalent to $2,400, even though at official exchange rates Soviet consumers have to pay as much as $7,300 for the same automobile. It is also worth noting that in their trade with the developed countries of Western Europe and Japan, where the Russians do enjoy MFN status, the pattern is not significantly different from what it has been in the United States without MFN. Soviet exports to these countries also consist primarily of raw materials, not machinery (see Table 2–3). Thus even with MFN treatment, the variety of Soviet goods being offered for export is not likely to expand in the foreseeable future.[23]

But while MFN treatment may not lead to a substantial increase in the sale of Soviet goods in the U.S., the Russians have still made it a major issue. The agreement to settle the Lend Lease debt was predicated on the U.S. extending MFN treatment to the Russians and making them eligible for Export-Import Bank credits. Indeed, if the legislation granting these two things had not passed Congress, then the Russians would have had to pay only $48 million (probably just enough to finish off their payments under the old pipeline agreement that they have been paying regularly since 1954; see p. 55) and nothing more toward the balance of $674 million on the basic Lend Lease agreement. (As we shall see, while Congress had passed and President Ford had signed a Trade Act which it was thought was acceptable to the Soviet Union, Soviet officials renounced the whole agreement in January 1975 because of what they considered to be discriminating provisions of the 1975 Trade Act. So as of this writing, the Soviet Union does not have MFN status, nor does it intend to repay its Lend Lease debt.)

Back on October 1, 1961, moreover, the Russians even introduced a double-column tariff system of their own just so they could have an additional bargaining counter to offer countries like the United States in exchange for MFN treatment. Under this system, the high-column tariffs would apply to those countries which did not extend MFN treatment to the U.S.S.R., and the low-column tariffs to those countries that did.[24] From all appearances this is the same procedure used by the other major trading countries. This made it possible for the Russians to say that they would not extend MFN treatment to American goods because we would not do the same for their goods.

But it is hard to see how anyone could be influenced by such a threat and indeed few Americans took it seriously. Tariffs are meaningless in the Soviet system, where state agencies are the only organizations authorized to import goods. Assume the Ministry of Foreign Trade has decided to purchase a machine tool from the United States. Next assume that the same Ministry of Foreign Trade decides to increase the tariff on machine tools imported from the United States. Will this make the machine tool so expensive that the Ministry of Foreign Trade, together with the Ministry of Finance, will rule against importation of that machine tool from the United States? Hardly. The decision on whether or not to import depends on the availability of hard currency. But since the tariff is collected in rubles and paid by the importer, the Ministry of Foreign Trade, it is difficult to see how the Soviet tariff could prove much of a deterrent, particularly when collecting it is really nothing more than an internal bookkeeping operation. When a decision is made to import a particular commodity, the government authorizes an increased allocation of rubles to the Ministry of Foreign Trade so that the ministry can pay the tariff. The tariff, in turn, is collected by another government organization which in effect recycles the money to the Ministry of Foreign Trade so that it can pay the tariffs for the next set of imports.

Unlike the situation in a noncommunist country, the Soviet tariff generally has no impact on the final price paid by the ultimate consumer—particularly when the purchaser is an industrial enterprise of the Soviet government. When imported items are intended for Soviet consumers, there is a high markup whether or not a tariff has been paid. This is done to hold down consumption of imported goods. It must be remembered that at best, consumer demand has only the most indirect effect on determining imports. In other words, tariffs in the Soviet Union are a paper shuffling exercise and do not serve to accelerate or dampen the flow of imports into the U.S.S.R.

The decision of the Soviet Union to import goods is ultimately determined by two things: 1) availability of foreign exchange; and 2) whether the goods are included in the state import plan. Indeed, other countries in Western Europe have insisted that the proper quid pro quo for extending MFN treatment to communist countries is for the planners in such countries to agree in advance to increase their foreign purchases by predetermined amounts or percentages. Although similar provisions were included in the first Soviet Union-United States trade agreements of July 1935 and August 1937, the 1972 American-Soviet agreement did not require any specific concession of this sort.[25] In sum, while the Russians insisted on MFN advantages for themselves they apparently were not prepared to offer any similar tariff privileges in exchange.

Tariffs are not the only form of discrimination that has been applied against Soviet imports in the past. In 1951, Section 11 of the Trade Agreement Extension Act added a provision which ordered a ban on further importation of ermine, fox, kalinsky, marten, mink, muskrat, and weasel fur skins from both the U.S.S.R. and China. That prohibition continues today. Similarly, until 1961, importation of Soviet crab meat was prohibited because of the ban on importation of goods made with convict or forced labor. Lobbying in 1959 also resulted in a ban on the use of federal government funds to buy school laboratory equipment from the communist countries, unless such equipment was unavailable elsewhere. At best it appears that adoption of such restrictions was due to more effective lobbying by some domestic interests than any considerations of military security or national defense.

PUBLIC PRESSURE AND THE SPECIAL PROBLEMS OF TRADING WITH THE U.S.S.R.

The Russians are not the only ones who have suffered because of the opposition of various groups in the United States to trading with the Soviet Union. American businessmen who have brought from or sold to the Russians have also been subject to harassment. What are the types of pressures that have been applied to American businesses, and what has been the effect of such tactics both here and in the U.S.S.R.?

As might be expected, conservative groups have consistently opposed commercial dealings with the Soviet Union and other socialist countries. During times of military confrontation, their cause is supported by others who may decide to take the opposite stance at times of détente. Thus the National Association of Manufacturers, which now supports liberalization of trade with the Soviet Union, opposed it as recently as 1966.[26] However, there appear to be some groups which never change.

The John Birch Society in particular has been extremely active

63

in opposing East-West trade.[27] For a period in the 1960s the society sponsored "card parties." Whenever it was discovered that a store was selling merchandise from communist countries, the "players" would place cards on the store shelves and in communist-made goods with the inscription, "Buy all your communist-made products at _____," with the name of the local store filled in the blank. Such methods were especially effective on the West Coast and in the South. Some merchants withstood the pressure and even managed to bring about enactment of laws forbidding such activities. In other instances, "card parties" led to laws banning the sale of goods made in communist countries. Thus in Montgomery, Alabama, the city commission passed a law in 1962 which ordered that all communist-made goods be removed from store shelves unless the merchant paid $5,000 for a special license and posted a sign which said, "This store sells communist slave-labor merchandise."

One of the earliest campaigns to be directed against an individual American corporation occurred in the late 1950s when the Ealing Corporation, a division of Baird Atomic Corporation of Boston, decided to import Russian-made educational equipment for use in the teaching of science. Immediately Ealing's noncommunist suppliers and customers were urged to boycott the company unless it stopped selling its Russian-made equipment. Similar pressure was placed on the parent company, which was a defense contractor. To avoid such situations, many companies (especially those vulnerable to consumer boycotts) have gone to unusual lengths to mask their participation in East-West trade.[28] Importers have rerouted textiles from Yugoslavia via Italy in order to put "Made in Italy" on them, or gloves from Czechoslovakia have passed through Holland in order to qualify for a "Made in Holland" label.

Such concern is understandable, for these campaigns can be a real threat. In 1964, as part of its campaign to encourage Rumania to broaden its industrial involvement beyond the communist bloc, the U.S. government actively encouraged the Firestone Company to build a $50 million synthetic rubber factory in Rumania. Egged on to some extent by the Goodyear Tire Company, which had lost the contract, the Young Americans for Freedom (YAF) began an active campaign of picketing Firestone stores and threatening a spectacular demonstration at the Indianapolis 500 mile race. YAF threatened to rent airplanes that would fly over the Indianapolis track with banners protesting Firestone's contract.[29] Under such pressure Firestone canceled its contract. Yet Universal Oil Products, which simultaneously had agreed to build a $22.5 million petroleum refinery, fulfilled its obligation. Undoubtedly the fact that Universal Oil Products did not sell in the consumer market where it could be exposed to pressure made it easier for the company to come to such a decision.

Emboldened by its success, YAF threatened to launch the same type of campaign against any company that engaged in trade with a communist country. To counteract YAF's pressure, to reassure American businessmen, and to encourage economic independence from the U.S.S.R. among the smaller East European countries, the secretaries of state, defense, and commerce finally took a firm stand. In 1965 they announced their support of the purchase of Yugoslav tobacco by six American tobacco companies. They agreed that they, not YAF, should determine whether or not such transactions were in the national interest. Still, administration efforts to liberalize East-West trade met some opposition in Congress. The late minority leader, Senator Everett Dirkson, opposed MFN treatment for Eastern Europe as well as Export-Import Bank credits for American suppliers of machinery to the Fiat plant in the Soviet Union. Referring to Vietnam, he lamented: "Is trade so sweet and profit so desirable as to be purchased at the price we now pay in death and agony?"

Another form of pressure was exerted by the International Longshoremen's Union at the time of the 1964 Russian wheat sale. Reflecting the traditional hostility of the American labor movement toward the Soviet Union for the way it had emasculated the Soviet labor movement, the longshoremen had adopted a policy of refusing to load cargoes destined for the Soviet Union. In order to get the longshoremen to agree to load American wheat, President Kennedy stipulated that at least 50 percent of the wheat would be sent in ships of the U.S. Merchant Marine. Since American merchant marine costs are significantly higher than those charged by other ship carriers, this automatically raised transportation costs on any U.S. wheat sales to the U.S.S.R. It was only in June 1971 that President Nixon managed to win labor's permission to alter this arrangement. (See Chapter 7.) It looked at the time that the Russians would otherwise never agree to buy any more American wheat as long as they had to pay the higher American merchant marine costs.

More than anything else, the visits of President Nixon to the Soviet Union in 1972 and 1974, and President Ford in 1974, and Secretary Brezhnev's visit here in 1973, have helped to make trade with the Soviet Union more acceptable and respectable. Yet though such visits diminished the opposition's base of support, the protests of fervent groups like the John Birch Society and YAF have continued. Among those companies which have had difficulty recently are American Motors, Pepsi Cola, and several of the firms which supplied machinery for the Fiat plant.

Occasionally the perennial opponents of American-Soviet trade are joined by other groups not associated with the ideological right wing. Thus in the early 1970s many intellectual groups such as the Committee of Concerned Scientists of New York, whose members would normally favor increased trade between the United States and the Soviet Union, allied themselves with those who normally oppose any kind of relationship in order to urge that Congress withhold MFN treatment from the Russians until the Soviet government ends the repressive conditions it imposes on its intellectuals. In the same way, Jewish groups have sought to pressure the Russians into easing the discrimination against Jews which exists in various areas of Soviet life, and relaxing emigration procedures for those relatively few Russians who want to leave for Israel.

The campaign against giving the Soviet Union MFN status was led by Senator Henry Jackson. His so-called "Jackson amendment" had over 75 supporters in the U.S. Senate. As ultimately passed by the House and Senate and signed by President Ford, the Jackson amendment, which was incorporated into the Trade Reform Act of 1975, would have required the president to deny MFN status and Export-Import Bank loans from the U.S. government to countries like the Soviet Union that: (1) deny their citizens the right or opportunity to emigrate; and (2) impose more than a nominal tax or fee for emigration or exit visas on those who express a desire to emigrate. (At one time Soviet authorities were taxing potential emigrants with advanced educational degrees as much as $30,000 per person for their visas.) While the terms seemed rather demanding, Secretary Kissinger indicated that the Soviet government had agreed to accept the conditions. Thus the Soviet Union was to have MFN status for 18 months after which time the President of the United States would have to make a determination that the Soviet Union had not reverted to its old policies in order to insure the continuation of MFN treatment. The intent was to maintain constant pressure on the U.S.S.R., for in the past the Russians have often given the appearance of agreeing to more relaxed emigration procedures only to close off emigration soon after they were granted a specific concession.

EFFECTS OF POLITICAL PRESSURE

What has been the effect of such protests, especially the campaign to use MFN treatment as a weapon to bring about increased emigration from the U.S.S.R.? Has this strategy had an impact on either Soviet or American policy?

The Russian response has been particularly instructive. They have bitterly protested attempts to interfere in their domestic policies and have insisted that they will not change their policies toward intellectuals or Jewish emigrants. On the contrary, they argued such tactics would only threaten détente and cause the Soviet Union to take its trade elsewhere.

Of course, Russian protests ignore similar efforts on their part to affect domestic affairs in other countries. Take the campaign they organized on behalf of Angela Davis during her trial in California. Each day during her trial, at least one major Soviet paper would carry a lead article about the case. There were Soviet-sponsored rallies and campaigns throughout the U.S.S.R. and other countries that sought to help win her freedom. There is no reason why the Russians should not do as they please in such matters, whether it be over Angela Davis, an end to atomic testing, or any of the countless other causes they sponsor from year to year. Nor is there anything wrong with the Soviet Union sending a dozen or so senior Soviet officials to the United States in February 1973 and again in February 1974 specifically to lobby in Congress together with representatives from the National Association of Manufacturers for MFN treatment. Such tactics are common in the United States and are recognized as a legitimate form of politics. It is just hypocritical when Soviet officials call foul when the same methods are used by others against them. (Significantly, while the Soviet government complained bitterly about efforts to influence their policies toward Soviet Jews, no such objections were heard when foreign conservation groups sponsored a boycott of Soviet goods in protest over Soviet refusal to curb its killing of whales.)

As this is being written, it is too early to predict what the ultimate outcome of the Jackson amendment efforts will be. After there seemed to be valid assurances that an agreement had been reached, the Soviet government announced in January 1975 that it had decided to reject the U.S.-U.S.S.R. Trade Agreement of 1972. Of course there had been strong hints throughout the intervening years that most Soviet officials were very displeased with the Jackson amendment. Yet for a time they did seem prepared to accept it. However their displeasure seemed to increase significantly when in addition to the stipulation about the emigration of Soviet Jews, the U.S. Congress also passed a law limiting the extension of Export-Import Bank credits to the Soviet Union to a total of $300 million over a four year period. This seemed to upset them more than anything else. The Russians have made no secret of their belief that they regard having access to American credits and technology as one of the main advantages of the policy of détente. At the same time, full participation by them in the 1972 U.S.-U.S.S.R. Trade Agreement requires that they repay $722 million of their Lend Lease debt. Undoubtedly they had hoped to obtain some of the dollars for this repayment from money they had expected to obtain from the Export-Import Bank. With a debt limit of $300 million over four years, their ability to arrange such refinancing would have been severely constrained. Finally senior Soviet officials including Brezhnev himself seemed particularly incensed about the way Senator Jackson used the White House itself as a stage for proclaiming Soviet acquiescence with a plan imposed on the Soviet Union by the United States Congress. While Soviet officials apparently were prepared to carry out the terms of the agreement, they felt that the manner of Senator Jackson's announcement was an attempt to humiliate the world's second largest power and this caused enormous resentment.

How the dispute will ultimately be resolved and whether or not it will affect American-Soviet trade significantly or cause an unbreechable rift in the path of détente remains to be seen. Yet despite the rejections of the accord, the Soviet response up to late 1974 does suggest that under the proper conditions economic pressure can be used to win political concessions, particularly when the Soviet Union is in economic need. The danger, however, is that it is hard to know when to stop and when the Russians may come to feel that they are being asked to concede too much. In retrospect, they were probably prepared to concede a great deal in 1972–1973 to obtain the wheat and feed supplies they so desperately needed. They did make major concessions—on issues ranging from suspending the emigration tax on Jews and allowing the emigration of 10,000–30,000 Jews a year to agreeing to a Lend Lease settlement and helping the United States achieve a peace settlement in Vietnam. Obviously the Russians are prepared to make political concessions when the need is great enough. Conversely their willingness to concede diminishes as their own economic position improves as it did once they began to collect large oil revenues after the Arab embargo in late 1973 and as the American economic position deteriorated as it did in the 1974–1975 recession. Clearly the trick is to ascertain just how much the Soviet Union is prepared to concede.

While it is hard to predict when the Russians will yield and when they will resist outside pressure, it is often equally hard to anticipate when an issue affecting a communist country will provoke a protest by some American group. It is often a matter of chance. (It is interesting, for example, that Americans who deal with the Chinese seem considerably less subject to such boycotts and protests. Following President Nixon's trip to China in 1972, American stores and newspapers were filled with ads for Chinese goods that had just been purchased. There seemed to be genuine excitement among both American businessmen and consumers. For some unknown reason, trade with China evoked interest, not protest. After his visit to China in July 1974, even Senator Jackson seemed to be in favor of more trade with China, despite the fact that the Chinese too have a communist form of government and restrictions on free emigration. Nothing comparable in the way of approval for the sale of Russian goods followed President Nixon's trips to the U.S.S.R.)

But political moods are ephemeral, particularly moods about American-Soviet relations. Consequently, there is a serious risk that the policy of détente may at any moment be superseded by one of hostility. Thus it would be shortsighted if, for example, the management of Pepsi Cola failed to weigh the costs of a boycott by American groups versus the rewards of tapping the potential of Soviet Pepsi drinkers. Moreover, there is always the possibility that if political conditions deteriorate, a firm like Pepsi, which is more exposed than most companies to consumer pressure, might have to endure a widespread boycott.

FROM HESITANCY TO EAGERNESS

Yet, in spite of all these obstacles, American businessmen have suddenly developed a great eagerness for Soviet trade. The reasons for this unprecedented excitement are not hard to explain. As long as the United States had plenty of markets elsewhere, there was no great concern if someone else catered to the Soviet market. Equally important was the fact that except for vodka and a few furs, no one could figure out what there was for us to buy from the Russians. With one or two exceptions, Soviet equipment and Soviet technology were not competitive, even at prices much lower than anyone else's. It may have made sense for the West Europeans and Japanese to trade with the Russians, since the Russians had vast quantities of raw materials to sell which were badly needed. But the United States, with its vast resources, had no such needs (or so it seemed).

As we saw earlier, the first significant swing of American public attitudes toward the Soviet Union, particularly among businessmen, appeared sometime in the mid-1960s. Surveys of businessmen conducted in 1964 by the Senate Foreign Relations Committee showed a majority in favor of increasing East-West trade. Yet, significantly, almost all those questioned chose to have their answers presented anonymously. Presumably they were fearful of suffering reprisals for rewards that were uncertain at best.

By the late 1960s, however, in a similar set of hearings, this time conducted by the Senate Committee on Banking and Currency, there seemed to be not only additional support from the business and professional community for trade with the U.S.S.R., but a willingness to stand up and be identified with such ideas.[30]

This was all the more remarkable for coming at a time of significantly increased U.S. involvement in Vietnam and growing popular resentment over Soviet support of North Vietnam.

Several factors accounted for the change, including a growing disenchantment with the cold war and our involvement in Vietnam. Perhaps more than anything else, it was the change in our international economic standing that provoked the most rethinking about our relations with the Soviet Union. In the late 1940s and early 1950s there was no large economic power for the Russians to deal with other than the U.S. All the other countries of Western Europe as well as Japan had been crushed or exhausted by World War II. Thus Americans were not losing much business by turning their backs on the Russians. The Russians were not much interested in buying outside Eastern Europe, and few non-American companies were interested or able to sell to them.

It was only a question of time, however, before the economies of Western Europe and Japan regained their prewar strength and began to compete with American manufacturers in areas where Americans once had the field to themselves. The speed of the recovery and growth of the economies of Japan, Italy, France, Germany, and even Singapore was somewhat unexpected. More and more it was not just a case of matching or even surpassing productive capabilities and products which originated in the U.S., but of driving them out of business. American firms were being underpriced not only in foreign markets, but in their home markets as well. In some instances the foreign competition came from the United States-owned subsidiaries relocated overseas, but with time, more and more locally owned industries began to assert themselves as well. Inevitably the refusal of the United States government to allow American firms to sell to the U.S.S.R. became a futile gesture. Of course, in areas such as computers and certain specialized machine tool products in which the United States had a monopoly, the East Europeans had to settle for second best or nothing. But increasingly, an American refusal to sell often amounted to little more than flag waving and less competition for the products of foreign manufacturers. One way or another, the Russians and the East Europeans found it possible to buy what they wanted—often from overseas subsidiaries of American firms.

Even though it hurt to see the West Europeans and Japanese have unencumbered access to Soviet markets, throughout most of the 1960s American firms did not feel they were sacrificing too much. After all, until 1963, the most that even the West Germans had sold to the Soviet Union was $207 million worth of goods, and that was back in 1962. Except for the Japanese (in 1966), no other capitalist country came close to matching that volume. If that was the most that such trade would generate, the United States did not appear to be missing much. In comparison to the $5 billion or so that the United States was selling to Canada, or the $1.5 billion to $2 billion the United States exported to the United Kingdom, West Germany, or Japan, the Russian market had little to offer.

But in the late 1960s uneasiness over losing out on sales to the communist bloc began to grow. First of all, the volume of deliveries from Western Europe and Japan to the U.S.S.R. started to increase rapidly. From 1967 to 1969, West German and Italian sales to the Soviet Union more than doubled, and those of France and Japan were up about 70 percent (Table 2–4). More important, some Soviet purchases, such as the Fiat plant and some of the chemical factories, were clearly once in a lifetime opportunities that caught the imagination of the American businessman, regardless of how meager the overall trade total might be.

The growing number of such lost opportunities coincided with the increasing difficulties of U.S. manufacturers in international and even American markets. There was no one specific point when everyone became aware of the seriousness of our foreign trade deficit. Except for 1957 and 1967, the United States had been carrying a negative balance of payments since 1950, but that was not regarded as particularly worrisome. Because of the dollar shortage, we wanted to pump out more dollars than we were taking in. What is more, although we were paying out billions of dollars in the form of military expenditures and corporate investments, our foreign trade surplus remained at about $4 to $5 billion from 1960 to 1967. That seemed to suggest that there was not too much to worry about, since we could still pay our way. But in 1968, while United States merchandise exports increased by a considerable amount, American imports jumped up by even more; the United States trade surplus was only $1.4 billion, a low seldom recorded in recent decades. From that point on the merchandise trade balance continued to deteriorate. In 1971 it actually was negative by $2.7 billion. Finally, in 1972, we imported about $7 billion more than we exported, an unsettling record.

Of course, many of our difficulties stemmed directly from the war in Vietnam and the accompanying inflation which made United States goods less competitive. Something had to be done to increase United States exports and thereby restore some confidence in the dollar.

Many businessmen now began to comment on the folly of discouraging exports to communist countries eager for U.S. goods at a time when American salesmen were finding it more and more difficult to sell to other countries. Such a policy seemed particularly futile when, as invariably happened, the rejected Russian buyers merely headed for Western Europe and Japan with their purchase orders. Thus when Henry Ford turned down an early feeler to build a large automobile plant on the Volga River, the Russians simply headed to Fiat with their $1 billion contract. The continuing sale of hundreds of millions of dollars worth of chemical plants by America's competitors also began to hurt.

American businessmen were not the only ones who sought a reorientation in American policy. Labor also became interested in Soviet trade as growing competition from foreign firms and the swelling flow of imports into the U.S. led to increased unemployment at home. It was one thing to support a boycott of the U.S.S.R. when there was plenty of work around. However, it required more principle than most workers could afford when it meant the loss of an American job to a German or Japanese worker who would profit by being able to fill the Soviet contract.

The change in labor's attitude became fairly obvious by 1970, when the unemployment rate climbed over 4 percent. It kept rising, moving past 5 percent in 1971 for the first time since 1964 and staying there until May 1973. It fell but rose sharply again 8 percent in 1975, unemployment at times exceeding 6 percent in 1971 and in 1974. Although the circumstances were nowhere near as desperate, it was possible to liken the attitude of American labor in 1971 and 1975 to the 1930s. During those depression years, exporters found themselves closed off from many of their traditional markets and so were led by need rather than ideology to bid for Soviet contracts. Americans were many times better off in the 1970s than they had been in the 1930s, but by 1970 there was no denying the change in labor's attitude.

Of course, there was still plenty of anti-Soviet feeling, but labor unions no longer were as vocal about boycotting Soviet shipping or as insistent that 50 percent of all American wheat shipments to the U.S.S.R. had to go in American ship bottoms. By the 1970s labor had come to agree that something was better than nothing, and that if the Russians would agree to send one-third, rather than one-half, of the wheat in American bottoms, that would be sufficient. In October 1972 they also agreed to end their ban on the loading and unloading of Soviet ships in American East Coast and Gulf ports. For the first time in years, Soviet ships were authorized by the U.S. Government to enter 40 ports in the United States.

Thus, by the early 1970s, a deteriorating economy at home had served to convert the attitudes of a surprisingly large part of the business and union communities toward increased trade with the U.S.S.R. Not only were sales to communist countries like the Soviet Union and China generating more jobs for American workers and farmers and more profits for American businessmen, but the one-sided nature of the trade flow enabled the United States to come close in 1973 to a positive balance in its overall trade dealings for the first time since 1970. At the same time, the diplomacy of Nixon and Kissinger with the People's Republic of China and the U.S.S.R. and the winding down of America's involvement in Vietnam also provided respectability for those who advocated closer relations between our own country and our communist antagonists. If Nixon, once one of the leading critics of communism, could find himself as much (if not more) at home in Moscow and Peking than in Tokyo or Paris, it was hard to criticize businessmen for adopting the same attitudes.

As has happened so often in the past, our hate for the Russians seemed once more to be turning to love, particularly among potential exporters. Certainly the future looked good to the exporters—but what about the importers? What do the Russians have to sell? How will the Russians be able to pay for all they want to buy and all that the Americans want to sell? These are the questions we turn to next.

PART II

HOW MUCH CAN THE SOVIET UNION PAY?

CHAPTER

4

Petroleum—

A New Ball Game

F O R years the traditional put-down for those who advocated increased trade with the Soviet Union has been, "There is no problem finding things to sell them, but what can they sell us?" Today, the question is no longer a put-down. Not many years ago, few would have thought that the large and rich United States would one day find itself short of raw materials. True, more and more American firms had found it necessary to seek supplemental sources of raw material outside the United States, but the nation was so large that we could always be assured of obtaining the bulk of our needs from within. Moreover, going outside the U.S. posed no problems. Since most of the overseas mining operations were in developing countries, the local residents seemed only too delighted to discover they finally had something that someone wanted to buy. Consequently, these supplemental sources of supply seemed secure for years to come.

Suddenly, however, many of our supplies of raw materials no longer look so abundant. Several forces have come to bear at once. After years of despair, the developing countries have finally discovered that they have some market power. This has come about mainly because the demand for resources has been growing faster than the discovery of new reserves. Led by the Japanese, countries from all over the world (including some that used to be considered developing countries) have joined the hunt for new and assured sources of raw materials to feed the growing appetites of their industries. Today, the United States and Western Europe are no longer the only ones looking for secure sources of supply. With demand for many resources growing 5 to 6 percent a year, it has become harder and harder for the industrialized consumers to play one supplier off against another. Today the long-range prospects for the raw material producing countries is very good. As long as countries like Japan, which is very poorly endowed, maintain the pace of their economic growth, and as long as countries like the United States continue to dig deeper into their slowly vanishing resources, those countries with raw materials in excess of their own needs can command better prices than ever before.

For the U.S.S.R. all of this is good news. As the largest country in the world, its raw materials resources are generally larger and more varied than anyone else's, including our own. With the change in world market conditions, and the exhaustion of many existing deposits not only in the traditionally mineral-short countries of Western Europe and Japan, but in the United States as well, the Russians now find their raw materials being courted by all kinds of new suitors.

The dramatic change in petroleum prices should go a long way toward satisfying those who question the Soviet Union's ability to pay for all it wants to buy. Yet, based on some calculations that were made before the change in oil prices (and some that were made subsequently as late as mid-1974), there are some analysts who have concluded that the Soviet Union had and probably will continue to have severe balance of payments problems. As these specialists in the State Department and the CIA see it, the Russians have been having great difficulty paying for what they have already purchased in Europe, and will have even greater difficulty paying for the $1–2 billion a year extra they want to buy from the United States, particularly as our prices begin to increase in response to the already increased prices of petroleum and other raw materials.[1]

Such questions become all the more urgent when it is realized that in 1969 U.S. exports to the Soviet Union were double U.S. imports; in 1972 our exports were five times higher, and the pattern continued into 1973 because of the wheat purchases. This seeming inability on the part of the Soviets to sell as much as they buy in markets like the United States should presumably create serious balance of trade and payments problems for them. As reflected in the warnings of Congressman Ben B. Blackburn of Georgia, the Soviet Union's "outstanding long-term (10 to 15 year) debt of $3.5 billion and their short-term debt of about the same amount (the two figures combined equal more than 200% of Soviet annual earnings of hard currency) represents an enormous dent in the U.S.S.R.'s balance of payments—and makes their ability to repay highly questionable."[2] Because of the harvest difficulties of 1972, the same analysts who provided Congressman Blackburn with his data calculated that the Soviet Union's hard currency deficit that year was $1.3 billion. (See Table 4–1.) And since the Russians continued to make major purchases in the West in 1973, Congressman Blackburn and other analysts estimated the Soviet Union's 1973 balance of payment deficit would be about $2.5 billion.

Presumably because most of the calculations used by Congressman Blackburn and the Department of State and the CIA were made before the Soviet Union raised its oil prices, a more recent set of calculations would show the Soviet Union to be in a radically different hard currency position. Yet subsequent studies by the CIA and Department of State suggest that the Soviet position has not changed much and that the Soviet hard currency shortage extends beyond 1973.[3] The specialists in the CIA and State Department who made these calculations have gone on to project a cumulative trade deficit of from $6 to $7 billion by 1980 with the

TABLE 4–1

The Pattern of Soviet Trade
(in millions of rubles; 1969 rubles for years prior to 1969)

	TOTAL		INDUSTRIALIZED [a] COUNTRIES	
	EXPORTS	IMPORTS	EXPORTS	IMPORTS
1946	588	692	209	282
1947	694	670	240	219
1948	1,177	1,102	420	259
1949	1,303	1,340	251	315
1950	1,615	1,310	236	204
1951	2,062	1,792	306	271
1952	2,511	2,256	347	388
1953	2,653	2,492	348	400
1954	2,901	2,864	426	528
1955	3,084	2,755	503	402
1956	3,254	3,251	553	540
1957	3,943	3,544	643	628
1958	3,869	3,915	632	591
1959	4,905	4,566	799	709
1960	5,007	5,066	913	1,004
1961	5,399	5,245	984	1,006
1962	6,328	5,810	1,023	1,175
1963	6,545	6,353	1,135	1,281
1964	6,915	6,963	1,181	1,587
1965	7,357	7,253	1,346	1,470
1966	7,957	7,122	1,581	1,601
1967	8,684	7,683	1,739	1,633
1968	9,571	8,469	1,887	1,965
1969	10,490	9,294	2,056	2,276
1970	11,520	10,559	2,154	2,540
1971	12,426	11,232	2,482	2,601
1972	12,734	13,303	2,441	3,441
1973	15,802	15,541	3,750	4,589

Source: Various issues of *VT SSSR*.
[a] As defined by Soviet Union.

hard currency bloc. At this rate, the Russians would have to desig-
nate about 25 percent of their total hard currency exports for debt
service. If such analyses are correct, they suggest that the Soviet
Union may not be a good credit risk. How good, then, is Soviet
credit? What are their hard currency exports and what new ways
are there for them to earn more hard currency?

THE SOVIET BALANCE OF TRADE

Determining the credit worthiness of the U.S.S.R. is no easy matter, since the Russians do not publish enough statistics for us to make the necessary calculations. Indeed, we cannot even be sure which Soviet transactions are made in hard currencies and which are not. Presumably most of their dealings with Western Europe, Japan, the United States, Canada, Australia, New Zealand, and Malaysia are in hard currency. But that does not hold for the bulk of Finnish trade or for some deals arranged on a barter or swap basis between the Soviet Union and some private corporation in one of the above countries.

It is virtually impossible to determine from official Soviet data what the balance of trade is for the hard currency countries alone. The Russians break down their trade statistics into:

1. Socialist countries (including members of CMEA and others.)
2. Industrially developed capitalist countries.
3. Developing countries.

Prior to 1971, all capitalist countries came under a single category. Unfortunately, it is difficult to ascertain just what countries the Russians presently include under "Industrially developed capitalist countries." Although the foreign trade handbook lists 12 countries in this category,[4] the list is clearly not all-inclusive, since these 12 countries accounted for only 20.8 percent of Soviet exports and imports in 1972, while the overall trade of the "Industrially developed capitalist countries" was 22.6 percent.[5] It is hard to determine what other countries should be included in the total, but presumably Denmark, Norway, Switzerland, Australia, New Zealand, and even Malaysia should be added. At the same time, Finland, which is included, should be excluded because, as mentioned earlier, the bulk of Finland's trade with the Soviet Union is in soft currency or barter.

To complicate matters even further, one's conclusion depends on whose foreign trade figures one uses. Thus the Soviet trade deficit looks much smaller if the figures of its trading partners are used. According to the statistics published by the British and Japanese, for example, both countries have had significant trading deficits with the Russians for many years. Thus the British trade deficit in 1972 was $400 million and the Japanese deficit was almost $100 million. (See Table 2–4.) In 1973 the deficits were even more pronounced. For the British it was $640 million and for the Japanese it was almost $600 million. Presumably these deficits should go a long way toward providing the Russians with the hard currency necessary to pay for their American exports.

Yet, according to the statistics issued by the Soviet government, the Soviet trade surplus with the United Kingdom and Japan may not have been nearly as favorable. The Soviet statistics for 1972 show that the Russians had a *deficit* of 50 million rubles with Japan (about $60 million at an exchange rate of $1.21 = one ruble), not the *surplus* of $100 million indicated by Japanese statistics. And they show a surplus of only 184 million rubles (about $222 million) with the United Kingdom, not the $400 million that British statistics designated. The 1973 statistics are not so diverse, at least for Soviet-British trade. Soviet statistics show a surplus of $520 million for the Soviet Union, $100 million less than is shown by the British. The Japanese deficit, however, is listed at only $200 million by the Russians—not the $600 million reported by the Japanese. Some of these disparities are inevitable. On occasion they may be due to the kind of bookkeeping problems that arise when, for example, the Russians ship goods in December 1971 which are not received and recorded until January 1972. Such discrepancies should balance off in the following year, yet countries like Japan and the United Kingdom consistently report higher deficits in their trade with the Soviet Union than do the Soviet statistics. To a minor extent, such disparities may also be explained by the fact that Soviet imports reported by the United Kingdom should total a higher pound sterling value than those same goods reported as exports by the Soviet Union. Great Britain (like most capitalist countries) includes the cost of freight and insurance (C.I.F.) in its import figures, while the Russian exports would be listed only free on board (F.O.B.). This makes Soviet trade *surpluses* when measured by British statistics look larger than they would in Soviet statistics. The overall impact of this effect is probably offset to some extent by the tendency of Soviet statistics to understate the size of the *deficit,* because the Russians record imports into the U.S.S.R. at F.O.B. the exporting country, and not at the higher C.I.F. price the Soviet Union actually pays.

Since the overall effect of such statistical discrepancies is probably minor, there must be something else to explain the often large difference in the figures. For example, the Russians consistently show their exports at almost $100 million less than what the British show they should be. More than anything else, this probably reflects Soviet omission of the gold and uncut diamonds which the Soviet Union sends to the United Kingdom. The Russians have always been squeamish about openly acknowledging such transactions, even though they add to the Soviet payment surplus.

This statistical digression is important because most of those who have been warning about the Soviet trade imbalances have been using Soviet figures which, as we saw, tend to understate Soviet trade surpluses. Thus, based on their own statistics, the Soviet Union reported a substantial trade deficit of 485 million rubles (about $540 million at the exchange rate of $1.11 to one ruble) in 1970 in their dealings with Western Europe (except for Finland), Japan, the United States, Canada, Australia, New Zealand, and Malaysia, instead of a minor deficit of only $40 million, according to the statistics of Russia's trading partners. More dramatically, in 1971 the Russians reported a 266 million ruble *deficit* (about $300 million), while data from her trading partners showed a *surplus* of about $150 million. In 1972, because of the grain crisis, the U.S.S.R. did indeed suffer a severe balance of trade deficit, no matter how the statistics are calculated. According to Soviet statistics, the deficit was 1,040 million rubles (or $1,260 million at an exchange rate of $1.21 to one ruble). However, using the statistics of her trading partners, the Soviet Union still had a deficit but it was a deficit of only $500 million. In 1973 Soviet statistics showed a deficit of 840 million rubles (or $1,126 million at $1.34

to one ruble), while the statistics of Russia's trading partners showed a deficit of only $300 million, or about one-quarter of that reported by the Russians.

Thus, part of the answer to whether or not the U.S.S.R. can pay its bills depends on which trade figures one uses. But no matter which figures give the most accurate picture, the Russians do have special means of keeping their external financing under control. If the balance of trade becomes too one-sided, the Russians can simply curb imports. Whereas in most capitalist countries this is done indirectly by either devaluing the currency or raising tariffs, in the Soviet Union it can be accomplished by simple administrative action. At least this is what seems to have happened in 1931. (See Table 2–1.) And lest there be some who suggest that the new age of advanced and interlocking technology makes it impossible to sever trade this way in the 1960s and 1970s, it should be noted that the Russians reacted in exactly the same way in 1963.[6] (See Table 2–4.) When the Russians realized that they were having difficulty with their grain harvest in the period 1963–1967 (Table 2–5), they cut back sharply on their imports from the United Kingdom, Germany, France, and Italy until about 1967. The only country to escape this retrenchment was Japan, and as we saw even her exports to the U.S.S.R. fell in 1967. Such cutbacks are relatively easy to accomplish when the state owns all the means of production and controls the distribution and foreign trade network. Of course, as foreign trade develops and as more long-term projects are undertaken, it may become harder to cut off foreign components so abruptly. Nevertheless, as long as the state maintains monopoly control over the import sector, the potential is always there.

ENTER PETROLEUM

But more than anything else, the Soviet balance of trade has been helped by the astounding transformation of its petroleum and natural gas export markets. Export sales of these items in 1973 and 1974 have gone a long way in providing the Soviet Union not only with a positive current trade balance, but with the wherewithal to service past debt. In some ways this is going according to plan, since much of the Soviet debt was accumulated to finance the natural gas pipelines which by 1973 had begun to operate and therefore to pay for themselves.[7] The big windfall for the U.S.S.R., however, was its petroleum.

Actually, Russia's role as an exporter of petroleum is nothing new. Oil shipments from Baku oil fields by the Nobel Brothers and several other Western-dominated firms made Czarist Russia one of the world's largest exporters of crude oil. Of course, by today's standards, the amounts involved were relatively insignificant, but at the time Russia was a major factor in the world market. It could play this role in part because the Russian economy had not yet developed much need for oil and because the massive quantities of cheap oil in the Middle East were as yet unexploited.

Apart from some brief interruptions brought on by World War I and the revolution, the export of oil from Russia (often to the United States) continued until just before World War II. When reconstruction was completed after the war and exports could be resumed, the Russians were less interested in trading with the nonsocialist countries. Thereafter, from the mid-1940s until the late 1950s, whatever surplus petroleum the Russians had was directed mostly to their East European allies and China. Following Stalin's death, however, the Russians again became much more venturesome and through a series of bold moves resumed their role in the world's petroleum markets.

Russia's initial efforts to reenter world markets were fiercely resisted by the dominant Western oil companies. Since the Western firms owned or influenced most of the noncommunist world's fields, tankers, pipelines, refineries, and sales outlets, most potential customers found it expedient to ignore the Soviet offers for fear of being cut off from their traditional sources.

But in the late 1950s conditions began to change. Aided by

such factors as revolutions in the third world and a willingness to undercut the prevailing world prices for oil, the Russians gradually broke into the oil markets of countries like Ceylon, India, Ghana, Guinea, and Cuba. At first, Western companies with distribution facilities in these areas refused to process or distribute Soviet oil. In the confrontations that resulted, nationalization or threat of nationalization was often the result. Drop by drop, Western firms came to accept the situation and Russian oil began to flow through their pumps not only in Africa and Asia, but in Western Europe.

The biggest breakthrough for the Russians came when Enrico Mattei, head of Italy's state oil company, ENI, decided to force his way into the West European oil market. Although he built his own refineries and filling stations, he still found himself dependent on the Western-owned oil fields for most of his crude oil. To overcome this dependence and despite the political and strategic complications involved, Mattei decided to sign an agreement to buy Russian crude oil. Italy had already been importing minor amounts of petroleum products from the U.S.S.R. as early as 1947 and crude oil beginning in 1951, but major deliveries began only in 1957 after the closing of the Suez Canal in 1956. By 1959 Italy had become the Soviet Union's biggest purchaser of crude oil, and remained that way until about 1970.

Once the Italians had demonstrated that no great harm would come from buying Russian oil, at least in the short run, the other countries in Western Europe soon began to follow Italy's example. By the mid 1960s, moreover, delivery procedures had also been improved. With the construction in 1964 of the Friendship (Druzhba) Pipeline linking Soviet oil fields to Schwedt in East Germany and the Baltic seaports, West European access to Soviet oil had become faster and cheaper. (See Map, p. 110) Oil exports jumped by about 20 percent in 1964 and 1965. The closing of the Suez Canal again in 1967 also served to boost sales, as difficulties in obtaining oil from the Middle East led some heretofore hesitant buyers to sign up with the Russians. Thus by 1968 Finland had come to depend on the USSR for 82 percent of its oil, Iceland for 65 percent, Yugoslavia for 44 percent, Austria for 15 percent, Sweden for 12 percent, and Italy for 11 percent. By 1971, when the United Kingdom finally agreed to import Soviet crude oil, all the major European countries, the United States, and Japan were importing Soviet oil, sometimes in substantial quantities.

It did not take the Russians long to discover that their oil was a highly desirable product. Total crude oil output in the Soviet Union was 394 million metric tons in 1972, and more than one-quarter of production was exported. In 1973 production increased by 7 percent to 421 million tons and exports rose correspondingly by 11 percent to 118.3 million tons. Although the sulfur content in some Soviet oil and gasoline is unusually high, the homogeneous nature of the product makes it easy to penetrate even the most anticommunist markets, especially if the price is low enough and other sources of supply scarce enough. Usually the buyer is unable to tell the difference between Soviet oil and oil from other countries, so the most immediate concern is price and availability and, at least until recently, the Russians have done their best to insure that they are competitive in these areas. Petroleum exports have been a particularly important factor in building up Soviet trade surpluses with most of the hard currency countries of the world. Of the 107 million tons of crude and refined oil exported by the U.S.S.R. in 1972, about 33 million tons were shipped to hard currency countries. These exports earned approximately $570 million for the U.S.S.R., or about $17 a ton (or about $2.30 a barrel). If petroleum exports to Finland are included as hard currency exports, this would boost the 1972 total to over $770 million. (See Table 4–2.) In 1973, despite or perhaps because of the Arab embargo, total hard currency exports rose to 36 million tons and average prices doubled to $35 a ton, so that petroleum export earnings to the hard currency countries (less Finland) more than doubled to $1.3 billion. (By the way, included in that total was $135.6 million, or 3.2 million tons of oil, sold to the beleaguered

TABLE 4–2

Production and Exports of Soviet Oil and Oil Products

	MILLION TONS		MILLION RUBLES [a]	
	1972	1973	1972	1973
Production				
Crude Oil	394	421		
Exports				
Hard currency				
countries [b]	33.8	36.2	483.2	949.6
			$580	$1271.
Finland	8.6	10.0	162.0	221.8
	42.4	46.2	645.2	1171.4
			$776	$1568
Soft currency				
countries				
bloc	60.0	67.4	935.1	1124.8
other	3.3	2.4	55.5	43.3
Subtotal [c]	104.9	116.0		
Reported total	107.0	118.3		

Source: VT SSSR 1972, 1973.
[a] 1972:1 ruble = $1.21.
   1973:1 ruble = $1.34.
[b] Includes West Berlin.
[c] Soviet statistical handbooks do not explain why there is a difference between the Reported total and the Subtotal derived by adding exports on a country-by-country basis. It may be due to the fact that some exports are omitted, such as those to the United States.

Netherlands. That was more than three times [$42 a ton] what the Netherlands had paid in 1972 and was collected in the face of Soviet denials that it was sending "enlarged" exports to the embargoed country.)[8]

There is no doubt that the hard currency receipts of the Soviet Union rose sharply in the aftermath of the Yom Kippur War and the ensuing jump in oil prices. Nonetheless, it was still a bit of a surprise to learn that in March 1974 the Finns agreed to a contract price of about $17 a barrel ($125 a ton). Of course the irony is that although the Iranians had managed to obtain prices that high a few months earlier, by March 1974 the world price had fallen to about $11 a barrel ($80 a ton) or less. When the Russians tried to charge their West German customers $16 a barrel ($116 a ton), the Germans balked and turned to other, cheaper suppliers. Although the Russians had originally worked their way into Western markets with the promise of cut-rate prices, the minute they saw the opportunity they (along with the Arab producers and the Western oil companies) rushed in to squeeze out as much profit as they could. (In their bitterness at Russian profiteering, the former German buyers also complained that the Soviet commitment to deliver oil had not been fully honored. Deliveries in 1973 turned out to be 15 percent below what had been promised.)[9]

Assuming the Russians were able to jack up their hard currency transactions to about $15 a barrel ($110 a ton), that would mean that in 1974 they were able to increase their earnings per barrel about sixfold from the approximately $2.30 a barrel ($17 a ton) they earned in 1972, which in turn would mean they had boosted their petroleum earnings in the hard currency countries from about $580 million in 1972 to about $4 billion. Even more realistic prices of about $10 a barrel ($74 a ton) would bring them revenue in 1974 of over $2.5 billion ($3.2 billion if Finland is included). These earnings will go a long way toward paying for the hard currency purchases of equipment and technology that the Russians have been making over the last decade. Small wonder that they are anxious to retain and expand their oil export opportunities.

SOVIET DOMESTIC NEEDS

As long as the Soviet Union and Eastern Europe deemphasized the production of automobiles and stressed the use of coal rather than oil and natural gas, the Russians could take advantage of these opportunities and divert a considerable portion of any increase in petroleum production to the hard currency export sector. Thus from 1960 to 1965 crude oil production increased by 60 percent. But because production of automotive vehicles grew by only 20 percent, the Russians were able to set aside a disproportionate amount of the increase in oil output for exports, so that crude oil exports increased by 140 percent during the first five years of the 1960s.

Beginning in 1965, however, several Soviet specialists began to warn that the Soviet Union could not sustain this pace. A variety of factors unfavorable for exports began to develop simultaneously. First, the rate of growth of petroleum production began to diminish. From 1965 to 1970, oil production increased by only 45 percent compared to 60 percent in the previous five years. Second and even more important, the Soviet planners concluded that they had made a mistake in assigning priority to coal over oil and natural gas in the country's fuel balance. The countries of the noncommunist world began to switch shortly after World War II. Belatedly the Russians saw that the reason for the switch was that oil and gas at pre-1973 prices were more efficient and cheaper fuels. In the decade of the 1960s, therefore, domestic consumption of both oil and gas in the Soviet Union rose sharply. Finally, in 1966, the decision was made to surrender to the automobile revolution. The Fiat plant was built and production of automotive vehicles accelerated by 50 percent in the years from 1965 to 1970. Combined with the relative slacking in the growth of petroleum production, the sharp increase in demand meant that inevitably there probably would soon be less available for export. Not surprisingly, oil exports for the 1965–1970 period rose by only 50 percent compared to the impressive growth of 140 percent in the earlier 1960–1965 period.

These pressures on exports were supposed to become even more pronounced in the period 1970–1975. According to the goals set out in the Ninth Five-Year Plan, production of motor vehicles in this period was to increase by 130 percent (production of automobiles alone was to grow by 270 percent), while crude oil output was to expand by only 40 percent. At the same time, the switch from coal to oil and natural gas continued. Thus it is logical to assume that the Soviet Union will have to set aside a larger and larger percentage of new oil production for domestic use, leaving less and less for export. Moreover, since the appetite for oil in Eastern Europe has been growing at the same pace as in the Soviet Union, an increasing percentage of the export surplus will have to be diverted to Eastern Europe and away from the hard currency markets. Unless there is a marked change in present trends and unless new sources of supply are found, the Soviet Union may someday be unable to satisfy its own needs and those of Eastern Europe, let alone those of Western Europe, Japan, and the United States.

It is ironic that just as the Soviet salesmen have managed to work their way into lucrative markets of the hard currency countries and the oil-importing countries of the world have found themselves desperately seeking assured supplies of petroleum, the stock available for export to the hard currency markets has begun to diminish. One way to cope with this might be to divert some of the shipments which presently go to Soviet soft currency partners in Eastern Europe. Unfortunately for the Russians, while their 1972 exports of oil and oil products increased by almost 2 million tons, that portion going to the hard currency countries fell by about 3 million tons. The situation improved markedly in 1973, when not only the quantity but, as we saw, the price of petroleum going to the hard currency areas went up significantly.

Even so, while exports to the hard currency capitalist countries rose by 3 to 5 million tons, shipments to the soft currency communist countries rose even more, by about 7 million tons. At the going prices of late 1973, that 7 million tons could have bought at least $500 million more in hard currency if it had been sold to hard currency countries. For that matter, if the Russians could have found some way to take the whole 68 million tons of oil they delivered to their soft currency allies in 1973 and divert it to hard currency purchasers, they could have earned themselves at least $4.5 to $7.5 billion over and above the $2.5 to $4 billion they did earn. As it was, it took enormous restraint for the Russians to keep their soft currency oil prices to the East Europeans at the levels agreed on in the Five-Year Plan for 1970–1975. Despite what was happening all over the world, until early 1975 the Russians did not change their prices to the East Europeans. Thus the average price to Eastern Europe in 1973 (except to Yugoslavia, where the average price almost doubled) held constant at the 1972 level of about 14 to 16 rubles a ton, which was a ruble or two less than what the Russians had charged in 1960. In contrast, whereas the Russians had charged the West Germans only about 10.5 rubles a ton in the 1960s, they were collecting about 38 rubles a ton in 1973. If in the 1960s the East Europeans were being overcharged and the West Europeans undercharged, by 1973 the situation had been reversed. That the Soviet Union was not content with this situation was indicated by complaints from Hungary and East Germany concerning the Soviet Union's insistence on higher prices in 1975 regardless of the existing contract. There were reports that soon after, the U.S.S.R. doubled or tripled its prices. This still left Soviet prices below world prices, but the Soviet Union may insist on another price rise in 1976 with the start of the new five-year-plan. Certainly the opportunity cost in hard currency (the dollars the Soviet Union was precluded from earning because it sold to Eastern instead of Western Europe) to the Soviet Union of such sales has been very high. Yet if the Soviet Union forces the East Europeans to pay world prices, such a sharp increase, whether payable in hard or even soft currency, could produce a series of serious crises in the already fragile economies of Eastern Europe. The problems of West European countries like Italy and Great Britain caused by high petroleum prices would appear almost simple compared to those likely to develop in Eastern Europe.

The diversion of hard currency-earning exports to soft currency allies also helps explain why the Soviets began to complain that their allies had come to rely too much on the U.S.S.R. The Russians have strongly urged other communist countries to move actively into the less developed regions of the world for their supplies of raw materials—particularly petroleum. As they repeat over and over again:

The steadily growing demand of the CMEA member countries for oil and the desire of these countries to improve their consumption can be met not only by deliveries of oil via the Friendship Oil Pipeline and expansion of their own oil production, but also from the developing countries of the Middle East and the African continent. Increased oil deliveries from these countries can be carried out at the cost of rendering technical assistance to the developing countries in establishing their national oil industries, and by engaging in other forms of cooperation.[10]

And the socialist countries of Eastern Europe have in fact begun to look elsewhere for supplemental supplies of oil.[11] For that matter, so have the Russians.

THE MIDDLE EAST

The most logical place for the East Europeans to supplement their oil supplies is in the Middle East. Precise information about the kinds and magnitude of the various deals is difficult to obtain, but it is possible to sketch out the general strategy. Wherever possible, the Russians and their allies have sought to avoid spending hard currency to obtain their supplies, although there is evidence that after the Yom Kippur War some Middle East countries began to insist on hard currency payments for their oil. But from the Soviet point of view a successful deal is one in which oil is obtained in exchange for a Soviet-produced commodity. Such an arrangement is preferred because it is often the only way the Russians can sell their goods. Since Soviet-manufactured products are generally regarded as inferior to those of the other developed countries of the world, the Russians have discovered that if they are to make a sale they normally have to offer long-term credits to the buyer in order to make it worth his while to take Soviet goods. In the same spirit, the Russians are then usually content to take commodities as repayment. Since such credits are usually extended for at least

95

12 years, they are often treated as foreign aid, although, for the most part, Soviet foreign aid might more appropriately be described as delayed barter.

Because of such deals the Russians have periodically found themselves wallowing in commodities like Cuban sugar and Brazilian coffee. Increasingly, therefore, they have tried to arrange projects in which repayment could be made in more desirable commodities such as oil or natural gas. This accounts at least partially for Soviet loans to Iraq, Iran, and Afghanistan of almost $500 million, to Algeria for over $400 million, and even to Egypt, where it has extended economic loans alone totaling over $1 billion. Shipments of billions of dollars worth of Soviet military equipment were to be repaid in the same way.

Some of these deals have already resulted in a direct payoff in oil and gas, or in the promise of such a payoff. The Iraqis assigned exploration rights to the Russians in the rich Rumalia and Kirkuk oil fields after these oil fields had been nationalized from British Petroleum in 1971 and Iraq Petroleum in 1972. As shown in Table 4–3, the Russians received 4 million tons (all measures are in metric tons) of crude oil from Iraq in 1972, worth 58 million rubles (about $64 million), and about 11 million tons in 1973, worth 185.9 million rubles (about $250 million).

The first Soviet imports of Middle Eastern oil apparently began in 1967, when the Soviets received 61,000 tons from Algeria. By 1969 the Algerians were sending close to 500,000 tons, worth about $7 million. This rose to 750,000 tons and $17 million in 1971. Egypt shipped over $9 million worth of oil to the Soviet Union in 1969 and about $15 million (2 million tons) in both 1970 and 1971. Shipments from both Algeria and Egypt ended or declined in 1972 and 1973, but these declines were more than made up for by the substantial shipments from Iraq as well as sales by Libya of about 1.8 million tons in 1972 and 1973. (See Table 4–3.) Libya's oil came primarily from the former British Petroleum concession in the Sarir oil field, which she nationalized in 1972.

As indicated in Table 4–3, "Reported total" Soviet purchases of Middle Eastern crude oil increased about 2 million tons a year from 1968 to 1972 and then in chaotic 1973 jumped by over 5 million tons. It is not known, however, if this figure accounts for all the crude oil transferred by the Middle Eastern countries to the U.S.S.R. It frequently happens in international trade that commodities are loaded aboard a ship with no intention of ever sending them to the port listed on the ship's manifest. The destination is often changed en route depending on how market conditions change. The Russians follow this practice with other commodities, and there is good reason to believe they do it with petroleum as well.[12] If so, it remains unclear how they classify such petroleum transfers in their foreign trade statistics. Although they may never show up as imports, such transactions can be very important to the

TABLE 4–3

Soviet Crude Oil Imports

	1967	1968	1969	1970	1971	1972	1973
Algeria							
1,000 tons	61.3	123.8	495.4	494.2	749	570	NOR [a]
Iraq							
1,000 tons	NOR	NOR	NOR	NOR	NOR	4,084	11,010
Libya							
1,000 tons	NOR	NOR	NOR	NOR	NOR	1,867	1,713
Saudi Arabia							
1,000 tons	NOR	NOR	19.7	NOR	NOR	NOR	NOR
Egypt							
1,000 tons	NOR	NOR	934.8	2,022	2,040	971	209
Syria							
1,000 tons	NOR	NOR	NOR	NOR	NOR	315	247
Sum total							
1,000 tons	61.3	123.8	1,449.9	2,516.2	2,789	7,807	13,179
1,000 rubles	796	1,612	14,797	21,743	28,703	107,794	220,265
Reported total							
1,000 tons	100	900	2,500	3,500	5,100	7,800	13,200
1,000 rubles				31,200	56,700	111,185	220,265

Source: Country figures—*VT SSSR 1968*, p. 264; *1970*, pp. 251, 262, 274; *1972*, pp. 237, 276, 282, 286; *1973*, pp. 237, 265, 274, 284. Reported total—*VT SSSR 1968*, p. 49; *VT SSSR 1970*, p. 49; *VT SSSR 1971*, p. 141; *1972*, p. 41; *1973*, p. 41.
[a] NOR—None Officially Reported.

Russians if they follow their usual practice of selling their oil exports for hard currency and paying for their oil imports with soft Soviet rubles or with materials supplied under the Soviet foreign or military aid program.

The Russians are less than forthcoming about such matters in their trade statistics, and the analyst finds himself faced with many unexplained gaps. For example, there is a figure showing the Russians' total tonnage of crude oil imports from 1967, when they first began importing crude oil, until the present time. But as shown in Table 4–3, Soviet statisticians do not always indicate where all of this crude oil comes from. Thus there is a gap between the official "Reported total" and the figure derived by adding together imports on a country-by-country basis. In 1968 the discrepancy came to 800,000 tons, in 1969 1 million tons, and in 1971 about 2.5 million tons. Although all of the imports are accounted for in 1972 and 1973, the question remains: Who else sold the Soviet Union crude oil from 1967 to 1971? Moreover, did the "total import" figures reflect Soviet oil shipments from the Middle Eastern countries that were subsequently resold, or were they limited to that crude oil that ended up in the Soviet Union itself and was not reexported?[13] (Nor do the Soviets always publish complete information about their exports. Thus the U.S. government reported it imported $76 million worth of petroleum from the U.S.S.R. in 1973, including $40 million received during the embargo. But Soviet statistics as of 1975 contained no hint of such a transaction.)

Regardless of how they handle the statistics, there is no doubt that when the Middle Eastern countries limit production or divert large amounts of oil from the traditional Western oil consumers, the Russians find it hard to resist the temptation to reroute their shipments to countries like the United States. So far the amount of Russian oil involved in such transactions has been too small to eliminate the problem for the United States. Nevertheless, because they are in need of dollars and hard currency, the Russians feel a much greater pressure to sell products to the United States, Western Europe, and Japan than do such traditional suppliers as Saudi Arabia and Kuwait. That is why, in the last few years, they have been intent on opening up new markets wherever possible, even at the expense of the Middle Eastern countries themselves.

This is exactly what happened in the aftermath of the Six-Day War when the Russians failed to honor the temporary embargo imposed by some of the Middle Eastern countries. Similarly, in 1971, the Russians saw nothing wrong with increasing their penetration of the oil markets in Morocco and Ghana even though it came at the expense of Algeria and Libya, respectively. In the aftermath of Iraq's nationalization of the Kirkuk oil fields, formerly a concession of British Petroleum, the Iraqis turned to the U.S.S.R. in 1972 in the hope that the Russians would take some of the oil off their hands. The Russians in turn extended concrete offers to sell this oil to American importers for delivery in 1973.[14]

Middlemanning it became particularly important for the Russians during the Yom Kippur War. While much of what happened during the petroleum embargo that arose during the war is hard to authenticate, there is good reason to believe that the Russians and the Rumanians used their intermediary status and the sudden world shortage of oil to increase their profits and dollar earnings.

The oil business has never been noted for its straightforwardness or aboveboard dealings. Yet the oil industry before October 1973 is simplicity itself compared to the intrigue that took place in the months that followed. It is likely that no one will ever be able to untangle exactly what happened during those traumatic months. What we do know is that the Arabs did not extend their embargo to the U.S.S.R. and Eastern Europe. This was important to some of the poorer Arab countries like Iraq which were anxious to take advantage of the sudden climb in prices. Unlike their richer neighbors in Kuwait and Saudi Arabia, the rulers of Iraq and Algeria had limited cash reserves on hand and wanted to sell while they could. Indeed, the Iraqis acknowledged that they had increased their daily output from 1.5 million barrels a day in 1972 to 2.1 million during the 1973 war, and that they had plans to increase that to 3.5 million by 1975, embargo notwithstanding. Yet the Iraqis and those with similar views sought to cover themselves by insisting that they were not sending any of this additional oil to the countries being embargoed. This meant that some other buyer had to be found. Intermediary countries like the Soviet Union and Rumania were obvious candidates.

Once the oil had been shipped, the Russians and Rumanians found they had considerable room to maneuver. In all (or at least partial) honesty, they could assert that they were observing the letter of the embargo by sending their increased shipments of Middle Eastern oil only to other CMEA members, as they were permitted to do by the Arabs.[15] Yet there is every reason to believe that without stretching the truth too far, the Russians and Rumanians managed to increase petroleum shipments to many old customers in Western Europe as well as to some new ones like the United States and Canada. For while the Russians were innocently enough directing their increased supplies of Iraqi oil to Hungary and Czechoslovakia, they were diverting the *Soviet-produced oil* originally intended for those areas to the hard currency bloc. In the same way, Alexander Trowbridge of the Conference Board in New York has concluded, the Rumanians had begun to supply the United States with substantial quantities of oil, made possible in one way or another by initial sales by Libya to Rumania. Canada received oil by means of similar manipulations. Thus it probably was more than just coincidence that the 5 million-ton increase in imports from the Middle East to the Soviet Union in 1974 also happened to approximate the increase in Soviet oil exports to Western Europe, Japan, and the United States. While exports to Eastern Europe also increased, it is logical to assume that any extra oil the Soviet Union had went to the hard currency rather than soft currency markets. There seems little doubt that Soviet oil imports from the Middle East, particularly Iraq, made it possible for the Russians to increase their overall petroleum exports by 11 percent in 1973, even though, as we saw, their domestic output of crude petroleum increased by only 7 percent and their domestic demand for petroleum continued to eat rapidly into any exportable surplus. Whatever the explanation, the increased sales of "Soviet petroleum" outside the CMEA bloc served to blunt the effect of the embargo and at the same time increased the hard currency earnings of Russia and Rumania and thus their purchasing power in countries like the United States.

EASTERN EUROPE

As indicated by the actions of the Rumanians, Russia's East European allies are pursuing the same strategy of seeking additional supplies outside of the U.S.S.R. Already 15 percent of East Germany's oil is imported from Middle Eastern countries. Egypt alone provides one-half million tons. Algeria is also a supplier, and they were joined by Iraq, which recently received an $84 million loan from East Germany which, as usual, is repayable primarily in oil. Czechoslovakia has also extended a loan of $32 million to Iraq and expects to receive up to 5 million tons of oil in exchange. Hungary and Bulgaria have also provided loans to Iraq. In 1970 Hungary extended $20 million and an additional $50 million in August 1972.[16] In exchange Hungary received 700,000 tons of oil in 1972, which was to be increased to 5 million tons a year by 1975. Shipments to Bulgaria were to start with 500,000 tons in 1974, grow to 1 million tons in 1975, and continue at that pace until 1980. In addition, the Yugoslavs signed a barter agreement with Iraq for 12 million tons of oil over a ten-year period.

Rumanian negotiators have focused on Iran, Egypt, Algeria, Libya, and Iraq. In 1972 Algeria agreed to sell Rumania 5 million tons of oil over an undisclosed period. Like the Russians, the Rumanians have also arranged to obtain oil from Libya's Sarir oil field. Initially they agreed to buy 1.5 million tons of oil a year, but this was increased to at least 2.5 million tons a year after the outbreak of the Yom Kippur War.

It is worth adding a special word about the Rumanians. Except for the Russians, they are the only Eastern European country with any major deposits of crude oil. Now, however, they are no longer self-sufficient so they also have to look elsewhere. Whether it is because of their past experience in the oil industry or just because they are Rumanians, their deals are more sophisticated than those of anyone else in the Middle East. They have arranged for larger imports of Middle Eastern oil than anyone else in Eastern Europe. They are particularly large purchasers of Iranian oil. The other East European countries would have trouble gaining access to this oil since it is difficult to ship through Iraq, with whom Iran is at odds, or through the ARAMCO owned pipeline. But Rumania has no such trouble. Partly as a by-product of their remarkably independent stance toward the U.S.S.R., the Rumanians maintain good relations with Israel, and Israel, by more than coincidence, happens to have a pipeline which serves as a major conduit through which Iranian oil moves to Europe. The Rumanians reportedly receive over 50 percent of their oil from Iran through Israel's Elat-Ashkelon pipeline. Although it is just a rumor, one reliable source reports that the Russians have also received oil through the Israeli pipeline.[17]

Like the Rumanians and Russians, the Bulgarians in 1972 also signed up for 500,000 tons of oil from the Sarir oil field in Libya and expect to buy 1 million tons a year thereafter. The Libyans also plan to sell about 5 million tons a year to the Yugoslavs.[18] Even Saudi Arabia is engaging in trade with Eastern Europe. There were reports of a deal with Rumania, presumably for cash, and the Saudis have agreed to deliver 1.8 million tons of oil to the Yugoslavs in exchange for two oil tankers.

Encouraged if not forced by the Russians to look elsewhere for their oil, some East Europeans have branched out further afield and in different directions than might otherwise have been expected.[19] Instead of turning to the East, they turned West. Thus,

Rumania made a deal with Shell Oil. Poland has agreed to the construction of a series of service stations jointly run by CPN-AGIP and it also has contracted with British Petroleum (BP) to build a refinery and supply it with 3 million tons of crude oil a year for 10 years at a price estimated to be close to $500 million. BP also has arranged to sell oil to East Germany. Hungary has negotiated oil purchases with AGIP, Shell, and BP.[20] Shell's, BP's, and AGIP's agreements with Hungary permit them to move directly to the retail level and to open up ten service stations. Mobil and Exxon have also contracted to provide oil to East European purchasers. Some of this oil will undoubtedly move through the pipeline which is to be built by 1976 from Yugoslavia's northern Adriatic coast at Omisalj, with one branch heading to Hungary, Czechoslovakia, and Poland and the other branch leading to Rumania. This pipeline, which Kuwait and Libya have offered to help finance, will carry Middle Eastern oil primarily from Iraq and Iran and should reduce the dependency of these countries on the U.S.S.R.

WESTERN EUROPE

Not to be outdone by their East European neighbors, the Russians have also shown considerable imagination and flexibility in their dealings with Western Europe. From being simply suppliers of oil to Western European companies and countries, they have begun to sell gasoline and oil directly to the West European automobile driver.

There are basically three types of approaches the Russians have used: direct sales, swap sales, and joint stock companies or direct operations. Direct sales of oil are made by tanker and through the Friendship pipeline to foreign companies, which then refine or sell the petroleum to their own customers. The original pipeline to

Czechoslovakia was completed in 1962. It now runs from Alme-
tyevsk near the Kama River, about 500 miles east of Moscow, to
Mozyr in Belorussia, where it branches to Poland and East Germany in the north and Czechoslovakia and Hungary in the south.
(See Map, p. 110) By extending their pipelines to Bratislava, Czechoslovakia, the Russians were able to arrange for the sale of both
oil and natural gas to Western Europe with a minimum of confusion. The pipeline lies entirely within the borders of Czechoslovakia. (The East Germans reportedly were particularly distressed by
this. Not only were they upset that the Russians could now deal
directly with the Germans without the chance of an East German
veto, but they were also bothered that until 1973, the Russians
had not even provided them with a natural gas connection.) There
is also a branch of the pipeline before Mozyr which swings north
within the U.S.S.R. and terminates at the port city of Ventspils,
near Riga in Soviet Latvia. This serves as a major distribution
point for consumers in Northern Europe. The completed pipeline
extends for more than 3,000 miles.

The Russians have also built a second parallel pipeline to supplement the original Friendship pipeline. Friendship 2, as it is
called, was completed through Hungary in September 1972 and
now makes possible an annual flow of 50 million tons of oil a
year.[21] The combined pipeline network has also been extended
1,200 miles to link up with the more recently discovered fields in
Samotlor in the Tyumen region of West Siberia. In anticipation of
increased volume of direct sales in the future, the Russians have
been dutifully increasing their tanker fleet, and also have plans to
enlarge the pipeline to Western Europe by 1975.

Swap sales were largely a result of the closing of the Suez Canal,
which not only made it more difficult for Western firms to ship
crude from the oil fields along the Persian Gulf, but created even
graver problems for the Russians in moving their oil from the
Black Sea ports to customers in Japan and other Asian countries.
Some Western companies were at least able to move their oil to
the Mediterranean through pipelines running through Syria,
Egypt, and even Israel. Unfortunately for the Russians, the flow of

oil in these pipelines is from east to west, whereas the Russians want to move their oil in the reverse direction. That is why it was an important step forward for the Russians when they were able to arrange with Western companies to swap oil supplies. For example, a Swiss company traded the Russians 3.5 million tons of oil in a Persian Gulf port for an equivalent amount in the Black Sea port. By by-passing the Suez Canal, the Russians were then able to fulfill their contracts in Japan and Burma on time and at a cheaper cost. At the same time, the Swiss company sold its Russian oil to a French company, which then delivered it to a group of Italian purchasers. BP has engaged in similar swaps with the Russians. BP exchanges Abu Dhabi crude, which eventually is sold by the Russians to the Idemitsu Kosan Company in Japan. In turn, BP takes Russian crude, which then is mixed into the regular BP marketing network.

Having gone this far, it seems only natural that the Russians should go on to establish operations directly in Western Europe. As long as they limited themselves to direct or swap sales, the Russians could do no more than make a profit on the sale of crude oil. Perhaps it was natural, therefore, that like others before them, the Russians eventually concluded that they could also profit from the refining and marketing of the product directly to the West European consumer by opening foreign affiliates that would refine and sell imported oil, just like Shell, Exxon, Mobil, BP, and ENI.

When embarking on an overseas investment, the Russians tend to follow the patterns established by other foreign investors. Frequently they form a partnership with indigenous businessmen. This helps to make the venture more acceptable to local authorities not only from a business but from a political point of view. Another strategy is to buy up an existing company. This makes it easier to establish a market foothold, especially when the competition and customers tend to resent foreign intrusion. They have used both tactics in operating their oil enterprises in Western Europe.

There are at least three oil markets that the Russians have selected. In partnership with ELF-ERAP, a state-operated oil company in France, the Soviet oil-exporting corporation Soiuznefteekhsport has announced plans to build a refinery which would possibly be located at Le Havre.[22] If built, presumably this refinery will not limit itself to French consumers but will sell to oil-marketing outlets throughout the Common Market. Certain to be included among the French refinery's customers is Nafta GB Ltd. of England, which is wholly owned by the Soviet Ministry of Foreign Trades Soiuznefteekhsport. Included among the French refinery's customers is Nafta GB Ltd. which is wholly owned by Soiuznefteekhsport. Actually, the sale of Soviet oil in the United Kingdom began before World War II. Then representatives from the Soviet Ministry of Foreign Trade opened up a gasoline service station network called ROP (Russian Oil Products) to sell oil from the Soviet Union. At one time, ROP had 10 percent of the petroleum market in Great Britain.[23] This marketing operation was sold, however, during World War II to Regents Oil which in turn was purchased by the Texaco Oil Company. In 1957, the Soviet Union reentered the market under the Nafta GB Ltd. name. Presently Nafta GB has 250 filling stations located in London and in the southeast of the United Kingdom. Pending completion of the Le Havre refinery, Nafta Ltd. has arranged for the refining of 150,000 tons of petroleum a year at BP's refinery on the Isle of Grain in Kent.

Nafta GB Ltd. could not import oil directly from the Soviet Union until 1971, when the British for the first time since 1941 decided to allow them to do so. Previously Nafta Ltd. imported most of its supplies from Finland. Since Finland's oil fields have not been particularly noted for their quality, much less their quantity, and since, as we saw, Finland received over 80 percent of its oil from Soviet suppliers, it is not altogether clear just how much the ultimate sources of supply for Nafta GB Ltd. will actually be affected by this new, more direct policy.

With their sources of supply assured, some Nafta GB Ltd. dealers have mounted an aggressive marketing campaign. It has been impossible to verify but at one time a story circulated that in an effort to build up sales, one station owner decided to hire female attendants and dress them in microskirts and see-through blouses. With the Exxon marketing campaign in mind, he then began to advertise, "After the American tiger, the Russian bare."

Perhaps the most ambitious Soviet undertaking is in Belgium, where the Russians seem to be experimenting with a little of everything. On December 1, 1967, Soiuznefteekhsport joined with two Belgian coal-importing companies, the Belgium Bunkering Co. and Antoine Vloeberghs Co., to form a diversified petroleum company which they gave the same name as the British company, Nafta B. Initially the Belgian partners contributed 40 percent of the capital, which was only $60,000. By 1971, however, the capital value of the firm had increased to $15 million and the share of the Belgian partners had fallen to less than 10 percent.[24]

Nafta was located in the port area of Antwerp, where a 60-acre site was equipped with Soviet-built storage tanks designed to hold 500,000 tons of crude oil and 750,000 tons of refined products. Much of this oil has come by way of the Baltic Sea from the pipeline connection in Latvia. Nafta B of Belgium has also tried to obtain a refinery. Its efforts were opposed by Belgian oil companies, which fiercely resisted Soviet incursions, however. Thus far Nafta B has purchased the site, but has not been allowed to build the refinery.

The operation of Nafta B of Belgium is highly suggestive of things to come. When convenient, the Russians will apparently continue to import crude oil directly from the Soviet Union. But they evidently see no reason to make their hard currency sales of oil dependent solely on the availability of oil for export from the Soviet Union itself. Like Exxon, Shell, Mobil, BP, and ENI, the Russians have begun to sell oil which originates outside the country where the home office is located. Like their Western counterparts, moreover, the Russians find nothing wrong with making money simply by acting as a middleman. Thus, in 1967, Soviet exports of crude oil to Belgium were 339,000 tons; that same year, Nafta sales in Belgium were 300,000 tons. In 1969, however, while the U.S.S.R. exported only 758,000 tons of oil to Belgium, Nafta sold 1,500,000 tons. The following year, although Soviet exports totaled 1,275,000 tons, Nafta's sales climbed to 2,500,000 tons.[25] The difference was presumably made up with oil from the Middle East. The Soviet oil dealer, therefore, like Exxon and BP, is serving as a middleman. He buys oil in one country (not necessarily his own), sells it in another (also not necessarily his own), and pockets the profit in hard currency.

NATURAL GAS

Almost everything that has been said about the emergence of the Soviet oil dealer onto the international market can also be said about the Soviet dealer in natural gas. Perhaps even more so, for the Soviet purchase and resale of natural gas epitomizes the Soviet Union's transformation from autarchy to independence in its trade relations.

Soviet export of natural gas goes back at least to the late 1940s, when the Russians exported small amounts to Poland. But it was only in 1966 and 1967, with the completion of Bratstvo (Fraternal), a natural gas pipeline from the Soviet Union to Bratislava, Czechoslovakia, that natural gas exports increased in any significant way. On September 1, 1968, with the pipeline built, the Soviets extended their sales to Austria. The Austrians supplement their purchases from the Soviet Union with some of the natural gas originally sold by the Soviets to the Czechs. The Czechs have also learned how to act as middlemen.

As was true in the case of Soviet oil, exports of natural gas began to rise dramatically in the late 1960s, just as the growth of domestic supplies began to slacken. Furthermore, with completion of a natural gas pipeline linking all the major cities in the Soviet Union, and with apparently larger untapped reserves of natural gas

than of oil, the U.S.S.R. moved even faster than with oil in sub-
stituting natural gas for coal.

In their effort to enlarge supplies, the Soviets responsible for the
sale of natural gas did exactly what their counterparts in the oil industry had done. They arranged to inject large quantities of
foreign natural gas into their distributive network. As we saw, the
U.S.S.R. extended large sums of foreign aid to Afghanistan and
Iran. In the established pattern, both countries have arranged for
repayment to be made in the form of natural gas which is fed into
the Soviet pipeline on the Afghan and Iranian borders from gas
fields that are cut off from the coasts and from possible sale to
hard currency countries. (See Map, p. 110) Afghanistan began its
deliveries in 1967, just in time to offset the start of Soviet deliveries to Czechoslovakia and Austria. Although by 1972 total exports of natural gas from the Soviet Union already exceeded 5
billion cubic meters, the Russians were never forced to divert more
than about 1 billion cubic meters from domestic production. By
1970 the Russians had actually become net importers of gas. (See
Table 4–4.) As of 1972 they were importing 2.8 billion cubic
meters from Afghanistan and 8.2 billion cubic meters from Iran,
for a total of 11 billion cubic meters. At the same time, since exports to West Germany had not as yet begun, the Soviet Union
only sold 1.6 billion cubic meters to Austria, 1.5 billion cubic
meters to Poland, and 1.9 billion cubic meters to Czechoslovakia.
Total exports were 5.1 billion cubic meters, which left the Russians with a 6-billion-cubic-meter net import deficit. Approximately the same pattern prevailed in 1973.

Not only have the Russians sought to protect themselves by off-
setting their exports with imports wherever possible, but they
have also tried to make money on the deal. Thus in 1972 they
paid Iran and Afghanistan about 5–6 rubles in soft currency per
1,000 cubic meters (about $.18–$.19 per 1,000 cubic feet). But
they sold it to Austria at 11.5 to 12.5 rubles per 1,000 cubic
meters ($.40–$.44 per 1,000 cubic feet) and to Czechoslovakia
and Poland at 13–14 rubles per 1,000 cubic meters ($.46–$.49

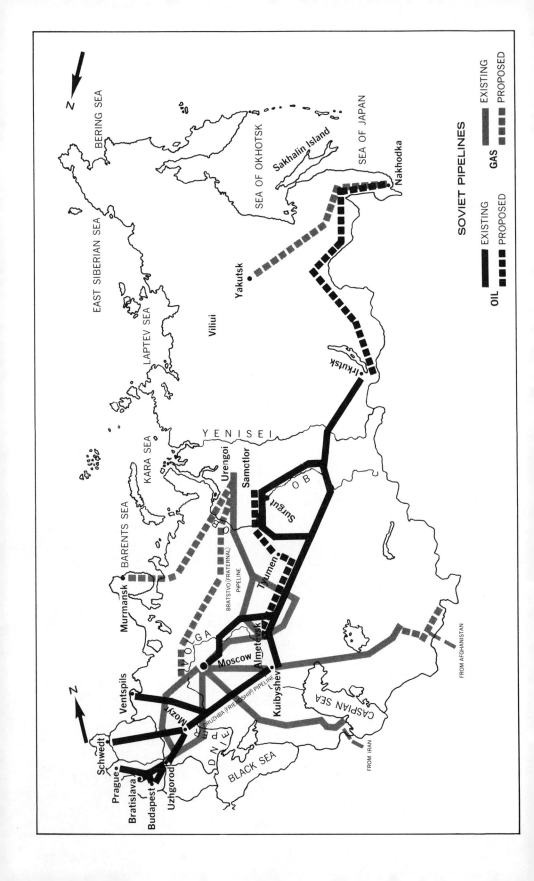

SOVIET PIPELINES

OIL
EXISTING
PROPOSED

GAS
EXISTING
PROPOSED

BERING SEA

EAST SIBERIAN SEA

LAPTEV SEA

SEA OF OKHOTSK

Sakhalin Island

SEA OF JAPAN

Nakhodka

Yakutsk

Viliui

Irkutsk

YENISEI

Urengoi

Samotlor

Surgut

OB

KARA SEA

BARENTS SEA

Murmansk

BRATSTVO (FRATERNAL) PIPELINE

O B

Tiumen

VOLGA

Moscow

Almetevsk

Kuibyshev

DRUZHBA (FRIENDSHIP) PIPELINE

CASPIAN SEA

FROM AFGHANISTAN

FROM IRAN

Ventspils

Mozyr

Schwedt

Prague

Bratislava

Budapest

Uzhgorod

DNIE PER

BLACK SEA

N

N

TABLE 4-4

Soviet Natural Gas Imports and Exports
(volume in million cubic meters)

	1965	1966	1967	1968	1969	1970	1971	1972	1973
IMPORTS									
Afghanistan			206.7	1500.	2029.7	2590.7	2513.	2849.4	2735
Iran			0	0	0	964.9	5622.6	8197	8680
Total			206.7	1500	2029.7	3555.6	8135.6	11046.4	11415
EXPORTS									
Austria	0	0	0	142	781.7	956.3	1428.4	1633	1622
Czechoslovakia	0	0	265.2	587.4	888.6	1341.4	1639.3	1937.3	2362
Poland	391.5	827.9	1025.3	999.7	993.8	1002.4	1487.7	1500	1710
Total	391.5	827.9	1290.5	1729.1	2664.1	3300.1	4555.4	5070.3	5694
Misc.[a]									1100
Combined total									6800
Net exports	391.5	827.9	1083.8	229.1	634.4	−255.5	−3580.2	−5976.1	−4615

Source: Various issues of *VT SSSR.*
[a] Miscellaneous exports to West Germany begin in October 1973 but are not officially reported in the statistical handbook.

per 1,000 cubic feet). The Iranians were very unhappy about these arrangements, especially after they found that they could sell their natural gas from other fields more accessible to the coast to the French and Japanese for about 9 rubles per 1,000 cubic meters, or $.33 per 1,000 cubic feet.[26] (In October 1973 they even agreed to sell some to the United States.) After a good deal of pressure from the Iranians, the Russians finally agreed in 1972 to increase their payments to Iran by 70 percent to $.30.7 per 1,000 cubic feet, or 8.7 rubles per 1,000 cubic meters. That satisfied Iran for a time, but after the explosion in energy prices in late 1973 she demanded a further 100 percent price hike to $.61.9 per 1,000 cubic feet, or 17.5 rubles per 1,000 cubic meters—which would have been even more than the Soviet Union was getting from its sales of gas to the West. After two weeks of intense negotiation, including a bluff by the Soviet Union that at such prices it would stop all purchases of Iranian gas, the U.S.S.R. and Iran agreed on August 8, 1974, on a compromise price increase of $.57 per 1,000 cubic feet, or 16.1 rubles per 1,000 cubic meters, retroactive to January 1, 1974. With the higher price, the U.S.S.R. was now paying about $.10–$.15 more than it was collecting from the Austrians for the sale of the same type of gas. To compensate, the Soviet Union will probably raise the price of its gas to Eastern and Western Europe. The U.S.S.R. indicated that it would also increase the prices on the material it was supplying to the Iranians as part of the initial barter agreement by a corresponding amount.

Because of their lack of alternatives (the Russians buy almost all of the natural gas produced in Afghanistan), the Afghans have been less dissatisfied than the Iranians. Nonetheless, an agreement was reached in 1974 to raise the price the Russians pay Afghanistan—5 to 6 rubles per 1,000 cubic meters to about 9.6 rubles per 1,000 cubic meters, or $.34 per 1,000 cubic feet (a bit more than half of what the Iranians will collect).

Despite these difficulties, there seems to be little doubt that the Russians are counting heavily on such infusions of imported natural gas to support an enormous expansion of exports. In the late 1960s they embarked on a massive drive to sell natural gas throughout Western Europe, which thus far has met with remarkable success. Extension of their natural gas pipeline from Czechoslovakia to West Germany in October 1973 has enabled them to supply increasing amounts of natural gas to West Germany, and by 1980 the flow is expected to reach about 9.5 billion cubic meters (which is equivalent to the total amount of natural gas consumed by the West Germans in 1970).[27] Starting in 1976, the French have agreed to purchase 2.5 billion cubic meters a year until 1980 and 4 billion cubic meters until 1996. With the opening of the Transaustna gas pipeline (TAC) in May 1974, the Italians began to receive their first Soviet deliveries. By 1979 they will receive 6 billion cubic meters a year. By 1980 Soviet deliveries will amount to as much as 70 percent of all the gas the Italians consumed in 1972. At about the same time, the Austrians are to receive an allotment increased from 1.6 billion cubic meters to 2.4

billion cubic meters. Finland and Sweden are reported to be seeking similar commitments. A natural gas pipeline to Finland was opened in January 1974. By 1979 Finland expects to purchase 1.4 billion cubic meters and, if the Russians agree, possibly 3 billion cubic meters of natural gas a year from the Soviet Union.[28] The Swedes hope to import their gas via Finland by 1978. For the non-socialist countries alone, the Russians have arranged to sell anywhere from 18 to 28 billion cubic meters of natural gas a year by 1980.

To make such deals, the Russians are prepared to negotiate some very intricate arrangements. As originally contemplated, the sale of Soviet natural gas to France would have had to wait until the Russians had time to add a French connection to their Friendship pipeline. Instead, the Russians engineered a four-party deal whereby they will deliver gas intended for France to Italy, which already has plans to tie in to the Russian network. In turn, the Italians will transfer their option for the delivery of natural gas from the Netherlands to the French. By means of such sophisticated transactions, extensive transportation was eliminated.

It is true that Soviet deposits of natural gas are among the largest in the world. Still, the U.S.S.R.'s ability to export 18–25 billion cubic meters of natural gas a year by 1980 to Western Europe and about 15 billion cubic meters to Eastern Europe will undoubtedly be helped considerably by the fact that at the same time they should be importing at least 13.5 billion cubic meters a year. Thus, shipments from Afghanistan are to rise to 3.5 billion cubic meters a year and continue until 1985. Imports of natural gas from Iran are to total 10 billion cubic meters a year in 1974, also as a repayment for Soviet aid. Reportedly the total flow of gas from Iran (not including that which the Germans are trying to buy from Iran via the U.S.S.R.) will actually total 20 billion cubic meters. The Russians presently have commitments of imports which will cover as much as one-half of their projected annual exports.

At one time it was claimed that these natural gas imports would be consumed in the Central Asian and Caucasian republic of the U.S.S.R. While this may be partially true, the natural gas pipeline in the U.S.S.R. makes it possible to move gas from one point in the system throughout the entire network. In fact, several deposits of Soviet natural gas are located in regions considerably more distant from the Bratislava outlet of the natural gas pipeline than those in Iran and Afghanistan. (See Map, p. 110) It would not be surprising if the Russians sought to secure other sources of supply from outside their borders to make possible even larger reexports.

RESELLING AND HARD CURRENCY

All of this contributes to the hard currency earnings of the U.S.S.R. Whether the Russians sell their own oil and natural gas or the Middle East's, the effect is the same, at least as long as the Soviet Union repays the Middle Eastern countries either with its own soft currency or with materials produced in the U.S.S.R. This point is missed by those who concentrate on the net export position of the Soviet Union. In dealing with Soviet (as opposed to other countries') foreign trade statistics and their effect on the Soviet ability to buy hard currency items, what counts is total exports to hard currency countries, not just net exports. Thus Robert Keatley in the *Wall Street Journal* notes that "the USSR is already a net *importer* of natural gas," implying that the Soviet Union will have or is having its own energy crisis.[29] On the contrary, for the Soviet Union, importation of natural gas is a decided asset. As we saw, at one time the Soviet Union was paying 5–6 rubles per 1,000 cubic meters for gas in soft currency (i.e., otherwise called foreign aid and/or delayed barter) and selling it for double the amount to Austria in hard currency and at almost triple the price to Czechoslovakia and Poland (albeit in soft currency). Even more important, this net import balance will last only briefly. Probably in 1974 and certainly by 1975 trade statistics will show the U.S.S.R. to be a net exporter of natural gas. By then the pipelines will have opened up to the hard currency countries in Western Europe, particularly Italy, West Germany, and France. It is to be expected that the Russians will do all they can to maximize the export capacity of their 30-billion-cubic-meters-a-year Trans-European pipeline. Then the U.S.S.R. will wish that it had even more imports that it could convert into hard currency sales. It really doesn't matter how much oil the Soviet Union imports, since its foreign exchange position will not suffer as long as: 1) it pays soft currency to the Middle East supplier (or pays with bartered industrial or military equipment); 2) it does not have to pay hard currency for shipping the oil to the Soviet Union; and 3) it increases its exports to the hard currency countries. Even if it has to pay hard currency to some of the Arab suppliers, the Soviet Union will not suffer financially as long as it can buy cheaper than it sells or it can offset such demands with equal demands for higher prices for its economic aid or for cash for its military equipment (which has been its major export to the Middle East). Reportedly the Soviet Union collected $2 to $4 billion in hard currency for its military equipment in 1973 and 1974.

In any case, however it obtains its oil or natural gas, the U.S.S.R. does not lack hard currency customers. Two of the most interested onlookers have been the United States and Japan. The Japanese have been purchasing oil from the Soviet Union for some time (3 million tons in 1971, 1 million in 1972, and 2 million in 1973, plus an extra 1 million tons in 1972 and 1973 that apparently came from a third country), and we have seen how the United States has also received oil from the Soviet Union in recent years. Such modest amounts could hardly be expected to satisfy the needs of either the United States or Japan, both of which imported about 300 million tons of oil in 1973. But in the new era of energy shortage, everything helps.

The question remains: How much oil will Russians be able to

export from within their own country in the future? Certainly their own energy needs are increasing. Yet their reserves, even if not thoroughly verified by Western specialists, are substantial. Although there is a good deal of dispute over just how large they are, the United Nations estimated Soviet petroleum reserves in 1970 as totaling approximately 8 billion tons.[30] Compared to the 40 or 50 billion tons thought to be in the Middle East, this is not very much. Yet it is almost double the amount of estimated U.S. reserves.

Whatever the size of the reserves, it has usually been assumed that the Russians had a strong desire to sell what they had. Recently, however, some Russians, including author Alexandr Solzhenitsyn, have begun to argue that the Soviet government should hold back its production for a future time when demand will probably be even larger than it is now and supplies will be the same or smaller. They have been joined by those who argue that Soviet pricing practices do not adequately reflect royalty, conservation, and pollution costs. Now it looks as if the Soviet Union may be able to have it both ways; that is, it can earn hard currency and still not exhaust its oil reserves. With prices as high as they were in 1973–1974, the Russians can sell less than they had planned, yet still earn three or four times more for each ton of oil they sell.

The Japanese found themselves directly involved in the Russian debate over conservation versus an increase in oil extraction. At a press conference on May 27, 1974, Soviet Minister of Oil Valentin Shashin seemed to suggest that the Soviet Union was no longer interested in supplying major quantities of petroleum to Japan. This caused considerable consternation in Japan, and the Soviet government issued an official denial that Shashin had made such a comment.[31] According to *Pravda,* the Soviet Union was still interested in selling oil to Japan. Naturally the Japanese were still interested in buying, despite the political uncertainties involved in becoming dependent on the Soviet Union for some of its oil. The Japanese need foreign oil desperately (they have to import over 95 percent of what they consume), and the Russians' large oil fields in Siberia are very tempting to them. Indeed, the only reason the Russians do not supply more of Japan's needs is that as yet there is no cheap or convenient way to extract and ship oil across Siberia.

Theoretically, given existing pipelines and working oil fields, the best way for the Soviet Union to supply Japan would be through the Black Sea. But as long as the Suez Canal was closed, this was impossible, and shipment around South Africa, either by way of the Black Sea or the Baltic Sea, was simply too costly. It was just such considerations which led to the early swap arrangements.

With or without the Suez Canal, however, the nearness of Siberia to Japan makes development of oil resources there more attractive. The main difficulty is that a pipeline through miles of frozen Siberia to the port of Nakhodka is both expensive and technically complex. On their own, the Russians have been building portions of the pipeline. Thus in 1964 they extended their 28-inch Trans-Siberian pipeline to Angarsk near Irkutsk. (See Map, p. 110) Originally this linked up the deposits in the Volga-Ural oil field to the west near Ufa to Kuibyshev. Subsequently, in 1972, the Trans-Siberian pipeline was linked up to the new and potentially richer Middle Ob fields at Surgut in West Siberia, and in 1973 to the Samotlor fields in the West Siberian Tyumen region. While this makes available enormous quantities of oil to Irkutsk, it still leaves a 2,000-mile gap in the pipeline between Irkutsk and Nakhodka on the Japanese Sea. Despite this obstacle, the Japanese firm Idemitsu Kosan signed a contract to purchase 1 million tons of crude oil from the Tyumen field in 1973.[32] Presumably the oil could be shipped by pipe to Irkutsk, but the reports indicated it would be shipped all the way by rail.

The Russians have been trying to induce the Japanese to lend them $1–2 billion to finance 4,000 miles of pipeline from Tyumen to Nakhodka. In exchange, the Japanese would receive 750 million tons of oil over a 20-year period. Armand Hammer and his Occidental Petroleum has proposed to Hiroki Imazato, president of Nippon Seiko KK, that his firm share in the finance and operation of the pipeline. Since half of it is already in operation, it would seem that the pipeline need only be built from Irkutsk to Nakhodka. The Russians, however, feel that the existing 28-inch line is not big enough to handle their domestic and foreign needs in spite of the fact it is larger than the vast majority of pipelines in the United States.[33] In any case, they want the Japanese to finance a separate Tyumen-to-Nakhodka line that would also enable them to ship oil destined for the U.S. through the same projected pipeline. Conceivably the Russians would also like this pipeline to provide fuel for their army and fleet along the Chinese border. At least this is the reason the Chinese have given for their opposition to Japanese participation in such a project.[34]

Similar strategy motivates Soviet thinking about natural gas pipelines. As with oil, they have opened some natural gas lines on their own, but are seeking loans to finance pipelines with enough capacity so that presumably they can be used for export purposes as well.

The Russians are primarily interested in opening up three natural gas fields: the Middle Viliui near Yakutsk, the Urengoi field in West Siberia, and the fields on Sakhalin. The Russians claim that the fields at Yakutsk contain over 1 trillion cubic meters (460 trillion cubic feet) of natural gas, but for a long time were reluctant to allow foreigners in to make their own geological verification. Permission was finally authorized in December 1973 for a two-week visit—hardly long enough for the American visitors to unpack, much less do geological work. Nonetheless, an American consortium made up of El Paso Natural Gas, Occidental Petroleum, and the engineering firm Bechtel Corporation went ahead and signed a provisional agreement with the Russians for the building of a 2,000-mile gas pipeline from Yakutsk to Nakhodka. The project would require dollar loans of $4 to $5 billion. This would be used for the pipeline, a gas liquefaction plant, and a fleet of 20 tankers which would carry the gas across the Pacific Ocean. The loan would be repaid by the importation of 1 to 2 billion cubic feet of liquefied natural gas a day over a 25-year period (10 to 20 billion cubic meters a year). This would amount to total shipments of about $10 billion over the 25-year period beginning in 1980.

To reduce somewhat the burden on the American partners, the American group led by Occidental Petroleum has been negotiating with some Japanese groups for joint participation in the financing and the use of gas. Of the total $4 to $5 billion the Yakutsk project is expected to cost, the Americans and Japanese would be responsible for financing the $2 billion for the special tankers. The Russians themselves would bear the cost of the pipeline and land facilities, but they would try to obtain another $2 billion in outside loans to finance the cost of imported equipment for this work.

In addition to the natural gas pipeline from Yakutsk, the Russians are also trying to encourage the building of a second pipeline from the Urengoi field in West Siberia to Murmansk, about 1,500 miles away on the Barents Sea. The gas would be liquefied at Murmansk and then shipped to the East Coast of the United States. The pipeline and liquefaction plant would cost about $3.7 billion and the 20 refrigerated tankers another $2.6 billion. This would also be a 25-year deal that would presumably make possible the shipment of 2 billion cubic feet of natural gas a day, worth about $23 billion over a 25-year period. (The Russians claim that the reserves in West Siberia total 12 trillion cubic meters.) [35] To build and finance the Urengoi-Murmansk deal, another consortium was formed consisting of the Tenneco Corporation, Texas Eastern Gas, and the engineering firm of Brown and Root. On June 29, 1973, this group signed a letter of intent with the U.S.S.R., conditional, among other things, on whether or not the consortium can obtain financing and government approval from the United States. Given the reluctance in Congress to extend large credits to the U.S.S.R., particularly for energy projects, the future of such ventures is very much in doubt.

The third and less spectacular gas and oil field the Russians are trying to develop is on the continental shelf on and around the island of Sakhalin. This would be primarily a Japanese project, although Gulf Oil has sought to become involved as well.[36] The Russians are asking for $230 million from the Japanese as an initial investment to start the project, but the Japanese have so far been reluctant to spend that much. One reason for their hesitation is that Premier Kosygin himself reportedly warned the Japanese that the natural gas reserves of Sakhalin may not amount to the 60 billion cubic meters originally estimated, but may be only 16 billion cubic meters,[37] which would not be worth exploiting. Nonetheless, if the project is agreed on, the Sakhalin oil and gas could go by pipeline or ship directly to Hokkaido, the northernmost Japanese island, or it could link up with the proposed pipeline from Yakutsk to Nakhodka.

Because of their magnitude, there are enormous risks connected with all of these projects. That is why the negotiations have been slow and uncertain. Remember that, as of this writing, Western or Japanese geologists have not had much opportunity to make their own geological tests in these remote areas of Siberia, and there are reports that the deposits in the Yakutsk field as well as on Sakhalin are not as large as the Russians would like the rest of the world to believe.[38] The claim is that there is enough to maintain a flow for 20 years, but it would certainly be an expensive mistake if the gas field was exhausted before then. In the hope that some additional information could be obtained, the United States and Japan agreed to put up $120 to $150 million to provide additional exploratory drilling in and around Yakutsk. (Close to $50 million is supposed to come from the Export-Import Bank.) Reportedly the Russians intend to repay this loan with 1.5 million tons of liquefied natural gas (LNG).[39] However, there is some uncertainty as to whether foreign geologists will be allowed to participate in such explorations.

Even if it is assumed that there are deposits in the expected quantity, the project will still necessitate extremely large commitments. Each pipeline will require a loan of approximately $2 to $3 billion. Reportedly, there are lenders eager to put up the money, and the Japanese are said to be willing to share the costs and proceeds of the Yakutsk project. But consider the hazards. Even under the most protected circumstances, $4 to $6 billion is a large sum and 20 to 25 years is a long time. The promoters hope that the Export-Import Bank will put up over $1 billion on each pipeline at 8.5 percent interest. Commercial bankers would then be asked to put up an equivalent amount at market rates, and the Soviet Union would put up several hundred million. Still, complications abound. As we saw in Chapter 2, even if Export-Import Bank credits are made available, United States banks are limited under American laws as to how much they can lend a particular customer. Thus, even if the 60 largest American banks joined together, the most they could lend Vnestorgbank, the Russian foreign trade bank, would be $1.5 billion. There is the possibility, however, that the loans could be made directly to various segments of different projects rather than to a single bank.

Even if a way could be found around U.S. law, would the detour be worth the taking? Will most American bank presidents be willing to tie up a hundred million dollars or so for 20 years in an investment in the Soviet Union? (The Japanese have been holding out for a repayment period of no more than five years.) [40] After all, a Soviet pipeline would not be worth much as collateral to a judge in a Cook County Courthouse, nor would a Soviet liquefaction plant. The best collateral would be the 20 refrigerated ships which have to be built for each project. Reportedly, however, the Russians are insisting on part ownership of these ships. Many of the American participants have staunchly refused to turn over what appears to be the only bargaining weapon they may have in the event of future political or economic conflict. (And even then, there is not too much a company can do with just LNG refrigerated ships.) Nevertheless, some other American firms are less steadfast and have apparently been willing to share ownership in the hopes that this will turn the Soviet decision in their favor and lead the Russians to award them the contract.

The price of LNG once it reaches the United States also raises another question. Obviously, if the LNG is too expensive, there is no point in worrying further about whether or not it can be brought here. True, many authorities agree that the price set by the Federal Power Commission (FPC) on gas produced in the United States is too low, and in 1973 there were clear signs that the FPC was beginning to take a more flexible attitude. Yet even with the gas price increases of 1973, prices would have to go a long way before Soviet gas would become competitive. Some Western specialists doubt this will ever be possible. As they see it, it should cost at least $.60 per 1,000 cubic feet to transport and freeze the gas at Murmansk, and another $.60 to ship it across the Atlantic. Based on Soviet experience in the mid-1960s, moreover, Soviet domestic shipping costs may be double or triple those of the United States.[41] To all that expense, the Russians presumably would have to add something to reflect the price of the gas itself. Thus, by the time it reached the American East Coast, the Urengoi gas would probably have to carry a wholesale price of at least $1, and more likely $1.50, per 1,000 cubic feet. This would make it three times the price of domestic gas as of 1973 and almost double the price of LNG from Algeria. Of course, natural gas prices have recently been going up rapidly, and if they keep rising, Soviet natural gas might conceivably be competitive someday. Even then it must be remembered that with all the risks and difficulties in integrating Soviet gas into the American market system, the total flow from both Soviet fields is expected to amount to only 4 to 5 percent of total American consumption as of 1972.

The cost, the payback period, and the physical and political risks make one hesitate. The fact remains, however, that the Soviet supplies could be an important supplement to petroleum from the Middle East. If nothing else, our experience in October 1973 should have taught us that the more sources we have from outside the Middle East, the better. Contrary to some natural gas suppliers in the Middle East, moreover, the Russians are in need of dollars, and want them, devaluation and all. Buying natural gas in the Soviet Union would not hurt the balance of payments as much as buying it in the Middle East since the Russians would turn right around and buy or pay for American goods much faster than would the Saudi Arabians or Kuwaitis. There is always the chance of a coordinated embargo by some of the Middle Eastern countries and the Soviet Union, but the more suppliers there are, the more difficult such embargoes become to coordinate.

The question remains whether it is wise to spend billions of dollars in order to increase American dependency on *any* foreign country for its energy supplies. The several billion dollars required for the Russians' pipelines will mean that much less available for the development of domestic American resources—be it for solar and atomic energy or oil shale. In other words, the diversion of billions of dollars to the Soviet Union involves real opportunity costs. At this juncture, unless the Russians can do something to increase their own stake in the enterprise, the prospective gains may not be worth the actual costs.

But whether or not the United States decides to finance a Soviet pipeline, the coming of the petroleum era has been a godsend for the Soviet Union at a most crucial time. It has brought, and will continue to bring, massive quantities of hard currency, for after Saudi Arabia, Iran, Venezuela, and Kuwait, the Soviet Union is today the world's fifth largest exporter of petroleum. But the Soviet Union has more than oil and natural gas to export. That is the subject of the next chapter.

CHAPTER

5

The Quest for Hard Currency—

Commodities, Gold, Credits,

and Joint Ventures

W I T H Western and Japanese markets opening wide to Soviet petroleum and natural gas, the Soviet balance of trade and payments position has improved far beyond what even the most optimistic planners would have dared hope as recently as early 1973. Nor need the U.S.S.R. depend solely on the sale of petroleum and natural gas for increases in her export earnings. On the other hand, significant increases in Soviet export flows are likely to continue to be primarily raw materials. Careful input-output studies by C. H. McMillan as well as a glance at Soviet trade statistics indicate that the Russians export few highly fabricated products to the industrialized countries of the world.[1] The ratio of Soviet machinery exports to Soviet machinery imports from Western Europe, Japan, and the United States is seldom better than one to ten and generally is about one to twenty or more. (See Table 2–3.) These disproportions are all the more notable because, as we saw earlier, the Russians still often manage to achieve overall favorable trade balances with such countries as the United Kingdom and Japan. (See Table 2–4.) Equally significant, although these machinery import to machinery export ratios have improved somewhat in the 1970s, essentially they are no different from what they were prior to World War I.[2]

For that matter, there has not been much change in the type of raw materials the Russians export to the advanced countries in order to pay for their machinery imports. As before the Revolution, the Russians still rely heavily on the export of timber and petroleum (and wheat when they have it). It is worth noting, therefore, that in 1973 the Russians exported $352 million worth of logs and timber to Japan. This amounted to over 30 percent of all Soviet export earnings to Japan that year. Timber and timber products were also an important export to England—$115 million—and to several other West European countries. (See Table 5–1.) Indeed, after petroleum, timber and timber products provided the largest flow of hard currency to the Soviet Union. In 1973 timber product earnings in hard currency totaled almost $700 million, compared to $1.3 billion (exclusive of shipments to Finland) for petroleum. Other major sources of hard currency earnings for the U.S.S.R. include exports of cotton, coal, fur, copper, and ferrous metals. (See Table 5–1.) A relatively new type of export for the Soviet Union is diamonds, both cut and uncut. As we have already noted, the value of the uncut diamond exports does not usually appear in Soviet statistics. Barry Kostinsky of the U.S. Department of Commerce concludes that the Russians exported about $240 million worth of diamonds in 1970.[3]

Soviet exports to the United States reflect the same general pattern. In 1973 American importers spent $76 million for Soviet petroleum products, $43 million for palladium, $14 million for platinum, $17 million for diamonds and other jewelry, and $3 million for furs.[4] Except for $1 or $2 million worth of manufactured goods, everything else consisted of raw materials.

To the extent that the terms of trade have swung in favor of raw

TABLE 5-1

Exports of Major Soviet Commodities to the Hard Currency Countries in 1973
(in millions of dollars) [a]

	ALUMINUM	OIL AND OIL PRODUCTS	TIMBER AND TIMBER PRODUCTS	COTTON	COAL	FURS	COPPER	FERROUS METAL	PALLADIUM	PLATINUM	PRODUCTS TOTAL	EXPORT TOTAL
France	6	122	50	51	20	1	—	—	—	—	250	365
Great Britain	12	23	115	24	—	35	23	8	—	—	240	724
Italy	—	205	44	4	29	4	6	59	—	—	351	415
Japan	21	55	352	96	47	1	29	39	—	—	640	833
Netherlands	—	182	24	5	—	—	46	6	—	—	263	349
United States	—	76	—	—	—	3	—	—	43	14	136	215
West Germany [b]	—	316	42	20	1	12	29	6	—	—	426	644
Other	1	324	58	16	33	2	11	33	—	—	478	782
TOTAL	40	1,303	685	216	130	58	144	151	43	14	2,784	4,327
Finland	3	297	51	9	32	1	8	20	—	—	421	556

Source: VT SSSR 1973 (Soviet); Bureau of East-West Trade (U.S.).
[a] 1 ruble = $1.34.
[b] Includes West Berlin.

material exporters, the Soviet Union will benefit. However, at this writing it is by no means clear whether this alone will provide the Soviet Union with enough foreign exchange to make it feel secure.

COPRODUCTION WITH WESTERN COMPANIES

In order to increase their export earnings even more, the Russians are looking for ways to expand the quantity and variety of goods they export. To help identify those goods and upgrade the quality of Soviet products in general, the Russians have begun to cooperate in joint ventures with foreign firms. The Russians and East Europeans have sought to improve the productivity of their export sector by bringing in foreign help and seeking technology transfer from the West and Japan. In Eastern Europe this has sometimes meant bringing in a Western firm and allowing it to share not only in the management, but in the profits as well. In Yugoslavia, Rumania, and Hungary, where this has gone the farthest (Poland passed similar enabling legislation in 1973, and East Germany is now doing the same), some Western companies have been allowed to assume 49 percent in return for putting up a like percentage of the capital or technology.

Yugoslavia first authorized these operations in 1967, and as of mid-1973 had authorized 79 such joint companies. For example, there is now the Fiat participation at Crvena Zastava, which manufactures cars, and the Klockner-Humboldt-Deutz Company of West Germany, which is working jointly with TAM of Maribor in Yugoslavia to make light trucks. Another example is the air-conditioning operation jointly financed and operated by the Italian firm Marlo and the Bosina engineering company Union Invest at Sarajevo.

Rumania has approved an equity arrangement with Falco, a textile combine from Turin, Italy, whereby Falco will have a 49 percent interest in a Rumanian synthetic fiber plant in return for technical assistance and capital. Similar arrangements have been made with Control Data of the United States and are being negotiated with Renke of West Germany. Rumania has also worked out an equity arrangement with Sumitomo Shoji Kaisha Ltd. of Japan under which the Japanese and the Rumanians will jointly supervise the production of petroprotein in Rumania.

It should be noted that in most of Eastern Europe, the mixed company that is formed to share in the profits is maintained as an entity separate from the East European enterprise that does the actual producing. Profits and royalties are paid by the East European manufacturer to the mixed company. After taxes are paid, the remaining profits can then be repatriated to the investors' home offices within certain specified limits.[5]

In other situations there is no surrender of equity and Western firms have simply settled for joint production and marketing arrangements. Here there is no sharing of profits. In the case of Spelling-Werke of West Germany, that firm provides the boilers to Gants of Hungary, which sends generators to Spelling-Werke in exchange. Each company then keeps the profits it earns from selling the boilers and generators to electric generating stations in its respective market. Similarly, the Bowmar Co. of Canada and the United States has arranged with Cooperative Telecommunications of Hungary to produce and market Bowmar minicalculators in East and West Europe. Payment to Bowmar will be partly in the form of the calculators themselves, which will then be sold by Bowmar in the West.[6]

Some of these arrangements have grown increasingly complex. Less and less are the operations limited to the home territory of the two participants. Thus the Austrian firm of Simmering-Grats-Pauker has joined with Komplex, a Hungarian organization, to build power plants in Lebanon and India. The Bulgarian firm Machinoexport has joined with the Italians to form a trading corporation in Switzerland that will sell grinding machines built jointly in Bulgaria and Italy. All of these arrangements make it possible for the East European firms to take advantage of Western administrative and marketing management and earn hard currency in the process.

The Russians have not been nearly as venturesome, especially when it comes to allowing Western companies inside the territory of the Soviet Union. Their boldest arrangements have been with their East European allies, who have been told they will have to put up labor and capital if they want to obtain the desired flow of raw materials. Thus in April 1963 the East Germans, Bulgarians, Czechs, Poles, and Hungarians joined with the Russians to finance and equip the phosphorus mine in Soviet Estonia at Kingissepsky.[7] In the same year the Poles lent the Soviet Union $78 million for the development of a potash plant in Belorussia. Other East European projects on Soviet territory include a Bulgarian enterprise which will develop and utilize Soviet steel ingots and cast iron; a Rumanian project which will exploit Soviet iron ore from the Kursk Magnetic Anomaly; a Czech arrangement which will provide the Czechs with nonferrous metals; and a Bulgarian and Hungarian operation which will provide them with cardboard and paper pulp in exchange for investment help on the project itself.[8]

These projects, especially those involving Soviet raw materials, are almost entirely under the control of the Soviet Union. Usually the East European participant agrees to accept repayment for its participation in the materials to be produced by the project (just like the proposed American and Japanese natural gas deals). Once repayment is completed, the arrangement ends. Only then are the Russians presumably free to divert the output of such enterprise to the hard currency countries.

Recently the Russians have become somewhat more daring. Because they have apparently had difficulty in increasing their timber output, they have offered concessions to a group of Bulgarians and North Koreans to develop remote timber tracts. In December 1967 the Russians agreed to turn over tracts amounting to 7,000 square meters in the Komi ASSR to 5,000 Bulgarian workers. Output was expected to be 1,500,000 cubic meters a year by

1975.[9] A similar arrangement offered to the North Koreans in the Far East would ultimately involve 7,000 Koreans. But from all indications, these arrangements are for a fixed period and are quite distinct from the profit and equity concessions offered Armand Hammer and the Harriman Brothers in the 1920s. If anything, one is struck by how few such arrangements there have been, given the profuse Soviet expressions of fraternal brotherhood and economic cooperation with their East European comrades.

Recently there have been some indications that the Russians might agree to Western participation if their needs are great enough. In a somewhat surprising departure from normal policy, the Russians have authorized the Finns to develop the Kostamus (Kostomuksha) iron ore deposits in Karelia. Utilizing up to 4,000 Finnish workers, the ore concentration center is expected to have an output of 8 million tons of iron ore pellets a year. The Russians have also agreed to pay the Finns 16 million rubles to build a railroad and highway from Kostomukha to the Finnish border and are allowing them to bring in not only their own labor, but some of their own materials and equipment as well.[10] The Finns are to be repaid in part with iron ore from the mine. True, the Finns have a slightly different relationship with the Soviet Union than do other capitalist countries. Thus the Russians have also decided to utilize the labor, machinery, and know-how of Finnish firms to build the Viru hotel in Tallinin, hydroelectric stations in Murmansk region, and the Svetogorsk pulp and paper mill in the Leningrad region. They are also helping in the cutting of timber in the Pyaozero lumber camp. By the time they are through, the Finns will probably be engaged in more activity on Soviet territory than any one of the East European communist countries.

But despite numerous requests and proposals, the Russians have so far denied other Western firms comparable working arrangements. For one thing, they are normally most reluctant to allow large contingents of foreigners from capitalist countries to work on Soviet territory. They do permit foreign engineers and technicians to come in to supervise construction and to instruct their Russian counterparts—as they did, for example, in the construction of the Fiat plant. But such workers are usually few in number; they do their supervising and then go home. That is what makes the Finnish case so unusual.

Something close to what the Finns are doing may result from a contract recently signed by Soviet and Japanese coal interests. As presently contemplated, the Japanese will help the Russians build a 250-mile spur from the extensive coal deposits in the Soviet Yakutian coal basin. The coal is then to be sent along the Trans-Siberian Railroad to the port of Nakhodka, from which it will be sent to Japan. The Russians already have started on this project and the Japanese have agreed to help them speed up the work on the railroad and mining area with a loan of $450 million. In addition, the Japanese will help build some towns in the area and supply much of the mining equipment. It is unclear whether the Russians will permit the Japanese to bring in Japanese laborers as well as technicians, but since Soviet labor is in short supply in the region, they may agree to this as they have with the Finns. Such an agreement would be a definite departure from past Soviet practice.

As the Finnish and Japanese examples indicate, the Russians may be experimenting. As we saw in Chapter 4, the Russians are also considering whether to make 20- to 25-year commitments to supply petroleum products to some of the NATO countries and Japan. Of course, in these instances, the Russians are the ones who finger the valve, and they can sever the pipeline or the flow of iron ore and coal any time they want—once they have obtained the development help they need so badly. Since in almost all instances repayment will be in the raw materials being developed, the Russians can stop shipments after the project is operating and there is very little the foreign lender can do. Of course, developers of projects wholly located in a foreign country have always run such risks. It is just that political relations between noncommunist countries and the Soviet Union have not always been so warm and friendly in the past, nor have the Russians engaged in such arrangements with noncommunist countries. Yet even if the Russians keep their fingers crossed behind their backs when they sign these contracts, the very fact that the Soviet government would contemplate deals of such long duration represents a departure from past practice.

The fact of the matter is that where the Russians can simultaneously increase their productive capacity and their hard currency earnings, they are apparently quite amenable to innovative arrangements. This is surely what they had in mind when they negotiated a 20-year deal for the yearly exchange of about $500 million worth (at 1974 prices) of Occidental Petroleum's superphosphoric acid from Florida. In return the Russians are to provide Occidental with 1.5 million tons a year of ammonia, the same amount of urea, and 1 million tons of potash. Material deliveries, slated to begin in 1978, will involve a total two-way exchange of about $20 billion during the course of the 20-year contract. According to the agreement signed in June 1974, another company, the Chemical Construction Corporation (Chemico), is to provide the technology and equipment for four fertilizer-producing factories worth $200 million on the Volga near Kuibyshev, which are to supply the ammonia, urea, and potash. At the same time, Occidental is to build two ports to handle the shipping and storage of the chemicals, one at Odessa on the Black Sea and one at Ventspil on the Baltic. The Soviet Union will pay for the fertilizer plants and the ports by shipping Occidental an extra 1.5 million tons of ammonia each year. The Export-Import Bank has indicated its willingness to provide $180 million of the amount needed for the factories and other facilities. Nine U.S. banks, led by the Bank of America, have agreed to provide another $180 million. In addition, the Russians are to put up $40 million of their own. It is anticipated that Occidental Petroleum will also build a pipeline which is to carry liquid ammonia from Kuibyshev to the Black Sea. Its partner, the Bechtel Corporation, will do the engineering for the pipeline.

Russian interest in such an arrangement is not hard to explain.

Their agricultural problems have increased their need for phosphate-based fertilizer. Since the Russians have often had trouble obtaining a satisfactory supply of phosphates and have frequently had to depend heavily on imports from North Africa,[11] they are naturally responsive to such deals. In comparison with the natural gas and coal deals, the fertilizer project is also better for Western companies. While the Russians will still end up with a fertilizer factory, ports, and pipeline on their territory which cannot be reclaimed as collateral, they will nonetheless feel some compulsion to honor their contract, because any unilateral abrogation by the Soviet side will cut them off from the flow of Occidental Petroleum's super-phosphoric acid. Thus, in the fertilizer exchange, unlike the liquefied natural gas project, the Russians do stand to lose if they do not abide by the contract.

THE RUSSIANS MOVE OUT

Although the Russians have been squeamish about allowing Western or Japanese firms to operate and share equity profits inside the territory of the U.S.S.R. (even the Occidental Petroleum and Pullman deals involve only the sale and barter of equipment and technology), they have no qualms about Russian firms engaging in such "unorthodox" practices in the West. As we saw in the case of the oil companies, the Russians have started to operate in Western Europe. Occasionally such ventures have been quite profitable and have proven a useful means of earning hard currency.

Without any centrally directed or premeditated strategy, at least so far as can be seen, and without stopping to worry about the ideological implications of what they are doing, the Soviets are forming international corporations comparable to those in the West. They buy services and even produce goods in foreign countries with the intention of selling or servicing the same or processed products in still other countries through overseas subsidiaries. Products from the mother country are sold wherever possible, but in many instances the home country only becomes involved when it is necessary to send out managerial personnel or to send home profits.

A prime illustration of this type of organization is the Soviet foreign banking network, which not surprisingly is structured very much along the lines of international finance capitalism. The Russians have formed a network of wholly owned banks spread across Europe. Perhaps the most important of these is the Moscow Narodny Bank Ltd. of London (MNB), which as of 1974 had resources of more than £835 million (about $2 billion) and net profits in 1973 of slightly more than $3 million. Though founded on October 12, 1919, shortly after the revolution, the Moscow Narodny Bank traces its origins back to prerevolutionary times. A cooperative bank by that name was formed in Moscow in 1911 and opened a branch in London in 1917. Its assets were taken over by the Soviet government in 1919. The London bank is the principal operation in a chain of nine Soviet banks that extends around the world. Depending on their origins and location, these banks have varying degrees of independence. One of the earliest branches was established in 1923 in Teheran when the Russian Iranian Bank was opened.[12] The Paris Bank, the Banque Commerciale pour L'Europe du Nord (Eurobank), originally founded as the Banque Commercial pour le Pays du Nord in 1925, is now one of France's ten largest banks, with assets of $1,790 million.[13] Other Soviet banks now operate in Frankfurt (Ost-West Handelsbank), Beirut (The Moscow Narodny Bank, Beirut's second largest), Singapore, Kabul, Zurich (the Wozchod Handelsbank), Vienna (Danube Bank), and Luxemburg (Banque Unie Est-Quest S.A.).[14]

These various banks make fairly sophisticated transactions. The London, Zurich, and Beirut offices have been particularly active in selling Soviet gold. The Paris bank is credited with creating the Eurodollar market in the late 1950s. Following on this lead, the Hungarian National Bank in May 1971 began to float bonds on

134

the Eurodollar market. The Hungarians were joined in borrowing on the Eurodollar market by other East European countries and even the International Investment Bank of CMEA, which is head-quartered in Moscow.

Actually, some East European banks have engaged in even more complicated arrangements. A West German bank, the Hessische Landesbank Girozentrale, announced that it had gone into part-nership with the Landlowy Warszawie bank of Poland to form a new bank in Frankfort called the Mitteleuropaische Handelsbank (Central European Trade Bank). Similarly, the Rumanian Bank for Foreign Trade in Bucharest joined with Barclay's Bank Interna-tional of England and the Manufacturers Hanover Trust of the United States to form the Anglo Romanian Bank in London. The Rumanians put up 50 percent of the capital, the British 30 per-cent, and the American bank 20 percent.

As yet, the Moscow Narodny Bank has not gone as far as the Poles and the Rumanians, but it has not been backward. It has ar-ranged for the dollar financing of the Intercontinental Hotel, lo-cated in Budapest, which will be paid for by the Foreign Trade Bank of Hungary. It has also been actively engaged in interna-tional financial consortiums. For example, it joined with Lehman Brothers, the Bank of America, and about 20 other foreign firms in a $40 million financing venture to build housing for—of all things—Iran's navy!

In their quest for increased sales and profits, the Russians have not let themselves be disturbed by ideological implications in-volved in establishing trading and manufacturing concerns over-seas. They have set up several trading corporations in the develop-ing countries and Western Europe, with ownership usually shared with local firms. In March 1967 the Ethso Trading Company Ltd. was established in Ethiopia, with the Russian agency, Energoma-sheksport, holding 51 percent of the stock. About the same time the Russians, through their automobile-exporting organization, Avtoeksport, took over an 80 percent interest in a Lagos, Nigeria, company called the West African Automobile and Engineering Co. Ltd. (WAATECO). A few months earlier, the Soviet machinery-exporting organization, Machinoexport, joined with Tissage-Bedamo of Morocco to set up the Marimexport Company. All of these African companies were to import and service Soviet equipment and export other goods. The Russians have also jointly launched a shipping line with the Egyptians and have offered to build a tractor assembly plant in Syria which would be largely Soviet-operated.

In the more developed countries, the Russians have tended to concentrate on a few selected types of joint stock companies specially designed to help Soviet products break into hard currency markets. By joining with local citizens and extending them an equity in the company, the Russians are able to harness not only the self-interest of local businessmen, but their familiarity with local business customs. The first and perhaps most promising category of joint stock company is the Soviet oil company discussed in the preceding chapter. The others sell automotive equipment, machine tools, and optical and camera appliances. In addition, a variety of miscellaneous companies have been created in response to local market conditions and peculiar Soviet needs. (See Appendix III.)

Next to oil companies, the Russians have expended their greatest effort on the companies selling automotive vehicles. Some are jointly owned and some are owned entirely by foreigners. Initially, these firms concentrated on Soviet automobiles, but gradually some have expanded to include Soviet trucks and tractors. The sale and promotion of automotive equipment in Western Europe is of great importance to the Russians because they regard it as a demonstration of industrial machismo—they feel it is a matter of pride that they keep up with the other industrialized countries. Even though the Russians had to turn to the Italian and French automobile manufacturers to improve the production of their own cars, they have set up a joint stock company in France with French partners who own one-third of the stock. This firm, Actif-Avto, services and sells Soviet automotive equipment, particularly tractors, throughout France.

The oldest and perhaps most successful of the Soviet foreign subsidiaries is Konela, the Finnish operation. Founded in Helsinki in 1947 as a Soviet-Finnish joint stock company, it started importing Soviet vehicles two years later for sale in the Finnish market.[15] Production of Soviet vehicles in those postwar years was not very high—total 1949 production of *all* vehicles was about 276,000, and of that automobiles constituted only 46,000.[16] In view of the immense needs at home and the limited production, it is amazing that the Soviet government should have decided to divert any Soviet vehicles to the foreign market. As is frequently the case in matters of Soviet export policy, however, the ultimate decision was little influenced by domestic economic considerations. From 1949 to 1952 the Russians exported 1,225 vehicles.[17] By 1971 Konela was averaging sales of about 5,000 vehicles a year. As the Fiat plant at Togliatti began to produce more cars, the Russians stepped up their overall export program, and in 1972 exported more than double the number of cars they had shipped in 1971. In 1973 world export of Soviet automobiles was 121,000.

Konela has expanded rapidly to keep pace with this increasing volume of business. In 1956 it opened a new head office. Six years later it moved into a 6,000-square-meter spare parts warehouse, and then in 1964 into a large central garage with about 8,000 square meters of floor space. In 1971 an import center was set up in the customs free warehouse zone of Raipo. Today the company has eight branches with showrooms in virtually all of Finland's largest cities. To service cars, a perennial problem inside the Soviet Union, Konela has established a network of district representatives and branches across the country. As of 1972, there were 34 large and 51 medium-sized garages. Many of these facilities are run by authorized agents who sell and service Soviet autos in more remote areas.

All of this contrasts sharply with the service available for Soviet cars within the U.S.S.R. In Moscow, for example, it has been estimated that there are only three repair stations to service approximately 100,000 privately owned cars.[18] Although the situation is apparently not so serious for the country as a whole, the estimate is that there is one garage for every 2,200 Soviet cars, compared with almost 1,000 cars for every garage wholly owned by Konela in Finland. Soviet officials know that service comes hard for them, and that is why the creation of joint stock companies which involve a partnership with local interests is a good way to overcome their shortcomings. While not entirely successful, joint stock companies like Konela have gone a long way toward improving service. What is unfortunate is that the lessons learned outside the U.S.S.R. flow so slowly back into the country. Indeed, the best place to have a Soviet car repaired is in Finland, not Moscow.

Except that it is larger and more successful, the administrative makeup of Konela is not much different from that adopted by subsequent Soviet joint stock companies such as Matreco-Bil in Sweden, Konela-Norge Bill in Norway, and Scaldia-Volga in Belgium, all of which also sell automobiles. Konela is divided into three departments: commercial, financial, and technical. It contracts with its Soviet joint owner, Avtoexport, the Foreign Trade Organization of the Ministry for Foreign Trade, for its automobile imports, and with Traktoexport for its tractors and highway-building equipment, Sudoimport for boat engines, and Radnoimport for tires. To conform with Finnish law, Konela pays cash on delivery for Soviet automobiles but imports trucks and spare parts on consignment terms for a period of one to two years.

Whether such joint stock companies are profitable is a closely held secret. Considering that almost all Soviet automobile equipment is supposed to sell at least 10 percent below the price of competing equipment, it is logical to assume that significant subsidies are provided somewhere along the line. Of course the Russians make no pretense of linking domestic prices to foreign prices. As we have already noted (see p. 60), Soviet cars are sold to Soviet consumers at a cost of 5,500 rubles ($7,300), or three times the price charged in Western Europe as measured by official exchange rates. For example, the Lada (the export model of the Zhiguli produced at the Fiat plant) sells for almost $2,400. But whatever the price and whatever the profit margin, it is hard to see how, given their small sales volume, some of the foreign-owned subsidiaries of the Soviet union can operate profitably. With sales of 12,000 a year, Konela in Finland is probably profitable. But the same can probably not be said of Konela-Norge Bill of Norway with sales of 1,200 in 1973, Scaldia-Volga in Brussels with sales of 2,800, and certainly not of Matreco-Bil of Sweden with sales of under 300. However, as exports of the Lada begin to grow, there should be less need for operating subsidies and more reliance on internally generated revenue.

While the Soviets seem to prefer to deal through companies in which they have an equity position, they do sometimes operate through companies wholly owned by Westerners. Occasionally this is done because the Russians do not want to bear the loss or because the local company may simply be more efficiently operated. For example, a non-Soviet company, Satra Motor Ltd., has the franchise for Soviet cars in England. In 1971 it imported 1,600 Soviet cars and in 1972 8,000. It sold about 14,000 vehicles in 1973 through a network of 268 English dealers that had increased from 150 to 223 a few months earlier. Although sales were below expectation in 1973, Satra hoped sales would double to 28,000 in 1974. Satra also sells Soviet tractors. In England, trucks are sold by a separate and wholly owned Soviet corporation called the United Machinery Organization Plant. Founded in 1969, it has concentrated on selling Belaz 15-, 30-, and 45-ton dump trucks. It had plans to sell 120 in 1973. Satra's parent company, Satra Corporation of New York, hopes to introduce Soviet cars, particularly the Lada, to Americans in 1975. Satra has also been given the Soviet car franchise for West Germany.

Demonstrating their flexibility, the Russians have formed a mixed Soviet-Canadian company called Belarus Equipment Ltd. in Toronto and Montreal. This, too, is a subsidiary of Satra Corporation of New York. It planned to sell 200 tractors in 1973. It also imported almost 700 into the United States in 1974. Since Soviet tractors are due to sell at prices $1,000 to $4,000 below those of comparable tractors made in Canada and the United States, Belarus may be able to meet its targets.

On occasion, however, operating as the marketing arm of the Soviet Union can be risky. In 1963 two Britons, Fanny James and her nephew, Rafael Hyams, began to sell Soviet radios and cameras. With time their firm, Technical and Optical Equipment Ltd., began to generate a following and ultimately it began to make a profit. At that point, in April 1968, the Soviet exporter Mashpriborintorg, by means of a series of political and economic pressures, forced the British owners out of their own company. Representatives of Mashpriborintorg took over Technical and Optical Equipment Ltd. and now run it as a wholly owned subsidiary. In 1972 the firm sold over 100,000 radios and an equal number of cameras. (Incidentally, as an illustration of the happenings sometimes associated with Soviet trade enterprises and missions, the British government on September 24, 1971, expelled over 100 Russians as spies, including a large number from Technical and Optical Engineering. Revelations from the investigation that followed led to the expulsion the following month of an additional 30 Soviet citizens from Belgium, including some employees of the Soviet-Belgium trade concern, Belso.)

Even though such ventures (as well as the ones listed in Appendix III) do not necessarily earn enormous quantities of hard currency, many of them do increase its flow and, more importantly, open up Western markets and marketing techniques to Soviet-manufactured products. This is terribly important to the Soviet Union. If Soviet industry is to sell more to the West, Soviet managers must learn to merchandise their goods more effectively and also to improve their maintenance and spare parts operations. Here their Western partners in the joint stock operations can help them. Until the Soviets learn how to deal with such matters, they are unlikely to become major sellers of sophisticated machinery to the West, even if they could earn enough hard currency through the sale of raw materials. And the Russians do want to sell such machinery. Apart from the machine products already mentioned, they want to sell road construction equipment, watches, hydrofoil ships, aircraft, especially the YAK 40 and the SST, and electrical generating equipment. Many of these were specifically mentioned in the Ninth Five-Year Plan as items suitable for export.

They also hope to offset the cost of the technology they are importing by exporting some of their own. Thus they were jubilant about the sale of a $15.6 million turbine for the Nelson River hydroelectric power project in Manitoba, Canada, in 1972. The Russians sold a similar turbine for the Mica River Dam in British Columbia in 1971. At times the Russians seem to outdo themselves in their eagerness to win such contracts. Their bid on the Nelson River project was $10.7 million below the next lowest bid. In 1974 their bid on an addition to that project was 50 percent lower than the Japanese bid. In much the same way, their $75 million contract to supply 12 turbine generator units for a large hydroelectric project at Salto Grande on the border between Argentina and Uruguay was $21 million lower than the next bid.

The Russians have even cracked the American market. Because of national security they were initially ruled out of the competition for the supply of generating units for the Grand Coulee Dam in 1967. In 1972 they were allowed to bid on the same project, but they overbid by $5 million. Yet the Russians did sign a contract to supply a 560,000-kilowatt transformer to Detroit Edison in 1972.[19] Still upset about their treatment at Grand Coulee, they and their partner in the 1972 Grand Coulee Dam bid, the Westinghouse Corporation, decided to protest their failure to win the contract. They argued that Allis-Chalmers, the winner, lacked the experience to build the big turbines needed. The Russians and Westinghouse then went on to underbid Allis-Chalmers at the Rock Island hydro project in Washington. The Russians have also been discussing sales of licenses to the Reynolds Metal Co. and the National Steel Corporation for a new method of producing aluminum. Other American firms which are using, or are negotiating for licenses to use, Soviet technology are listed in Appendix II. Most of the transactions thus far deal with the acquisition of improved methods in either ferrous or nonferrous metallurgy. Even more impressive are Soviet sales of metallurgical equipment to steel producers in Japan, Sweden, Norway, France, and West Germany. Similarly, Mitsui of Japan will take delivery of a Soviet rolling mill in 1974, and a French company has purchased about $2 million worth of Soviet blast furnace equipment for their Solmer steel mill in the Fos-sur Mer district near Marseilles, France. Finally, in what may be an indication of things to come, the Russian Foreign Trade Organization, Machinoexport, has joined together with Blaw-Knox and Thyssen Inc. of the United States to bid on a 1.2 million-ton steel slabbing mill and a 400,000-ton steel plate mill for the San Nicolas Steelworks near Buenos Aires.

Such sales and bids should not be considered as exceptional. The Russians have made impressive progress in increasing the productive capacity and technology of their heavy industry (as opposed to electronics, computers, and chemicals), and they have long exported such items to the developing countries and to the CMEA bloc.

Yet despite these impressive gains, there is some reason to question whether the Russians are channeling their efforts in the right direction. Certainly it is more prestigious to point to sales of their technology to advanced Western firms. But their export efforts heretofore have been more effective in other areas—those where there is a heavy natural resource content to the exports. In addition to the raw material sales already mentioned, the Russians are also selling naphtha and nickel to American firms, electricity to Finland, and nuclear fuel to France. Extensive research by C. H. McMillan and Steven Rosefielde indicates that Soviet exports to poorer countries contain a large percentage of capital input, while exports to the richer countries contain a large percentage of labor input.[20] In both cases, however, they also rely heavily on their natural resource base, and that seems the most logical path to follow.[21]

GOLD

The Russians are clearly trying to increase their export earnings. Because they have not been as successful as they would like, they are slowly beginning to experiment with new products and new institutional forms, although as yet they have not gone as far as have some of their East European allies. But if, despite all their experimentation, they still cannot export enough to pay for their imports, they can always sell some of their gold hoard on the world market. Apparently they did just that in 1963–1965 when they sold over $1.5 billion to pay for their large wheat imports.[22] Sales resumed again in 1972 at considerably higher prices.

The figures are not precise, but some specialists estimate the Russians have reserves of about 2,000 tons of gold. (See Table 5–2.) At the market prices that prevailed in mid-1974, that would be worth approximately $8 to $9 billion. That is almost triple the size of the most conservative estimate of the debt referred to at the beginning of the preceding chapter. Even though the Russians may be reluctant to take their gold out of the vault, the point is that as long as the gold they have equals or exceeds their debt, they are good credit risks. Banks are going to be more willing to lend Russians money with that kind of collateral than they would without it.

One way or another, therefore, Russia's ability to pay for hard currency imports is not as bleak as some skeptics suggest. With gold reserves easily approximating $8 billion or more, with the natural gas pipeline to Western Europe open and running, with the price of raw material exports rising rapidly, with windfall earnings of an extra $2 billion or so from their oil exports alone, and with hard currency sales of billions of dollars worth of munitions to the Arabs, who in 1973 started to pay in dollars instead of soft currency, the Russians suddenly seem to have developed an admirable ability to pay for their annual $4 billion or so of hard currency imports. Indeed, there is reason to wonder if they really

TABLE 5–2

Soviet Gold Sales and Reserves
(in millions of U.S. dollars)

	GOLD SALES [a]		GOLD RESERVES [a]	
	AMOUNT	TONS	AMOUNT	TONS
1960	$200	180	$2,555	2,270
1961	300	270	2,365	2,100
1962	215	195	2,250	2,000
1963	550	500	1,800	1,600
1964	450	410	1,495	1,330
1965	550	500	1,095	975
1966	b	b	1,265	1,125
1967	15	14	1,425	1,265
1968	12	11	1,590	1,415
1969	b	b	1,765	1,570
1970	b	b	1,945	1,730
1971	b	b	2,135	1,895
1972 [c]	250–300	150	d	1,950

Source: JEC 1973, p. 702.

[a] Calculated at the official rate of $35 an ounce for sales in 1960–1968 and for reserves 1960–1971. Reserves are end of year. All gold figures are based on Bank for International Settlements figures cited in David Floyd-Jacob and Peter Fells, *Gold 1971* (New York: Walker and Co., 1972), except reserves for 1960–1963, which are estimated from assumed net production of 100 tons per year.

[b] Negligible.

[c] Preliminary estimates.

[d] Valued at about $2,400,000,000 at the then official price of $38 an ounce, but worth considerably more at current free market prices.

require the large credits for which they are asking. Presumably they prefer to finance their projects with someone else's capital, particularly when the lenders take pleasure in vying with one another to see who can offer the lowest interest rates. But everything seems to indicate that the Russians are now in a position where they could finance the bulk of what they want to purchase by themselves.

But if the Soviet Union is not the world's poorest credit risk, neither is it necessarily the best place to make money. Considering the size of the likely Soviet market compared to similar markets in Western Europe or other parts of the world, and considering past trade practices of Soviet foreign trade representatives, there is reason to wonder if Western businessmen, and Americans in particular, are using proper judgment in making as many concessions as they have. This seems especially significant now that the dollar and the goods it buys have become better bargains.

In our desire to open up new markets and deal with people who have been our "enemies" (at least ideologically) for several decades, some American businessmen seem prepared to offer terms and make concessions they would never dream of making to our older and more traditional trading partners. As before, it seems to fit the manic phase of our manic-depressive relationship with the Soviet Union. What else explains our decision in 1972 to embargo soybean shipments to countries like Japan and France while continuing to sell grain to the U.S.S.R.? Similarly, one sometimes wonders whether some large American corporations and bankers really know what they are doing when they fight with one another to provide the Russians with billions of dollars worth of machinery under terms that allow the American corporations only the most tenuous forms of protection. The Russians seek to pay for the machinery with the raw materials or the products to be produced after the machinery is in place. That means that the first repayments will not be made until five or six years after the Russians have had use of the machinery. In some cases it will then take about 20 years for the whole loan to be paid back. Such a repayment period would be considered long even if it were between two firms in friendly countries. And as we discovered in 1974, it may be that the U.S. manufacturer will occasionally find himself with an overabundance of products which were produced in his factory. Consequently, the last thing he wants is yet another batch of Soviet raw materials or equipment to sell. In addition, the collateral for such loans will consist primarily of equipment such as a pipeline which will be firmly installed within the U.S.S.R. There is little consolation in the fact that the pipeline is in good Russian black earth. If the Russians ever decide not to adhere to the terms of the agreement, it will take immense ingenuity to repossess or even to mount a meaningful threat to repossess the collateral.

Until the General Accounting Office of the United States Congress called a halt and induced a tightening of lending procedures, even the Export-Import Bank seemed to have been caught up in the excitement and euphoria of it all. What else explains apparent readiness as of July 1974 to extend $469 million worth of loans and $113 million worth of guarantees to the U.S.S.R. without insisting upon and receiving the always-required data on balance of payment statistics, independently determined geological surveys, and financial statements? There have been rumors, subsequently denied, that Henry Kearns, former head of the Export-Import Bank, was pressured into relaxing some of the normal criteria by Secretary of State Henry Kissinger's office, or at any rate Senator William Proxmire reported that Mr. Kearns had qualms about such loans.[23]

Nor are the Export-Import bankers the only ones who no longer seem to be acting like bankers. How else can one explain the willingness of some banks to lend money to the U.S.S.R. at rates below the prime rate offered customers in the United States? Ironically, in June 1973, after Gabriel Hauge, the president of the Manufacturers Hanover Trust Company in New York, publicly criticized other banks for engaging in "dubious banking" in Eastern Europe by offering loans at rates below those offered commercial borrowers in the United States itself, his own bank turned around and bid only ⅞ percent over the Eurodollar rate on a loan to Rumania, while the banks he was criticizing submitted bids at a more responsible rate of 1.5 percent over the Eurodollar rate.[24] Otherwise stable bankers and businessmen have even complained that the government-subsidized credits of the Export-Import Bank were noncompetitive at the then prevailing bargain rate of 6 percent (at a time when the Federal Funds Rate—the most sensitive commercial rate—was 10 percent), since the French government was sometimes lending money to the Russians at less than 6 percent!

Moreover, how can the three largest banks in the United States justify the opening of expensive offices in the Soviet Union when most of the activity of their bank representatives involves negotiating with the Russians over the size of their apartments or posing for advertisements which are then inserted in the *Wall Street Journal?* Most bankers reluctantly concede that the business generated by these offices is unlikely to cover the cost of their operation.[25]

It appears, moreover, that very few in authority have been unduly distressed with the one-sided way some American-Soviet agreements have been implemented. Thus despite pledges of equal facilities, the Russians have found excuse after excuse as to why it has been impossible to find street-floor offices for the American Express Company, so that it can move out of its backroom suite at the Metropol Hotel. American Express was even prepared to take a second-floor location at the new Intourist Hotel as long as they could use the first-floor windows for advertising. In the meantime, of course, Intourist, the Soviet travel agency, has opened up a comfortable two-story street entrance office of their own on East 49th Street, between Madison and Lexington Avenues. The Pan Am-Aeroflot promise of equal accommodations has been handled in a similar way. The Russians have stuffed Pan American offices in a remote corner of an upper floor of the Metropol Hotel in Moscow, while Aeroflot has taken a prime office on the corner of East 45th Street and Fifth Avenue, one of New York's busiest locations. Pan American generally adheres to the standard air tariffs, while Aeroflot has been caught pirating passengers away from Pan Am by illegal procedures for ticket issuance.[26] In all, the American Civil Aviation Board has found that Aeroflot has violated American air transportation laws more than 100 times. For instance, Aeroflot has frequently sold cut-rate tickets at 50 percent discount in violation not only of bilateral American-Soviet agreements, but of international air tariff commitments. Once it overbooked 50 such cut-rate travelers. To have allowed them to switch to Pan Am would have forced Aeroflot to make up the 50 percent difference in fares with dollars. To avoid this, the 50 passengers were forcibly locked in Aeroflot's Hotel in Moscow and told they would have to wait for three days until Aeroflot's next scheduled flight to New York. After a day of protest, Aeroflot allowed the English and Americans to fly out on Western airlines, but held the Indian, African, and Iranian citizens the whole time. Again, to earn as much in the way of hard currency as it can, Aeroflot also makes it all but impossible for foreigners to change their booking from Aeroflot to Pan Am once they are in Moscow. Such tactics are largely responsible for the fact that Aeroflot carries twice as many passengers between New York and Moscow as does Pan Am.

It is also difficult to understand the eagerness of many businesses to offer unusually favorable terms to Soviet trading companies, despite reliable reports that Fiat officials lost money on their $1 billion deal with the U.S.S.R., and that Krupp in Germany almost went bankrupt because of some of their fancier transactions. (Dr. Bertholdt Beitz, the chairman of Krupp, has personally denied that such deals were unprofitable for Krupp.)

Finally, in the euphoria of the moment, many seem to have forgotten just how arbitrary and unpredictable the Russians can be. In the 1920s and 1930s, the Russians closed out some American investments in the U.S.S.R. as the Soviet political mood changed. Such practices have continued into the post-World War II era. Because its international position had changed, the Soviet oil export company, Siouznefteeksport, abruptly canceled its contractual agreement with Jordan Investment Ltd. of Israel.[27] The Russians terminated wool purchases from Australia when the Australians granted asylum to a Soviet official, and withdrew credit from Yugoslavia when Tito began to criticize the U.S.S.R. The Chinese were similarly abandoned in the early 1960s.

Nor is Soviet arbitrariness due only to political pique. Although they promised to supply the West German firm, Veba AG, with three to four million tons of oil during 1973 at a fixed price, when the Germans refused to pay the higher price suddenly demanded by the Soviet exporters, the Russians refused to deliver more than 500,000 tons. In similar fashion the Russians raised the price of the petroleum they sell to Eastern Europe, again in disregard for their contract. And like the United States the U.S.S.R. cancelled some of its grain contracts when prices had moved against it. Furthermore, at a time of maximum political harmony between the United States and the Soviet Union, the Soviet government in mid-1973 unilaterally announced cancellation of its contract with Alaskan Airlines for flights into the U.S.S.R. because the United States and the Soviet Union could not agree on amendments to the bilateral air agreement. Similarly, the Soviet Union abrogated an existing and valid contract with International Weekends which called for the sending of about 16,000 Americans to the Soviet Union on budget terms. As far as anyone knows, both contracts were canceled because the Russians had decided that they were not going to make as much money on the deals as they had originally anticipated, especially after the dollar had been devaluated. At least one American importer of Soviet rugs found in 1973 that the dollar price contracted for on one day was arbitrarily increased two days later when it was announced in the interim that the ruble had been revalued.

In conclusion, the hazards of dealing with the Russians are not limited to whether or not they have the ability and the commitment to pay their debts. They have the ability to pay and, for the most part, their repayment record and contract performance has been very good. But there are exceptions, and the trick is to be sure that the exception always happens to the other guy.

PART III

HOW—AND HOW NOT—TO DEAL WITH THE RUSSIANS

CHAPTER

6

A Trader's Guide

T H O S E who hunger for a piece of that $1 billion in annual contracts (even if only $200–$300 million is for industrial products) will find that there are two ways of conducting international trade—the usual way and the Soviet way, which means extra time, money, and ulcers. For those who are nonetheless prepared to do it the Soviet way, there are a number of new lessons in pricing and working conditions both here and in Moscow to be learned.

PRICING

The first task is to try to understand the Soviet pricing system. Unfortunately, Soviet pricing methods are quite unusual. As we have already seen, Soviet export prices usually bear no relationship to the prices of counterpart goods sold within the Soviet Union. In fact, it is a point of pride with them (if with no one else) that Soviet domestic and foreign prices are independent of one another. The same principle applies to rubles used in domestic and foreign transactions. Indeed, it is illegal to take rubles out of the U.S.S.R.

At home Soviet prices are supposed to cover the costs of production. This is interpreted to mean the full labor costs involved in direct production as well as the labor spent in producing raw materials and machinery (depreciation). Until the so called Liberman reforms of 1966, adherence to Marxist tradition meant that interest and rent costs would be inadequately covered or not included at all. Since then increased acknowledgment has been made of the real costs involved in the use of land and capital, but even so Soviet domestic prices still tend to understate the real economic costs involved in producing a product, particularly those utilizing substantial inputs of land and capital. Because of the Soviet practice of adding a "turnover tax" to wholesale prices, moreover, goods destined for consumers as opposed to goods intended for manufacturers have often been overpriced. This excise or sales tax often results in the doubling of the price of consumer goods. In 1971 the turnover tax amounted to approximately 35 percent of the total government and cooperative retail trade revenue.[1] Thus, Soviet domestic prices have a meaning unto themselves.

In approaching foreign markets, the Russians normally operate with a minimum of inhibitions when it comes to pricing. Like Western businessmen they normally try to earn as much as they can when selling and pay as little as possible when buying. Goods such as Russian caviar are not subject to much competition and therefore they can command their own price. But the Russians recognize that they cannot claim premium prices for goods that compete with established Western brands. Most often they have to maneuver around the market price, particularly when they are trying to sell in new markets. Fortunately, since there is no firm connection between Soviet domestic prices and currency and foreign prices and currencies, this poses no great dilemma. In the Russian system of calculation, they are normally prepared to lower their price as much as necessary to make a sale. Their costs, after all, are in soft Russian domestic rubles. When they export to the United States, their revenues are in hard currencies which will allow them to purchase foreign equipment that otherwise would be unavailable to them. Therefore, cost parities and foreign currency exchange rates are usually of little importance. What does matter to the Russians is that they get a foothold in the market. Eli Goldston, the late president of Eastern Gas and Transmission of Boston, recounted that no matter how low his firm set the price of the coal it sold to Japan, the Russians always equaled or slightly underbid his price. Once he proposed to some Russian officials in Tokyo that the Russians set their prices first. They responded by saying they had already set their prices—at whatever Goldston's price turned out to be.

Obviously such a policy can lead to misallocation of resources, and it has. Most East European countries also engaged in such pricing fancies. After considerable study they discovered that all too frequently they had exported what they should have imported, and vice versa. It should come as no surprise that apparently the Russians have made similar mistakes.[2]

Until recently, the Russians have almost always taken the prevailing international dollar prices as a starting point in their negotiations. This is still their practice in arranging purchases, but in the wake of the devaluations of the dollar that have taken place since December 1971, there have been some variations. As we saw earlier, in at least one instance the Russians contracted for a price in dollars for the sale of Russian rugs and then raised it days later after the dollar had been devalued. Because the ruble-dollar rate held constant from 1961 to 1971, there was no occasion for such incidents earlier.

Normally the only ones bothered by the official rates of exchange between the dollar and the ruble are visitors to the Soviet Union. Such rates bear no necessary relationship to actual supply and demand conditions; the Russians set them unilaterally. Thus, while the official rate as of August 8, 1973, was $1.46 to 1 ruble, the unofficial black market rate in Moscow was $1 for 3 rubles. Since December 1971 the Russians have raised the price of the ruble in step with increases in the value of the German mark. When the dollar started to regain strength in 1973, the Russians initially appeared to take no notice. To have done so would have meant a devaluation of the ruble. Ultimately, however, in November 1973, they did lower the value of the ruble relative to the dollar, and the ruble continued to fall in terms of the dollar until it was worth $1.27 in February 1974. Subsequently, as the dollar in turn began to weaken again, the Russians raised the price of the ruble. Thus for the first time in decades the Russians have started to make month-to-month adjustments in the international exchange rate of the ruble. While such changes do not necessarily bear any relation to the market value of the ruble, they do indicate that foreign exchange rates have taken on a greater significance for the Soviet government.

WORKING CONDITIONS

Preparing oneself to deal with the Soviet pricing and currency system is only the first step. Even if Soviet officials seek out the prospective American businessmen, and even if the price negotiations are in dollars, everything else is still likely to be more complex than it would be if the Americans were dealing with Western Europeans or Japanese. Except for major transactions, the American buyer or seller usually has no contact with the ultimate seller or customer in the U.S.S.R., even if it is a factory. For that reason, it often becomes very difficult to discover who it is on the Soviet side who has the ultimate decision-making power. Letters and cables are sent and telephone calls are made, but there is never any assurance that they will be answered.

Actually, things have improved significantly in recent years. This is due primarily to the dramatically improved political conditions which followed the Moscow and Washington summit meetings in 1972 and 1973. In typical Soviet fashion, this new era was institutionalized on October 18, 1972, with the formal signing of an American-Soviet trade agreement and several subsidiary agreements which, in addition to the proposed Lend Lease and MFN concessions (see Chapter 3), contained several other clauses intended to facilitate trade. In exchange for permitting the Russians to establish a trade representative in Washington, the U.S. was authorized to establish a commercial office in Moscow. In principle, the Russians agreed that the Moscow facility would provide American businessmen with introductions to Soviet ministries, market information, bilingual stenographer service, and communication to the United States.

The Russians also agreed to permit some American firms to open their private offices in Moscow and to employ Soviet personnel, acquire telephones, a Telex, copying equipment, calculators, furniture, appliances, and automobiles. They agreed to provide a large office-hotel-apartment trade center as well as an exhibition hall in Moscow for Americans and other foreigners. Based on a contract signed by Armand Hammer on September 18, 1973, this $110 million center is to have a 600-room hotel, 400 offices, 650 apartments for representatives of foreign companies in Moscow, a 2,000-seat conference hall, and a parking lot. In exchange, the United States offered to assist the Russians in setting up a New York office for the purpose of purchasing equipment for use in the Kama River truck plant.[3] The trade agreement also provided for continuation of the work of the Joint U.S.-U.S.S.R. Commercial Commission which was set up at the May 1972 Moscow Summit. This commission is made up of an American and a Soviet section and meets jointly at least once a year.[4] It has served as a useful vehicle for improving Russian working conditions and trade relations for American businessmen. Indeed, most of the provisions of the October 1972 trade agreement were hammered out by various task force groups of the joint commercial commission.

By providing for a continual flow of ideas and interchange of efforts at the highest level, the joint commission creates the kind of built-in flexibility which may make possible continued progress toward somewhat more normal commercial relations between the

157

two countries. The American side has thus far found itself somewhat at a disadvantage because of the rapid turnover in personnel coming out of Washington. While Foreign Minister Patolichev and his staff have been involved in the U.S.-U.S.S.R. negotiations from the beginning, the Americans were first represented by Secretary of Commerce Stans, who was replaced by Peter Peterson, who was replaced by Frederick Dent, who was replaced by Secretary of the Treasury George P. Schultz, who in turn resigned in mid-1974. The only constant on the American side was the executive secretary of the commission, Steven Lazarus, the deputy assistant secretary of commerce, and even he resigned in March 1974 after less than two years of service.

Yet in spite of the rapid turnover in personnel, the governmental joint commission has worked so well that its work has been supplemented by the creation of a somewhat similar organization at the nongovernmental level. Cochaired by V. S. Alkhimov, the Soviet deputy minister of foreign trade, and Donald Kendall, chairman of PepsiCo, this new U.S.-U.S.S.R. Trade and Economic Council's membership includes such influential businessmen as Howard Clark, chairman of American Express, A. W. Clausen, president of the Bank of America, Benjamin F. Crane, of the law firm of Cravath, Swain, and Moore, and Samuel B. Casey, president of the Pullman Corporation, as well as representation from 24 other major American financial and industrial organizations.[5] Located on Park Avenue in New York, the joint council or glorified chamber of commerce is run on a day-to-day basis by its president, Harold B. Scott, a former Assistant Secretary for Domestic and International Business in the Department of Commerce. (See Appendix IV.) This is the fourth such joint Soviet chamber of commerce or council and is similar in nature to those formed by the U.S.S.R. with France, Finland, and Italy. What the group lacks in staff, it makes up for in political clout, and it too can be looked to by American businessmen for help and advice.

OPERATING FROM THE UNITED STATES

All of this makes life considerably simpler than it used to be for Americans who want to trade with the Soviet Union. Yet whatever the improvement in negotiating climate or the promise of improved facilities in Moscow, most American businessmen will still find it easier to conduct their negotiations in the U.S. itself or in Western Europe.

Where is the best place to begin? Since the 1930s the Russians have maintained what are presumed to be buying and selling offices at Amtorg in New York City, first at 355 Lexington Avenue and now in the New York World Trade Center. (See Appendix IV) But there is a good deal of uncertainty as to just what Amtorg people actually do, and the recent experience of most American businessmen seems to indicate that Amtorg has not had much to do with facilitating actual buying and selling. But it is one place to start.

More business is likely to be done at the offices of the Temporary Purchasing Commission for the Kama River truck plant set up by the Russians in the General Motors Building on Fifth Avenue in New York, or with the 50-man Kama River truck plant staff in the Mellon Bank Building in Pittsburgh. Indicative of the improvement in American-Soviet trading relationships is the widely accepted acknowledgment in England that the best way for British machine tool manufacturers to sell their merchandise to the U.S.S.R. is to fly to Pittsburgh rather than to Moscow.[6]

The next best choice after the Kama River office would be to try in Washington at either the Soviet Embassy or the Soviet Trade Representative Office, authorized by the U.S.-Soviet Union trade agreement of 1972. Soviet personnel at these other offices often speak with more authority than Amtorg officials. At the Kama River office, for example, they have the authority to make decisions. And while the Embassy people and the Trade Representative Office have diplomatic immunity, and so in theory are

159

precluded from negotiating or executing transactions, they nonetheless pursue a remarkably active role. Inevitably, there is still an enormous amount of referral back to Moscow for the simplest decisions, but at least there is less buck-passing than at Amtorg.

Rather than take on the Russians themselves, many Americans will prefer to seek advice and sometimes help from other countrymen or even from West Europeans or Japanese who have already experienced the rigors of Russian trade and are not embarrassed to admit it. For those seeking assistance from the U.S. government, the place to begin is at the Bureau of East-West Trade in the Department of Commerce. Formerly· headed by Steven Lazarus, the same official who was executive secretary of the American section of the Joint U.S.-U.S.S.R. Commercial Commission, the Bureau of East-West Trade has put together an impressive amount of material and has proven to be helpful both for those seeking insights into broader political and economic trends, and for those who want help with specific projects. The bureau works closely with U.S. personnel in the commercial office which was recently opened in Moscow at 15 Chaikovskiy (there are now similar offices in Bucharest, Warsaw, and Vienna).

Governmental and semigovernmental organizations of this type can play an important role because, unlike the custom in most noncommunist states, a foreign salesman or buyer in Moscow cannot just walk in on prospective trading parties. It is often necessary to seek help from someone who has already established connections with Soviet agencies. If, however, one prefers the private sector instead of government agencies, the logical and probably cheapest place to start is with one of the three U.S. banks that have opened Moscow offices. (See Appendix IV) True, it is not yet clear what, if anything, bank representatives can do in Moscow. They are not authorized to carry on any banking functions in the U.S.S.R itself. They can, however, make referrals to the home office and they can to a limited degree help establish contacts within the U.S.S.R. There are several reasons for going to an American bank for this kind of intervention. First, it is less likely that a bank will charge a commission, since the bank is usually satisfied to make its money by handling the finances involved. Second, most of the banks (particularly the Chase Manhattan) have set up East-West research and business development departments which may be able to provide important advice. For that reason, it is likely that the non-Soviet facilities of these banks may prove more helpful than the Moscow office. Actually, it may be just as useful to consult similar departments established by banks such as Chemical and Manufacturers Hanover, which do not have a Moscow office, but which have had dealings with Soviet organizations. In a coup of sorts, Manufacturers Hanover has opened an actually operating branch in Rumania which is also expected to do business with the Soviet Union.

Another approach is to seek help from American industrial firms which have managed to open offices in Moscow. (See Appendix IV) Again, they may be no more helpful than the bank officials there, but if relations between the American company and its Soviet counterpart happen to be good at the moment, the American company may be quite helpful. If nothing else, such offices have secretarial translation and Telex facilities available. Moreover, since the cost of operating an office in Moscow is very expensive, the likelihood is that they will normally be quite anxious to increase their revenues by providing services for a fee or some involvement in future contracts. The Pullman Company, for example, has indicated that it is interested in broadening its revenue base in this way, and has in fact served as a representative for other firms. Thus when Raytheon had to send a small team to Moscow to conduct technical discussions in December 1973, Pullman provided it with office space and a translator from Pullman. On several other occasions, representatives from corporations have found that a call from Pullman's man in Moscow has helped to open heretofore closed doors.

Several companies have been created specifically for the purpose of aiding American businessmen in dealing with the Russians and East Europeans, even though they have no accredited offices in

Moscow. (See Appendix IV.) In some cases, such as Cyrus Eaton, Jr.'s, Tower International in Cleveland or Ara Oztemil's Satra in New York, the companies trade on the warm relationship between the American principal (or his father, in the case of Cyrus Eaton, Jr.) and senior Soviet officials. Other firms, such as the International Affairs Associates of Washington, run by James A. Ramsey, build on the experience of former American foreign service officers who have had extensive dealings with the Soviet brueaucracy. Then there are companies like Intertag in Chagrin Falls, Ohio, that have been created for the purpose of tapping the knowledge of specialists who have dealt extensively with the Soviet Union in fields ranging from business to law. Other companies, like Media Engineering of Cambridge, Massachusetts, have limited themselves to the specific task of translating and providing Russian texts for companies which want to advertise or convert their documentation into Russian. Other companies such as Associated Translating Services of Pittsburgh concentrate solely on translating technical documents. All of these organizations are run by Americans and can be dealt with as one would deal with any other company in the United States. This is an advantage that is not to be ignored.

DOING BUSINESS IN MOSCOW

Then there is always Moscow itself. Most Americans would be wise to follow in the steps of those who have already established some kind of working relationship with Soviet officials, even if it be only through the official U.S. commercial office there. However, for those who like challenges, there is nothing to prevent a businessman from trying to establish contact on his own. The challenge will be to induce the Soviet officials to open their doors so the businessman can present his proposals. This requires some understanding of how the Soviets conduct their foreign trade.

To help ease the way, some effort should be made to obtain assistance from the All Union Soviet Chamber of Commerce. The chamber and its president, Boris A. Borisov, have the ability to head an American in the right direction. However, sooner or later the visiting foreigner is going to have to make contact with some agency of the Soviet Ministry of Foreign Trade, which almost alone is authorized to buy and sell in foreign markets on behalf of Soviet industry. The first trick is to get in the building, a closely guarded Stalinesque skyscraper which also houses the Ministry of Foreign Affairs. But this can only be done if authorization is issued to the guards at the door. Thus, the second task is to find out which ministry or official is interested in your product and will authorize the guard to let you in.

The Ministry of Foreign Trade is subdivided into a series of 50-odd foreign trade organizations (FTO), each headed by a president who tends to concentrate on one production line. Authorization to import or export stems ultimately from these FTOs, which in turn are supposed to coordinate their efforts with the final user or supplier. Since each organization has its own set of targets by which it is judged, coordination between them sometimes leaves something to be desired. For example, the importing Soviet factory would like the best and, therefore, often the most expensive equipment available, since the more durable and productive the machinery, the more likely it is that the factory will be able to increase its future production at low operating costs. After all, the foreign exchange for the purchase does not usually come out of the factory's own account. The FTO, on the other hand, is interested in buying as cheaply as possible so that its limited supply of foreign exchange will be spread as far as possible.

While it certainly would be nice if a Soviet factory manager could be induced to send through a request for a special product from a specific American factory, it is usually most difficult for the American businessman to establish contacts with individual Soviet factory personnel. The Ministry of Foreign Trade normally acts as a filter between foreigners and factory managers. Consequently anyone interested in trading with the Russians will sooner or later have to deal with the FTO of the Ministry of Trade. Indeed, given the Soviet system, this may be an efficient way of doing business, particularly for an American firm trying to buy something in the U.S.S.R. The FTO serves as a purchasing agent, and it can cut through Soviet bureaucracy in a way that a foreigner would find extremely difficult.

For the American seller, however, dealing with the FTO is likely to be a less than satisfying experience. The FTO often takes some time to ascertain if a factory somewhere in the U.S.S.R. needs or wants what the American has to sell. If the FTO refuses to cooperate, there is no such thing as moving down the street to the next factory. Therefore, it is necessary to prepare well in advance for the Moscow visit.

The American businessman bound for Moscow should prepare his way by seeking the help of all the Soviet agencies in the U.S., be they in Pittsburgh, New York, or Washington. American organizations with Moscow contracts should be checked in the same way. In addition, the president of the relevant FTO in Moscow should be sent material in the hope of evoking an interest on his part. Such material should include professional journal articles and technical reports prepared by the American firm's research staff, as well as any other material prepared by the firm that might not have appeared in professional journals.

Another means of gaining entrée is to offer to conduct seminars in the Soviet Union to selected groups of technicians and researchers. Often this can be done in conjunction with the trade fairs and scientific exhibitions the Russians are so fond of holding. Initiative for such events usually comes from the Russians and they extend open invitations to companies in the field. Occasionally, however, the initiative comes from the American side. That is what happened with the aviation and space industries in mid-1973. The American Institute of Aeronautics and Astronautics first obtained permission from the Soviet authorities to sponsor such a show, and then solicited American firms for their participation. Westinghouse Electric, Bendix, United Aircraft, Collins Radio, Texas

Instruments, Boeing, Lockheed Aircraft, and Raytheon were among the firms that proposed exhibits. The show was apparently successful, since the same group was invited to put together another exhibition in 1975.

Such exhibitions are highly regarded in the U.S.S.R.—particularly if they have some official U.S. government support and participation—and invariably an effort is made to send the best Soviet specialists to see what other firms around the world are producing. The Russians rely heavily on exhibitions to demonstrate the best of their own products, and at the same time they also rely on them to see what other countries have to offer. In many ways the exhibitions fulfill the same functions as a salesman in this country.

Trade fairs in Eastern Europe—for example, in Leipzig in East Germany, Poznan in Poland, and Brno in Czechoslovakia—play much the same role and are also a way of breaking into the Soviet orbit. But tangible results from such exhibitions may be slow in coming. PepsiCo exhibited for ten years at Leipzig before it finally obtained a contract for East Germany.

In the U.S.S.R. the scope of such general exhibitions is already wide, and it is growing. In a magazine interview, Kristofor G. Oganessyan, chief of the Department of International and Foreign Exhibitions of the Soviet Chamber of Commerce and the man in charge of such events, reported that in 1972 the Soviet Union held two international and 11 specialized foreign exhibitions.[7] The Russians also agreed to hold 128 special shows in response to requests of foreign companies. A total of 143 exhibitions were held in 1972, compared to 94 in 1970 and 121 in 1971. Subjects of past shows have included electrical engineering, farm machinery, machine tools, optical mechanics, container transport and food industry machinery, automobile service, timber and woodworking machinery, microbiological processes and equipment, electronic control of measuring equipment, electronic printing equipment, paper manufacturing equipment, obstetrical and gynecological equipment, and computers. The program for 1975 calls for exhibitions of equipment for the television and movie industries, pumps and compressors, communication systems, aluminum manufacturing, sports equipment, fishing industry, plant protection techniques, office mechanization, livestock handling, physics, and geology.

While it does not provide much notice, *Ekonomicheskaia Gazeta,* the weekly economics paper, publishes a list of exhibitions for the following month in the last issue of each month. And in its quarterly report, the Bureau of East-West Trade of the Department of Commerce also publishes a list of "Promotional Events in East-West Trade." [8] The Trade Representative Office of the Soviet Embassy should normally have longer-range information available, or be able to obtain it from Christofor Oganessyan at the Soviet Union Chamber of Commerce's International Exhibitions Department.

Other approaches open to an American manufacturer are limited only by the imagination of the seller. Some foreign companies, including Sharp and Hitachi of Japan and Gillette of the U.S., have inserted ads in Soviet journals. Theoretically, it is even possible to advertise on Soviet radio and television. While not particularly effective, the rates for such ads are remarkably low. (In 1968, for example, a minute of Soviet television time cost only $2000.[9]) Among the American firms that have established working arrangements with *Vneshtorgreklama,* the Soviet advertising agency, are Marsteller Inc. New York and Black-Russell-Morris of Newark. Each company thought it was the first American firm to have worked out such contracts, even though it happens that the S. S. Koppe Co. of New York had made a similar breakthrough in 1964.[10]

Despite all such efforts, more often than not there will be no response. As has happened so often in such cases, the visiting American may find himself waiting patiently in a Moscow hotel room for a call that never comes. As a minimum, an effort should also be made in Moscow to call the offices of the respective FTO, which is no easy matter. Even Moscow phone books or directories of official business offices are often hard to find, although they are usually available through the Intourist travel bureau located in the hotels assigned to foreigners. (The U.S. Embassy and commercial offices also have copies.) The visiting salesmen may also need someone who can speak Russian well enough to explain the purpose of the call. Intourist translators are frequently reluctant to make unofficial phone calls like these. Moreover, Russians are usually uncommunicative over the phone. Anyone forced to use the Soviet phone system can easily appreciate why. Not only is it difficult to hear, but usually long-distance calls to both Soviet and foreign locations must be reserved a day in advance. Moreover, the caller must also specify exactly how long the call will last. Russians regard answering the phone as an onerous chore to be avoided or, if that is impracticable, to be concluded as soon as possible. Russians say hello but not goodbye on the phone, so one never knows when the call is finished. In addition, Russians are loath to take or pass on messages, so there is never any assurance that it is worth taking the time to leave a message. Besides, since secretaries (male or female) are not as numerous in Soviet offices as they are elsewhere in the world, there is often no one even to answer the phone.

OPENING AN OFFICE IN MOSCOW

For some, the way to overcome such obstacles may be to open their own office in Moscow. This will not be easy or cheap. Obtaining permission to open an office in Moscow is difficult enough, but it is usually only half the battle. The other half is to run it efficiently. Finding help is one major problem. All Soviet employees hired by a foreign company must be recruited and screened by a branch of the Foreign Ministry called Administration for Services to Diplomatic Corps (UPDK by its Russian initials). Such personnel are chosen for their language ability and reliability as viewed primarily from the Soviet side.

Then there is the problem of office space. Obtaining ordinary office supplies is hard enough; getting office space can sometimes involve major diplomatic confrontations. The Russians have a housing shortage. Consequently, although it is less common now than it was a few years ago, foreigners will sometimes find themselves living in the same room that serves as an office.

Despite such uncomfortable quarters, the cost of operating a Moscow office is very high. According to Albert Wentworth, manager of Chase Manhattan's office, it costs the bank about $150,000 a year above and beyond his salary to maintain a presence in Moscow.[11] Since salaries for Americans assigned to Moscow run about $50,000 a year, the Chase Manhattan must spend at least $200,000 on its Soviet facility.

As yet there is no such thing as a commercial office building in any Russian city. Unlike the Kama River Purchasing Commission, which had its pick of commercial office space in Manhattan, the Chase Manhattan Bank decided to settle for a demobilized hotel room in Moscow's Metropole Hotel. It could have been worse. The Metropole is centrally located and an elegant if old hotel, where Chase employees happily boast they can walk the few floors when elevators are not working or are under repair. Other foreign businesses have not been as fortunate.

As more housing has been constructed, Russians have begun to set aside apartment building complexes for the use of foreigners as both offices and apartments. But there are no Russians in such facilities, which in fact are guarded 24 hours a day to keep away ordinary Russian citizens. (Even cars driven by foreigners are required to carry special distinguishing license plates. Russians have license plates that are black with white letters, while foreigners must use white plates with black letters.)

As mentioned earlier, one of the provisions of the October 1972 U.S.-Soviet Union trade agreements calls for construction of "a large office-hotel-apartment trade center." All indications are that this complex will be isolated in much the same way as existing facilities. Building one special complex makes it easier for the Soviet government to contain foreign influences.

Certainly the concept of special quarters for foreign businessmen in Moscow predates the current influx. Back in the sixteenth and seventeenth centuries, Muscovite rulers set aside a special quarter, the *Nemetskaia Sloboda,* for foreign traders.[12] Later the *Kitaiskii Gorod* was used for the same purpose. Both ghettos served the dual function of providing an area where foreigners could "do their own thing" and yet not contaminate the Moscow populace in the process.

STATE COMMITTEE ON SCIENCE AND TECHNOLOGY

One of the few places in Moscow where there is somewhat more openness in meeting foreign businessmen and where business methods are slightly more comparable to those in the East is the State Committee on Science and Technology (SCST). This state committee, even more than the Ministry of Foreign Trade, has been the prime mover in trying to upgrade technical competence in the U.S.S.R. Its research capabilities are impressive, as is its ability to get things done in the usually frustrating bureaucratic atmosphere of the U.S.S.R. As mentioned earlier, this may be explained by the fact that its chairman, V. A. Kirillen, is also deputy chairman of the Council of Ministers of the U.S.S.R., while its vice chairman, Dzerhman Gvishiani, is not only very able, but also Premier Aleksei Kosygin's son-in-law. Gvishiani (Gerry, as he has become known to his American friends) is highly conversant with Western technology and methods and is a frequent visitor to the U.S. and other capitalist countries. Most Americans regard him as one of the most knowledgeable Russian officials with whom they have negotiated.

Although it is sometimes encumbered with bureaucratic over-work, the SCST can play a leading role in sponsoring special seminars and trade exhibitions for foreign firms. It also serves as a point of contact for any American corporation that wants to invite a group of Soviet specialists to make a presentation in this country. This may be effective, but it may also prove to be expensive. One American company spent between $75,000 and $100,000 to bring Soviet specialists and officials to the United States to examine factory equipment for possible purchase, only to have the whole deal collapse.

Going beyond technological agreements, seminars, and trade exhibitions, the SCST has also sought to establish bilateral technological exchanges with individual foreign corporations in the hope of developing a more formal and longer-lasting relationship. The first American firm to enter into such an agreement was the Joy Manufacturing Company in July 1972. (Other American companies that have since signed such pacts are listed in Appendix II.) The Russians hope that such bilateral technological agreements will enable them to increase the flow of advanced technology to the Soviet Union, and to do it "on the cheap." The foreign corporation hopes that such relationships will pave the way for large-scale sales of plant and equipment. It is hard to see how *both* expectations can be fully realized.

From everything that can be gathered about the agreements so far, many of them are often little more than fishing expeditions. Indeed, looking at the list of firms involved in these agreements, there is the strong suspicion that the Russians are particularly interested in military technology. The list of companies reads like the aristocracy of the military-industrial complex. Moreover, since there is no guarantee that any firm commercial contracts will follow from such agreements, other advanced technology companies like the Pullman Corporation, which have also been approached, have refused to enter into such pacts. While interested in dealing with the Soviet Union, they are not interested in the talk and publicity which sometimes is the main result. Of course in some instances, as with Monsanto and Occidental Petroleum, these technological alliances have been followed by significant contracts. But so far, the majority of such alliances have not resulted in much more than cordiality and great expectations.

Why, then, have so many American companies actually taken the initiative in seeking out the SCST? What do they hope to get out of these agreements? First, they hope that the bilateral protocol will subsequently lead to large contracts—including some for the sale of obsolete equipment, at least as seen by the American firm. To a lesser extent, other corporations have rationalized their participation by pointing to the high degree of achievement shown by Soviet scientists. The Soviet Union has the capability and the facilities to develop some of the most advanced research in the world. The main problem, however, has been to move the research from the laboratory into the factory and into the marketplace. American firms have not been entirely successful in this kind of activity, but their record has certainly been much better than that of Soviet enterprises. It would seem, therefore, to be a natural match-up (even more so than with West European companies): Soviet enterprises should try to link up their research abilities with American practical production and marketing techniques. In addition to the Soviet ability in the laboratory, there have also been many developments at the factory level and in applied technology, particularly when the Soviets devote much effort in high-priority areas, be they industry, space, or military production. The Soviet problem has been that there are only so many areas that can be declared priority and that can receive the attention that seems needed in such efforts in the Soviet Union.

Whether or not the U.S.S.R. is prepared to share or sell this kind of technology and expertise, it is there, and any firms that can obtain such capabilities would find it both in their private and in the national interest to get them.

The Singer Company's technological agreement with the SCST illustrates the general pattern of relationships sketched above. As of this writing, Singer has not negotiated many major contracts with the Soviet Union. Even so, the company feels it has benefited from signing the pact.

Actually, Singer's relationship with Russia goes back some decades before the revolution. By 1914, Singer's Russian subsidiary had a sales force of 27,500, as well as several manufacturing plants with a total productive capacity of more than one million sewing machines a year. They had also built up a network of 50 agencies and warehouses, which in turn serviced 3,000 individual outlets which handled the sale and repair of sewing machines.[13] All these facilities were ultimately nationalized in 1917, at a loss that the company put at about $100 million.

After that experience, it took until about 1960 before Singer put aside its resentment over past treatment and started a corporate effort to reenter Eastern Europe and the Soviet Union.

To coordinate its campaign, in the spring of 1972 Singer created a special department for socialist country activities development. In addition it retained the services of International Affairs Associates in Washington and Vienna to guide Singer in its efforts to break into the Soviet circuit. Because of their long prerevolutionary connections, the Singer people felt it would not be too difficult to reestablish contact. But while their old ties did help, it took some while for the Soviets to respond with much enthusiasm.

The first move was to send the president of Singer, Donald Kircher, and other senior Singer officials to Moscow, after an exhibition and seminar in Warsaw. At the conclusion of the visit, Singer scheduled a reception in the Intourist Hotel to which 200 key officials were invited. Only 50 people showed up. Many would consider this a successful response, since the Soviets are often reluctant to request permission to attend such public affairs. Nonetheless, the Singer executives were disappointed and decided on a new approach.[14] In the early fall of 1973 they signed a technological agreement with the SCST. No major contracts followed immediately, but Soviet doors did open more readily.

The Singer staff now decided to try for another visit to Moscow. This time the main attraction would be a seminar put on by some of Singer's research and development people, with SCST serving as host. At a cost of about $100,000, Singer sent 35 of its people to

Moscow in September 1973. Two weeks before the seminar, some Singer executives and their consultants went to Moscow to arrange a site and an invitation list for the seminar. The SCST provided some help, but the Singer people had to do a considerable amount themselves.

A series of four seminars were held, each half a day in duration. Most were well attended by from 30 to 115 people. Following the seminars, Singer once again scheduled a reception. This time, in contrast to their experience the year before, 115 of the 135 people invited came. Sponsorship by the SCST made the difference. With the imprimatur of the SCST, everyone knew that Singer had become an acceptable foreign organization. In fact, Singer officials became so welcome that the Russians arranged to take them to see their old factory at Podolsk.

As cordial as the Russians were, however, there were still certain barriers that could not be penetrated. In an attempt to direct their future efforts at the ultimate user of their products, the Singer people tried to find out who was attending the seminars. As they do at such meetings in other parts of the world, Singer brought with it follow-up cards. If filled out, the addressee would be sent additional material by Singer. To the frustration of the Singer officials, their cards were confiscated and not returned until after the seminars had been held. In what seemed at the time like an adaptive response, one Singer executive decided to pass out a sign-up sheet. Again those who signed up were promised they would be sent technical materials. Out of the 65 people attending the seminar, only three signed the sheet.

All of this contact with Western firms suggests that the SCST is considerably more sophisticated and pleasant in its dealings with foreign groups than most other Soviet organizations. There is a certain irony here if we recall that the SCST is also a supersecret and sensitive research group. Oleg Penkovsky, America's superspy, served as a senior official in the SCST until he was arrested. Thus the same organization that encourages technological intercourse with the West also conducts supersecret technical research.

Needless to say, this has resulted in a somewhat schizophrenic atmosphere found disconcerting by some who have come in contact with it.

MARKET RESEARCH

Before we could worry about what it was the Russians wanted to buy or sell, we had to learn something about Soviet pricing policies, who to deal with, and where to deal. Obviously, it is still necessary to do some preliminary market research. It is generally safe to assume that the vast majority of industrial products manufactured in the West could find a market in the U.S.S.R. The problem, however, is that the Russians limit the amount of foreign exchange available at any one time for such purchases. It is therefore necessary to ascertain their order of priorities or find how they might be induced to include another product in that preference schedule. While a persistent businessman can occasionally convince the Russians of their need for his product, usually the more fruitful approach is to try to find out what areas the Russians are emphasizing in their present purchasing plans. Although the Russians do not as a rule make such information publicly available, there may be ways to approximate what their goals might be.

Some Western observers claim these can all be anticipated by studying Soviet five-year plans. Since the Soviet Union has a planned economy, everything (in theory at least) is spelled out five years in advance. Therefore, if provision is not made for construction of a particular factory, there is no hope of selling the machinery that would go in it. Similarly, if the plan does not provide for the production and setting aside of certain materials for export, it is often assumed that it will be impossible to buy such goods.[15] While there is an element of truth in such reasoning, and indeed many purchases and sales are sketched out in advance in the yearly and five-year economic plans, a study of Soviet foreign trade habits suggests that the Ministry of Foreign Trade operates in a remarkably extemporaneous fashion.

Some have argued that until we signed bilateral trade agreements, as we did in October 1972, American exporters and importers would not be included in Soviet plans and our Western and Japanese competitors would grab the major share of the market.[16] Such reasoning is contradicted by the fact that the U.S. became the second largest noncommunist exporter to the Soviet Union in 1972 and the largest in 1973. Signing of the bilateral treaty could not have been provided for in the Ninth Five-Year Plan, which was announced in 1971. Nor could the yearly plan for 1972 have included an allowance for the fact that the grain harvest for 1972–1973 would turn out to be so poor. In other words, foreign trade, particularly in commodities, is frequently a spontaneous affair.

Construction projects like the Kama River truck plant are suited for long-range five-year plans. Often, however, even major decisions, such as to build up a chemical industry or to proceed with a project as soon as possible (the Fiat plant), are made in the middle of an existing five-year plan. When new technological innovations that the Soviets want are announced in the West, they seldom wait for the five-year plan to be drawn up to buy the processes or equipment. The plan, in other words, should be regarded as a guide to prospective exports and imports, rather than an inflexible or limiting program.

Because technology is changing so fast, a five-year plan becomes dated shortly after it appears in print. Consequently in addition to examining the official plan, it may be just as useful to try to compare other societies and observe the directions they have moved in when they were at a similar stage of economic development. Presumably the Soviet Union will have somewhat similar needs in the future. Thus it is reasonably safe to assume that Soviet planners are or will soon be interested in such things as materials-handling equipment, highway construction and maintenance equipment, tools and parts for servicing automobiles, automobile accessories, synthetic fibers and plastics, do-it-yourself appliances and tools, convenience foods and the processing equipment to prepare such foods, and marketing and distribution equipment.

Another approach along the same lines is to analyze the periodic progress reports about yearly plan fulfillment. Invariably the Central Statistical Agency devotes a few paragraphs to discussing which industrial ministries have lagged behind expectations. Presumably some of these shortcomings could be corrected by infusions of Western technology. Thus it is not surprising that in 1973 Soviet trade officials negotiated with companies engaged in making equipment for oil exploration and drilling, chemical production, and pulp paper and timber processing. All these industries were having difficulty fulfilling their 1973 targets.[17]

Such an approach has its limitations. Some industries, such as the timber industry, have been having trouble fulfilling their targets since the inception of the yearly plan system. Sometimes, moreover, it is more a question of ill-suited incentive and plan procedures rather than outmoded machinery. In addition, industries for which some of the largest Soviet purchases have been made have never shown up on the delinquent list. Thus the automobile and truck industries have seldom been criticized for plan underfulfillment, yet the largest import projects have been for automobile and truck plants. The plans were generally fulfilled, but the plans themselves were inadequate, since the production capacity for automobiles and trucks was simply not very large. The only way this could show up would be in criticism of the machine tool industry, but such criticism is too vague to be helpful or suggestive for most American exporters.

Perhaps the best indicator of all, at least for the majority of future Soviet purchases, is the Soviet-sponsored exhibitions discussed earlier. The theme of the exhibition is usually chosen because the subject is of particular concern at the time. While the Russians do hope to sell some of their own products at these exhibitions, more often than not they regard such affairs as a unique opportunity to compare rival models of products they ultimately want to buy.

BARTER AND FINANCE

For those who like to live dangerously, there are other, less conventional ways of conducting trade with the U.S.S.R., some of which have been necessitated because the Soviet ruble is not convertible. Thus while almost all foreign trade is monopolized by the Ministry of Foreign Trade, the government has permitted some barter transactions by regional organizations that by-pass the controls of the Ministry of Foreign Trade in Moscow. For example, it allows three border areas in the northwest, in Central Asia, and in the far east to deal directly on a barter basis with firms in the adjacent countries of Finland, Norway, Iran, Turkey, Japan, and North Korea. Presumably some American firms might find it worthwhile to participate in such arrangements by joining with some of the Finnish or Norwegian firms and extending the barter process one stage further. Local Soviet officials in these border areas can do more or less as they please and exchange whatever suits them without interference from Moscow's Ministry of Foreign Trade. In principle, there is nothing wrong if American goods enter these barter and trade streams as long as Soviet goods flow out in return.

The governing principle in such operations is to exchange as much as possible as long as no hard currency has to be sacrificed. If they had their way, Soviet trade officials would probably never spend any hard currency. One example of a barter deal involving an American company is the Pepsi-Vodka arrangement. Soviet officials have agreed to match their Pepsi Cola purchases with sales of Soviet vodka in the United States by a PepsiCo subsidiary. However, the Russians appear to be trying to do more than settle for simple barter. They are attempting to make hard currency on the deal as well. Thus they are diverting large quantities of their locally produced Pepsi to the hard currency "Berëzka" shops in the Soviet Union, where they can sell it for dollars and pounds. This way they hope to profit above and beyond the original framework of the agreement. They are now earning dollars on a product (Pepsi) obtained in exchange for something that cost them only soft currency—vodka.

Generally the Russians have tried to be as innovative as possible in their barter operations. Where feasible, they have moved beyond simple barter and have attached prices to the goods being exchanged so that bilateral clearing arrangements can be created. In this way each side can trade a more varied collection of goods, with the provision that each side should try to purchase approximately the same amount so that by the year's end neither will owe anything to the other. In principle, this should assure a balance, but in fact there are often imbalances when one side is unable to find anything worth buying.

Despite the superficial simplicity of bilateral trade, the non-Russian members of CMEA have complained bitterly about the unsuitability of the goods they have received in exchange, the uncompetitive prices they have had to pay, and the unspendable credits they have accumulated which they have no way of utilizing. Over the years this has become the source of considerable friction. For example, among the Czech grievances during their abortive renaissance of 1968 was the complaint that they had accumulated claims against the Soviets of about 10 billion crowns, or $1.4 billion, which they could find no satisfactory way to spend.

Even the Russians have come to have misgivings about bilateral trade and barter. In the years 1958–1965, the Soviet Government accumulated a surplus equivalent to $891 million (from barter deals) which they could not spend. Because of such problems Russian critics have acknowledged that, after a point, bilateral clearing, instead of causing an expansion, may lead to a curtailment of trade. There is likely to be a holding back when one of the partners decides to demand the settlement of unbalanced clearing accounts in gold or hard currency, or when a debtor seeks an extension of his debt, which in effect then becomes a form of "technical credit."

Even though members of CMEA and the developing countries have become increasingly reluctant to involve themselves in bilateral and trilateral clearing arrangements, Western businessmen have sometimes been willing to take a chance. In their eagerness to sell to the communist countries, some Western firms have agreed to accept such payment in kind or in soft currencies because they thought they could resell these goods or credits at a discount in Western markets for hard currency. To compensate for the discount, they have generally tried to mark up the prices of their own products, hoping to provide themselves with a margin of safety. Occasionally even this has not been enough protection.

The fact that different state trading organizations (in Eastern Europe) and private organizations (in Western Europe) often have claims on goods for which they have no particular use has created an opportunity for alert businessmen and arbitragers. For a fee, such specialists will offer to *swap* these goods and currencies for other goods and currencies that might be more useful. Technically this is called "switching" and it has become a multimillion-dollar operation. Switching is also a logical prelude to convertibility, as in fact it turned out to be in Western Europe after World War II. In effect, it means the parties to the switch are prepared to accept the East European currency, but only at a discount. This is equivalent to a de facto devaluation. Depending on the goods and countries involved, switching can be a complicated process.

Actually, it is not a game for dabblers. On occasion, a member of CMEA may even end up competing against another member. For instance, one Boston chemical exporter reports that on several occasions he has found himself buying chemicals from the Soviet Union and then reselling them directly to East Germany. Since Soviet trading agencies obviously could have done this by themselves, why did the Russians permit an American to come in when they knew their goods were being bought and sent directly to their communist allies? As explained by the American exporter, once the Russians had met the terms of their bilateral trade agreement with East Germany for the delivery of chemical products, they still had some left over. They wanted to sell these chemicals for hard currency if at all possible. Although members of CMEA use only soft currency in their trade with one another, the American exporter knew that the East Germans were willing to pay hard currency because they were in urgent need of more of the chemical. Thus the American was able to sell to a communist country for dollars what he had bought from a communist country with dollars. Marxist purists would probably frown at the unorthodox nature of such transactions. But to the increasingly pragmatic traders in the Soviet Union, the important question is: Were the goods sold and did the Russians make a profit in dollars in the process?

Barter and swap sales are primarily designed to accommodate Soviet importers who want to buy but do not have hard currency. This means that the American businessman who wants to buy from the U.S.S.R. and pay hard currency for his purchase may be in a particularly advantageous position. His most logical course of action is to find some American exporter to the Soviet Union who is being pressured to accept something in exchange for the product he wants to export. If the American exporter is being loaded with goods that happen to satisfy the needs of the American importer, the importer can do the exporter a favor and at the same time probably obtain his Russian merchandise at lower prices than if he bought it directly from the Russians. Once the Russians find out about such arrangements, however, they will do all they can to insist that the American importer buy from them directly and pay hard currency for the privilege.

TRADITIONAL FINANCE

While these more exotic forms of finance appeal to some who feel they can expand their trade beyond the limits of what they would otherwise be able to do, most American businessmen prefer to be paid in the more prosaic and traditional manner normally used elsewhere in the world. For that matter, the Russians often do pay cash or use commercial credit. Wherever possible, however, they seem to prefer, for reasons that are not hard to understand, to use the services of the Export-Import Bank (Eximbank). The Eximbank lends money at a subsidized rate. Congress voted it this power in the expectation that the availability of such credits would increase American exports. Congress was prodded in this direction by the realization that other countries were providing similar services. For example, England has its Export Credits Guarantee Department (ECGD), France its Compagnie Francaise d'Assurance pour Commerce Exterieur (COFACE), Italy its Instituto Mobiliare Italiano, and Germany its Ausfuhrkredit-Gesellschaft (AKA). If the United States did not offer similar subsidies, American exporters would undoubtedly lose sales to those countries which did. Thus until early 1974 the Eximbank was lending money to purchasers of American products, Japanese as well as Russian, at rates of 6 percent. This was at a time when commercial borrowers in the United States were paying rates of 10 percent or more. In response to critics both at home and in Germany, the Eximbank finally raised its interest to 7 percent and in some instances to 8½ percent in the hope that the counterpart institutions in England, France, and Italy would similarly reduce their subsidies.

Eximbank procedures are usually not complicated. When a country is the borrower, the Eximbank insists on examining the country's balance of payment position and its stock of currency reserves. Like any careful lender, it wants to assure itself of the borrower's ability to repay. Unlike most noncommunist countries, where such information is a matter of record, most of the communist countries treat such information as classified material. In addition, the Soviet Union says that the Eximbank does not need such information because the Vnestorgbank, the Soviet Bank for Foreign Trade, which does all the borrowing for the Soviet Union, has the full resources of the Soviet government behind it. In a departure from established procedures, the Eximbank has accepted this argument so far and lent the Soviet Union $469 million as of July 1974. Such loans have generated a good deal of criticism from Congress. Apparently Algeria has also borrowed Eximbank money based on such guarantees, but such arrangements are unusual, especially when the collateral is in a fixed plant or pipeline which cannot be attached by the creditor or taken out of the country.

In taking out a loan, the Russians usually work closely with an American commercial bank. The Chase Manhattan Bank has been particularly active in such partnerships. As of April 1974 it had loaned about $150 million for just the Kama River truck plant. The usual practice is that the Eximbank is asked to put up the first 45 percent of the loan. The American commercial bank then puts up the second 45 percent at commercial rates. However, the Chase Manhattan, as well as some of the other lenders, have been accused of extending unusually low rates, below the prevailing prime rate charged American customers. Thus apparently in 1972 Chase provided Moscow with a loan at 7⅛ percent for its initial contract with Pullman at the Kama River truck plant. This was at a time when the Federal Funds rate (the rate banks charge one another) was about 7.5 percent.[18]

Most borrowers then ask the Eximbank to guarantee the second 45 percent, but the Russians have recently decided not to do this on all their loans. They assume that participation of the Eximbank in the first 45 percent is enough protection for the commercial bank that also signs the loan. By not asking for the guarantee, the Russians save themselves the extra percent the Eximbank would otherwise charge.

Finally, the U.S.S.R. pays the remaining 10 percent of the purchase price in cash. Thus in the trade center and hotel deal negotiated by Armand Hammer, the Eximbank agreed to put up $36 million, the Chase Manhattan the other $36 million, and the Soviet Union the final $8 million. This will take care of the $80 million in foreign currency the $110 million project is expected to cost.

Even though it was originally created to finance American trade with the Soviet Union, the Russians are not the only ones to use the facilities of the Eximbank. In fact, as of 1974, only 1.7 percent of the bank's total loans and guarantees outstanding had been extended to the Soviet Union. Nonetheless there are many in Congress who have had persistent doubts about the wisdom of subsidizing major purchases for the U.S.S.R. In 1973 and 1974 Congress forced the Eximbank to suspend the issuance of new loans to the Soviet Union for a time just because of such concerns. A move that infuriated Soviet officials, as we saw earlier, was the law passed by Congress limiting loans to the U.S.S.R. to $300 million for four years. Lenders in other countries have had similar doubts. The Germans have been reluctant to provide highly subsidized credits for some major Soviet projects, and their urging was a factor in the Eximbank's decision to raise the rates to 7 percent. In particular, the German government refused to subsidize the $2 billion direct reduction steel plant German firms were offering to build at Kursk. The Soviet Union tried for almost two years to obtain a German government subsidy. The German commercial rate at the time was close to 11 percent. Ultimately the Soviet purchasers agreed to pay the Germans cash for the whole $1 billion dollars worth of imported equipment called for by the project. At the same time, of course, the French have had a tendency to go to the other extreme. In 1974 they set aside an extra 1.5 billion francs ($300 million) for loans to the U.S.S.R. In the recent past the French have often charged less than 6 percent for such loans although they also raised their rates to 7½ percent in late 1974.

NEGOTIATIONS

From the nature of the transactions discussed thus far and the difficulty of arranging for meaningful bargaining, it should be evident that negotiations with the Russians can be demanding. The Russians pride themselves on their reputation as tough bargainers. Interspersed with their threats and bluffs will be professions of peace and friendship lubricated with enormous quantities of vodka intended to weaken the firmest convictions. One official of a large American corporation insists that he will not include anyone on his negotiating team who cannot hold his or her liquor. About the only way to avoid drinking and yet not have one's virility challenged is to plead stomach trouble or pregnancy. Yet a night of solemn pledges of warmth and companionship may often be followed by a morning of coolness and stand-offishness. The Russians may then stall for months and then announce that they are turning instead to a foreign or other American competitor.

The use of such tactics by the Russians reportedly cost the Caterpillar Corporation thousands of dollars. When Caterpillar refused to bear the financing for the equipment they were trying to sell, the Soviet negotiators are supposed to have turned to International Harvester, which did agree to such terms in hopes of winning the contract. The only way Caterpillar could regain the Soviet contract was to accept similar expenses. Needless to say, there is nothing sinister about such tactics; American firms will usually try to win the same concessions in the same way. This just demonstrates that the Soviets are as adept at these practices as the Americans.

Among other tactics, the Russians will sometimes insist that the negotiators fly to Moscow immediately and then let them sit and cool their heels in a hotel. The expectation is that such practices will so frustrate the American that he will be more anxious to sign and go home.

One method used by some of those interviewed to cope with such strategy is to arrange to be in Moscow for a short but specified period of time as part of a longer business visit through Western Europe. If contacts in the Soviet bureaucracy have been established in advance, these Soviet officials should be notified of the impending visit and of the limited amount of time available. If the Russians are serious they will arrange to accommodate the visitor's needs. There is always the possibility, however, that no meeting can be arranged for the time specified, in which case the businessman must always be prepared to leave Moscow with nothing but frustration. Another strategy is to try to negotiate several different deals with several different foreign trade organizations at one time. Obviously only a conglomerate or a corporation with markedly different products can pursue this technique. Where it can be adopted, however, the likelihood is increased that at least one potential Soviet customer will be willing to negotiate while the others are stalling.

Once negotiations do begin, they often tend to drag on much longer than would be the case elsewhere. Thus Armand Hammer's fertilizer deal with the Russians required that he sign four distinct agreements. The first step involved signing a *protocol,* which provided status for his company and made it easier to obtain visas for his staff at Occidental Petroleum. The second step was to sign a *letter of intent.* The third stage was a *global agreement* setting out the principal terms. Finally, after two years and approximately $1 million of negotiating expenses spent both here and in the Soviet Union, he signed an *implementation* agreement which set out the final contractual terms.[19]

Having to go through all these phases inevitably adds to the cost as well as the frustration of such dealings. In an effort to accelerate some of the process, the Singer Company has sought to anticipate as many as possible of the counterproposals the East Europeans are likely to make and to work out its reactions in advance. In this way there should be less need to return home for future instructions. The Singer people also bring with them the decision makers, so if need be, most unanticipated matters can be decided on the spot. But Singer goes a step further. A perennial problem is that the original contract proposal must be continually revised in order to reflect all the bargaining changes that take place. That may also necessitate trips to the West. Therefore, Singer brings not only its decision makers, but its secretarial staff as well. They carry everything from Scotch tape, to staples, to screwdrivers, to paper, to typewriters, not to mention the secretaries themselves. When compromises require adjustments in the original draft, the secretary is called in, and changes are dictated and typed out immediately. In a New York lawyer's fashion, they will work over the contracts through the night and have them ready the next day.

One of the Russians' usual counterproposals is that they have an aversion to paying more than 6 percent interest. The way to handle this is to increase the basic price, which surprisingly does not seem to bother the Russians as much as paying high interest. The Russians may also refuse to authorize any payment until all the equipment is installed and operating. This can be partially dangerous because the Russians love to cannibalize the parts of any piece of equipment, particularly if it comes from the West. On large installations there is almost no way to insure that what is shipped first will still be intact by the time the last piece is put in place. Some Scandinavian paper and pulp machine manufacturers have had a particularly hard time in this respect.

Many American businessmen are concerned about patent infringements by the Russians. The Russians have made some gestures toward conformity with international practice by taking the first steps toward acceptance of an international patent convention and by adhering to copyright procedures. But their licensing practices still vary significantly from those followed in this country, and they have not shown undue hesitation in pirating others' processes in the past. The best protection against such theft is to keep inventing and changing models.

Russian lack of appreciation for the proprietary concerns of capitalist firms sometimes leads to unusual actions. One American company that had become a favorite of a Soviet FTO was asked to submit a bid on a major Soviet undertaking. To the dismay of the FTO, the bid of the favored American company was several million dollars higher than that of its American rival. In order to help their American friends, they turned over to them the specifications and estimates that had been submitted by the low-bidding American rivals. Soviet officials hoped that this would make it possible for their high-bidding but surprised friends to see how they could improve their own design work and thus lower their bids and be awarded the contract.

In fairness to the Soviet Ministry of Foreign Trade, its record of observing the strict letter of its contract is good, particularly when the U.S.S.R. is the buyer. Ministry officials can be expected to bargain hard and refuse certain demands, such as adherence to American patent law. But with some exceptions, once a contract is signed, they tend to follow through. Of course, there are times when interpretation of contract terms does not conform to the American practice. Therefore, it is very important that the contract and its terms be carefully worked out so that nothing is left to future good will. This is particularly true for those who are selling to the Soviet Union. In one reported instance, the Soviet side insisted that its contracts always obligated the supplier to provide line drawings, not only for the equipment to be imported from the United States, but also for the standard equipment to be supplied by Soviet industry as well. This meant that the American company's draftsmen would have to draw specifications for ordinary off-the-shelf items like nails and nuts and bolts, an activity that would have required hundreds of thousands of extra drafting man-hours and would have made a profitable project unprofitable. Luckily the issue was finally resolved, but only after many anxious weeks. Nothing in the contract should be taken for granted.

While general observance of contract terms by the U.S.S.R. when it is the buyer is good, recently there have been reports that the Soviet negotiators do not adhere as strictly to contracts when they are the sellers. Apparently, disputes have arisen frequently over "the unreliability of Soviet deliveries and the failure of delivered products to live up to the samples on which the purchases were made." [20] As seen in our discussion of the internal operating problems of the Soviet economy, the Russians have great difficulty with such things as meeting delivery commitments and insuring quality and supply of spare parts. It is all but inevitable that these shortcomings will sometimes spill over into their external economic dealings as well. In such instances Western businessmen should be prepared to press as hard as Soviet officials do when contracts are violated by the Western partner.

Fortunately, the negotiator's tasks have been eased somewhat by the United States-Soviet Union trade treaty. In a marked divergence from their usual practices, Soviet officials have agreed in the treaty to settle commercial disputes by submitting them to arbitration under the arbitration rules adopted by the Economic Commission for Europe. Assuming that the treaty is ultimately accepted fully by both parties, this means that such arbitration can take place in a third country under arbitrators picked by an authority in a country other than the Soviet Union and United States.[21] Usually the U.S.S.R. insists that foreigners agree to arbitration by the Soviet Foreign Trade Arbitration Commission, which sits in Moscow and is made up entirely of Soviet citizens. The new treaty conveys authorization for the more impartial arrangement, although the ultimate procedure is still to be negotiated in each contract. At least the Russians can no longer insist that there is no precedent for outside arbitration.

The U.S.S.R. has also agreed to a unique antidumping provision. This is useful because although Soviet officials insist that they always seek the highest price possible and thus they never dump, sometimes their highest price must be below the prevailing market rate before anyone will agree to buy Soviet goods. Moreover, as we saw, since there is no direct link between their domestic and foreign prices, the Russians are prepared to manipulate their prices. But whatever it is called, their efforts to break into new markets with low prices has the effect of disrupting traditional market relationships. As a result, they have at various times been charged with dumping pig iron, tin, titanium sponge, and aluminum scrap.[22] To prevent such conflict in the future, Article 3 of the trade agreement contains a provision under which the Russians agree to cease the export of products to the United States which the United States feels will "cause, threaten, or contribute to the disruption of its domestic market." [23] The Soviets have the same privilege as regards United States exports to the Soviet Union.

Of course, no one expects that such rules will be interpreted in an excessively rigorous way. Moreover, the Joint United States-Soviet Union Commission and the U.S.-U.S.S.R. Trade and Economic Council can serve as useful avenues for facilitating commercial relations. The improved political climate can provide more impetus for "yes" rather than "no" answers than any number of long negotiating sessions. Not only has this been indicated by Soviet governmental actions, but by United States governmental actions as well. American firms may worry about contending with the obstinacy of Soviet bureaucrats, but they still have to deal with the United States government. American exporters must still obtain licenses for most equipment they sell to the Soviet Union. Nevertheless, conditions here have improved enormously since the start of better Soviet-American relatons. For example, the Gleason Machine Works reported in 1971 that it took them only six to eight weeks to obtain a license for equipment which in 1969 required a wait of two years. In 1972 Swindell Dressler received in days a license for equipment which had taken months the preceding year.

A SMALL COMPANY

All of these changes have been particularly beneficial for smaller companies which seek to trade with the Russians. The big obstacle for these companies in trading with the Russians is the expense required to solicit and win the contract. As we shall see, it is not unusual for some American corporations to spend as much as $200,000 to $300,000 on the preparation and presentation of the proposals they show the Russians. Since very few small companies can afford such sums, anything that can be done to facilitate negotiating procedures between the United States and the Soviet Union means that more American companies may be able to try their luck.

Still, no matter how much bargaining conditions improve, many smaller companies will feel that they have no choice but to seek the help of an intermediary or export-import broker like Satra or Tower International. But this is decidedly not the best approach. The Russians display openly their distaste for brokers and consultants and the extra fees they feel they will have to pay because of such middlemen. The Russians fail to realize that many firms often have no alternative if they want to deal with markets as remote and peculiar as the Soviet market. However, if the opportunity presents itself, there is another safer and usually more profitable alternative. Many small firms are invited by the prime contractors to ride piggyback on the major negotiating team, with the prime contractor bearing most of the overhead. Once ties are established this way, the smaller firm can call upon these new contacts in the Soviet Ministry of Foreign Trade or the FTO whenever it seeks to embark on new projects, without having to bear the expense involved in establishing the initial introductions.

One relatively small company which did this was the Holcroft Co. of Livonia, Michigan, a subsidiary of Thermo Electron in Waltham, Massachusetts. Holcroft managed to avoid most of the initial expense and trauma suffered by those without invitations who try to put their foot in the door of the Ministry of Foreign Trade. In a sense, Holcroft's foot was carried kangaroo-style by the Fiat Company in 1968. Fiat had used Holcroft heat treating furnaces in its plants in Turin for some years. Thus it was only natural that Fiat would turn to Holcroft for equipment in the plant Fiat was building at Togliatti.

With Fiat paving the way, Holcroft executives had many occasions to meet with officials in the Ministry of Foreign Trade and the automotive ministries. Actually it was more a reacquaintanceship than a new meeting, since Holcroft had sold the Soviet Union 35 heat treating furnaces back in 1935 for the Gorky automobile plant. Thus engineers in the Soviet automobile industry had a longstanding familiarity with Holcroft products.

This established association with Holcroft paid off when the Russians started on the Kama truck plant. Soviet officials called Holcroft in search of bids for furnace designs for "an automotive plant." [24] Holcroft received no more information than that. Ultimately five proposals were presented, and each time the Russians provided a little more information about their intentions. Holcroft officials claim that such procedures do not upset them since at no time did they attach a price to their project proposals. Therefore they could keep changing their specifications without penalty.

Holcroft officials consider their working relationship with the Russians to be excellent. The disputes they have had so far have been worked out amicably. There is give and take, but if the Russians ask for something that Holcroft feels was not covered in the contract, Holcroft simply asks for more money. The Russians have so far been flexible. One Holcroft vice president attributes their success to the fact that, as he put it, "We leave our lawyers home." It is easier to settle arguments when the parties to the dispute are not in an adversary position.

Holcroft people are proud of the fact that their contracts with the Russians are very short. Each new one (there are 13 so far) refers back to the original contract. This is not to say that all negotiations are easy. The Russians always come well prepared. Whenever Holcroft presents a proposal, the Russians immediately compare current prices to prices quoted on earlier contracts. They know how much the overall price index has risen as well as the prices of specific alloys, and they expect and demand that contract prices rise no higher than that. The Russians can be quite insistent. Occasionally there have been deadlocks. When this happens,

Holcroft officers have sometimes found it necessary to suspend contract talks.

Throughout all the negotiations, however, Holcroft's relations with their Soviet counterparts have remained cordial. For that reason Holcroft has been able to avoid unreasonably large negotiating costs. As the Holcroft people see it, the investment they make in securing the Russian contracts is not much larger as a percent of final sales than the money they spend on soliciting West European or American business. Of course Holcroft contracts with the Russians have been substantial. Their sales on the Kama truck plant total over $20 million. Many *large firms* would be happy with comparable sales. For Holcroft, though, this represents 50 percent of the parent company's total sales in 1972. The fact that Holcroft and its parent, Thermo Electron, are really small companies has not inhibited them in their efforts to sell the Soviet market. This is not surprising. When a Holcroft official was asked if his company had made money on its dealings with the U.S.S.R., he responded in what can only be described as a cheery tone, "Our profits with the Russians are satisfactory."

Certainly, trading and negotiating conditions have changed enormously for both the United States and Soviet bargainers. Institutional arrangements have been devised which should make it possible to retain a certain momentum even if political moods do not always remain as harmonious as they were in early 1973. Still, American-Soviet trade negotiation is not a sport for amateurs. The wheat deal is a good illustration of just how hazardous American-Soviet trade can be.

CHAPTER

7

How Not to Trade
with the Russians:
The Great Grain Robbery

N O one ever claimed that dealing with the U.S.S.R. would be easy or that the United States would always come out ahead on every transaction between the two countries. It was always assumed that negotiations for sophisticated equipment and advanced technology would prove to be especially hazardous. In contrast, the sale of standarized commodities such as grain was thought to be a relatively straightforward matter. How wrong such reasoning was we now know. Yet in analyzing what went wrong with the 1972 wheat deal, a transaction which cost the United States Treasury several hundred million dollars in subsidies and the world (except for the Soviet Union) significantly higher bread and beef prices, it turns out that our bureaucrats in the U.S. government were as much if not more to blame than the Soviet purchasers.

Because the events move so fast once the analysis begins, it is important to set out the basic facts of what happened. In a few months' time, the Russians bought over 19 million tons of U.S.

grain worth $1.2 billion. This consisted of approximately 433 million bushels of wheat, 246 million bushels of corn, and 37 million bushels of soybeans. At the same time the Russians also arranged to buy 5 million tons of grain from Canada, 1 million tons from Australia and France, one-half million tons from Sweden and Rumania, and lesser amounts from West Germany, Belgium, and the Netherlands.[1] For all intents and purposes this was the largest purchase of grain in history, and almost all of it was bought at rock bottom prices. Virtually the whole Soviet wheat purchase from the United States was contracted for at an average price of $1.61 to $1.63 a bushel, which was $.01 or $.02 below the prevailing market price.[2] Within a short time after the Soviet purchase, however, the international price of wheat had doubled. By August 1973 the price had risen, temporarily at least, to over $5 a bushel. Hard as it is to believe, senior officials in the Department of Agriculture still insist for the record that the size and speed of this purchase, as well as the price changes, came as a complete surprise to them.

In fairness to the Russians, let us emphasize that it is incorrect to attribute the whole increase in grain prices to the Soviet purchase alone. The drought in China, India, and Africa and the disappearance of anchovies off the coast of Peru had their effects as well. Yet the Soviet grain purchase was a major factor in setting off the commodity inflation that began in the early 1970s. Moreover, it illustrates almost everything that can go wrong in American-Soviet trade, so it is important to understand exactly what happened to insure that we do not repeat the experience, as we almost did in October 1974.

HISTORY OF SOVIET-AMERICAN GRAIN SALES

The 1972–1973 crop year sale was not the first major postwar purchase by the Soviet Union. We saw earlier how the Russians had been forced to purchase 1.8 million tons of grain from the United States in 1964. In 1971 they came back to buy 3 million tons of corn and other livestock feed for $136 million. Moreover, for much of the last decade they have been purchasing large quantities of grain on a regular basis from Canada and at times from Argentina, Australia, and France. Starting in 1963 the Russians found it necessary or expedient to purchase at least 1.5 million tons of grain a year from Canada in every year but 1968 and 1969. Apparently it was frequently easier and cheaper to supply Siberia and their grain-deficient ally, Cuba, with grain from Canada rather than from the European ports of the U.S.S.R.

But prior to 1972, the United States did not share in most of these transactions because the Russians found it politically more embarrassing to deal with the United States than with Canada. They were also deterred by the extra shipping costs they had to pay each time they purchased American grain. As we saw in Chapter 3, American regulations required that 50 percent of each bushel of grain sold to the Soviet Union be shipped in American ships. This automatically meant that the overall net price of American grain sold to the Soviet Union would be higher than grain purchased in Canada or Australia at the "same world price," because American labor, and therefore U.S. Merchant Marine rates, are as much as 30 percent higher than those prevailing in the world market.

Actually, at the time these higher shipping costs were imposed, they were regarded as a device to expedite rather than hamper trade. Throughout most of the 1950s the International Longshoreman's Association refused to load or handle products destined for or coming from the Soviet Union. To weaken labor union hostility to the 1963–1964 sale of American grain to the Soviet Union, President Kennedy promised that henceforth 50 percent of any grain or flour sold to the U.S.S.R., China, or Eastern Europe would have to be shipped in American flag vessels. Even though this increased the final price to the Russians, it did bring about the end of the longshoremen's boycott and meant that American grain could finally be sent to the U.S.S.R. In 1964 the Russians accepted such terms because there were not many alternatives. Normally, however, they went elsewhere.

In an effort to make purchases of American grain more competitive, President Nixon issued an executive order in June 1971 setting aside the 50 percent stipulation. This action was applauded by almost everyone. U.S. farmers, who were then suffering from low prices and overloaded grain silos, were especially pleased, for they hoped that this act would bring the Russians back into the American market and thus reduce feed grain stocks in the Midwest. A cynic might say this was a clever gesture for the support of American farmers, especially since it came just before a presidential election campaign. The Russians, however, were less concerned about the politics of wooing the American farmer and more concerned about the impact of such an action on American maritime workers and longshoremen. Having experienced effective and determined opposition to United States-Soviet trade in the past, the Russians did not believe that a simple executive order would by itself induce the unions to end their boycotts. Indeed, it took another five months, until November 1971, for the Nixon administration finally to win the cooperation of the unions. Even then the stimulus was not increased trade with the U.S.S.R., but the promise of a ten-year package of subsidies to enable domestic shipping to compete with all foreign flag ships, not just those in United States-Soviet trade.

Once they were sure of compliance by American unions, the Soviet Union acted quickly to place orders for 3 million tons of feed grains worth $136 million, to be delivered between November 1971 and June 30, 1972. Even then (in late 1971) there were rumors that the Russians would probably be back for more.[3] Their new five-year plan had placed great emphasis on increasing livestock and poultry herds in order to make more meat and chicken available for individual consumption. Thus egg, beef, and pork production were to increase over 20 percent. To fulfill these targets, Soviet farmers would need large quantities of corn. Unfortunately, because of inadequate rainfall and cold weather, Soviet growing conditions are ill suited for growing corn. If the Soviet

Union was to obtain this corn, it would probably have to increase feed grain imports for years to come. Since Canada, its favorite source of grain, was stronger in wheat than in corn, a large portion of such imports would probably have to come from the U.S. Throughout all of this there were no rumors of the disaster that was even then taking place in Soviet fields.

HOW IT HAPPENED

With the 1971 grain purchase the Russians had presumably prepared themselves for a regular, nonemergency type of relationship. The initial opening, however, could be expanded into something considerably larger if need be. While the Russians themselves were probably unaware of the potential disaster that lay ahead, their "preliminary planning" had the effect of establishing precedents which served nicely as camouflage for what eventually turned out to be massive rather than moderate purchases.

One thing is certain: Soviet grain buyers played their cards with great skill. That more than anything explains the ease with which they carried off the grain deal. At the same time their efforts were facilitated by incredible ineptness on the part of the Americans with whom they were dealing. In turn, this ineptness was a result of poor economic analysis and an irrationality provoked by politics, greed, and questionable if not dishonest business practices.

EARLY WARNINGS

Although it is always easier to evaluate blunders after rather than before they occur, there were numerous early signs of trouble in Soviet agriculture. There were also signs that the world market for grain had hardened and that buyers could not have their pick of surpluses as they had in the past.

Thus the U.S. General Accounting Office, in a study of world market conditions, found that as early as January 1972 American wheat was virtually the only wheat being offered for sale on the world's main grain market located in the Netherlands.[4] According to reports reaching Washington at the time, prospective buyers in the Netherlands were being told that there would be little or no wheat coming from Australia or Russia in 1972. That the Russians would not be selling became clear on February 28, when the Canadians announced that they had sold the Russians about 3.5 million tons of wheat (130 million bushels) for delivery after July 1972, with an option to buy another 1.47 million tons (55 million bushels).

Since the February 1972 agreement was in some ways similar to a previous Canadian-Soviet contract for the sale of a like amount in the 1971–1972 crop year, it aroused little attention. Yet the agreement not only indicated a Soviet need; it also exhausted all Canadian stocks. In March 1972 the Canadians, along with the Australians, withdrew from the market and did not come back in a major way until after the fall harvest of 1972. The U.S. General Accounting Office has published numerous letters from officials in Canada and Australia to our Department of Agriculture suggesting that the United States Department of Agriculture take advantage of the situation and sell its wheat at a higher world price.

But the Secretary of Agriculture's response was that the United States could not raise its export prices because it was necessary to protect United States export markets. Indeed, there were widespread suspicions that the Canadians and Australians were cleverly trying to inveigle us into increasing our export prices so that we would price ourselves out of the market. Alternatively, it was feared that high export prices would make the profits so tempting that other countries would expand their crop acreage and intensify what the Secretary of Agriculture already regarded as a glut on the market.

From the Secretary's very political viewpoint, that would be the wrong thing to do—especially in a presidential election year. Indeed, to earn farmer support he was determined to reduce grain stocks, not increase them, and to do this he was determined to keep foreign prices low. In this way he hoped that American grain exports would expand, which in turn would empty out American storage silos, which in turn would cause domestic grain prices for the farmer to rise. To show that he had the faith of his poor economic but good political convictions, he increased the wheat acreage to be set aside by farmers from 20 to 25 million acres in 1972. With less land planted with wheat, there would also be less wheat harvested and less wheat offered for sale. This would help reduce in turn the exceptionally large grain surpluses. If this could be done, then farm prices both at home and in foreign markets might rise and the farmers would be happy. Of course this would cost money, but Secretary Butz was prepared to spend $1 billion in subsidies for American farmers so they would not grow wheat.

Indicative of how insensitive Secretary Butz was to the economic changes that were occurring is that he held to his stand on acreage reduction throughout the remainder of 1972. Not until early 1973, after the price of wheat had more than doubled, did the Cost of Living Council get him to change his stand. Even then he insisted that some 7.4 million acres be set aside. Only in June 1973, after wheat had soared to $4 and almost $5 a bushel, did he agree to drop all acreage restrictions. With such insensitivity for market trends, it should come as no surprise that Secretary Butz chose to ignore other equally significant events.

If the Canadian wheat sale to the Soviet Union in February 1972 did not warrant a reevaluation of Soviet grain prospects, a series of subsequent events should have. A study by the Department of Agriculture's own Foreign Agricultural Service (FAS) in April 1972 indicated that the world market for grain was tight and that if the Russians had to look abroad for grain, they would have trouble finding it.[5] "In the short-run, therefore, if the USSR were to enter the world market looking for a large tonnage of grains in addition to the wheat which it has already purchased from Canada, it would have to be content with relatively small quantities from several different suppliers, unless it were to buy from the United States."

There was good cause to speculate about Russian interest in additional purchases of grain. The Russian winter had been unusually severe. Compounding the problem, the snowfall had been unusually light, so there was no blanket of insulation to protect the maturing plants or preserve the soil's moisture. The deep cold not only meant a reduced winter crop, but a belated spring sowing, since the soil could not thaw as rapidly as normal. Agricultural officials in Washington were kept fully informed of all this by an agricultural attaché in Moscow. According to the General Accounting Office, at least six reports describing the extent of the problem were filed between February 18 and June 26, 1972.[6] (Another report was requested on June 29 and received July 5.) The attaché generally reported that he thought as much as one-third of the winter grain acreage had been devastated by the severe winter. Moreover, a dry spring and hot June had made it difficult to recoup the winter losses with the spring planting.

In any bureaucracy, especially one the size of the Department of Agriculture, there is always the possibility that an important piece of information may never filter through the massive flow of information received every day. But even if this is what happened, there can be no doubt that Secretary Butz was personally aware of the seriousness of the Russian crop situation. If nothing else, Secretary Butz saw for himself when he was invited to the U.S.S.R. in April 1972. One of the purposes of his trip was to arrange for the future sale of feed grains to the U.S.S.R. While there he made an inspection trip through Soviet farms in the southern part of the U.S.S.R. Officials traveling with him, including Clarence D. Palmby, assistant secretary of agriculture, and Clifford G. Pulvermacher, general sales manager of the Export Marketing Service of the Department of Agriculture, reported, according to the *New York Times,* "that the damage to the Soviet winter crops had been more severe than they had previously thought. Earlier estimates that 30% of the crop had been lost were now termed conservative." [7]

As a minimum, Secretary Butz declared the Soviet Union would probably purchase $200 to $250 million of grain and soybeans over a five-year period. [8] Whatever the actual figures ultimately would be, it was clear that Secretary Butz felt he was on the verge of solving a domestic political dilemma. [9] The expected sale of more grain to the Soviet Union would reduce our overflowing surplus and in the process improve the farmer's view of the grain market and, by happy coincidence, of the Republican Party. The Nixon administration, with guidance from Secretary Butz, had worked hard for this political plum. They were entitled to enjoy the fruit of their efforts. That it turned sour was partly their own doing.

THE DEALING

On June 28 a delegation of Soviet trading officials arrived secretly in the United States. Only those Americans who "needed to know" were made aware of the visit. Reportedly, some of the secrecy was at the request of the Russians. Knowing they were about to embark on a massive buying spree, they presumed that any publicity about their trip would stimulate a rise in grain prices and make their visit considerably more expensive. (Not all Russians felt the need for such secrecy. By chance, officials in the Soviet Embassy in Washington mentioned to me on Friday, June 30, 1972, that a Soviet trade delegation had just arrived in Washington. Later in the afternoon when I inquired about this mission at a meeting of senior Department of Commerce officials working on the American-Soviet trade agreement, I was told there could be no comment or even an acknowledgment about the visit.)

It remains unclear why the U.S. felt it so necessary to maintain such secrecy. The debacle that followed might have been avoided if more news had been provided about the Russian visit. While commercial dealings between private American firms are often shrouded in secrecy, until recently American government dealings have been more open. Given the atmosphere in Washington in mid-1972, just after Watergate, however, such secrecy apparently had become a way of life in government offices. Fortunately for the Russians, it was just what they wanted. If nothing else, we should know now that the risk of serious error increases when we fail to insist on playing "the game" in our own way, and instead agree to go along with "Russian rules."

Because the scenario moves so rapidly, it may be wise to summarize first what the Russians managed to do. While one group of Russians stayed in Washington to negotiate with government officials, another group headed for a series of meetings with American grain exporters in New York, Memphis, and Minneapolis. By July 20 the buying missions had signed contracts for 8,050,000 tons of wheat, two-thirds of their ultimate purchase, and gone back to Russia. As Table 7–1 shows, they returned to the United States a week later on July 29 and 30, and by August 9, 1972, had signed contracts for the final 3,750,000 tons.[10]

It turns out that the Russians did not obtain all the concessions they sought, but they came remarkably close. In a few weeks' time they cornered one-quarter of the U.S. wheat crop with such dexterity and skill that they managed to buy almost all of it below the market price of $1.61–4.[11]

Exactly how it all happened is not known, and the full story will probably never be precisely clear. There are numerous contradictions as to who did what and when, but something like the following emerges:

While one contingent of the "secret" Russian visitors busied itself in Washington trying to arrange favorable credit terms, the other, led by Nicolai Belousov, the chief of Exportkhleb, the Soviet Union's grain importing and exporting company, immediately started to buy up grain. By July 5 the Russians had already secretly contracted for the purchase of 4 million tons of wheat and 4.5 million tons of grain from Continental Grain Company. (See Table 7–1.) While there were rumors that the Russians were purchasing grain as early as July 3, senior officials in the Department of Agriculture insist they were left in the dark.[12] Whether or not the Assistant Secretary and the Secretary of Agriculture were

TABLE 7–1

The 1972 Sale of Grain to the Soviet Union
(millions of tons)

COMPANY	WHEAT		CORN		SOYBEANS	MISC.
	JULY 5 TO JULY 20	AUG. 1 TO AUG. 9	JULY 5 TO JULY 20	AUG. 1 TO AUG. 9	AUG. 1 TO AUG. 9	AUG. 1 TO AUG. 9
Continental Grain						
July 5	4.		4.5			
July 11	.5					
July 20	1.					
August 1				1.75		.2
Cargill						
July 10	1.					
August 9		1.				
Dreyfus						
July 10	.75					
August 1		1.5				
Cook						
July 11	.6					
August 4		.3			1.	
Garnac						
July 20	.2					
August 2		.35				
Bunge						
August 2		.6				
Sub total	8.05	3.75	4.5	1.75	1.	.2
Total wheat	11.8					
Total corn			6.25			
Total grain	19.25					

Source: Committee on Government Operations, United States Senate, *Russian Grain Transactions* (Washington, D.C.: U.S. Government Printing Office, July 20, 23, 24, 1973), p. 218.

as uninformed as they now claim has become a matter of some dispute. Everyone agrees, however, that the general public and the wheat farmers in particular were kept ignorant.

For people in a tough spot, the Russians apparently played a remarkably cool hand. Despite evidence of a mounting agricultural crisis, the Russians initially showed no interest in buying any additional grain from the United States unless they were offered U.S. government credits at ridiculously low interest rates. At the April 1972 meeting in Moscow, the Russians insisted that the Commodity Credit Corporation of the Department of Agriculture provide them with a 2 percent loan for ten years. Since no other country was being charged less than 6⅛ percent nor given more than three years in which to pay off the loan, the Russians were told no. Incredibly on May 9, as harvest conditions continued to deteriorate, Deputy Minister Vladimir Alkhimov of the Soviet Ministry of Foreign Trade sought an appointment in the Department of Agriculture in Washington to ask again for the same low terms. It was only during the July 4 weekend that the Russians finally agreed to pay the same as everyone else. Moreover, as late as July 10, the Russians rejected offers of 600,000 tons of American wheat from the Bunge Corporation because the "price was too high"![13]

Based on their earlier purchases of November 1971, and the targets of the Ninth Five-Year Plan, everyone expected the Russians to be in the market for animal feed grains. However, on their first approach to the grain dealers in July, they immediately indicated that they would like to purchase wheat as well. In some cases they indicated they wanted only wheat.

In every instance, however, the American exporters were urged to keep their knowledge about Russian purchasing activities secret from everyone else. There was nothing unusual about such a request; grain dealers always tend to be secretive in dealing with one another. The grain dealers properly feared that if there were leaks, the market price would move the wrong way. In any case, massive purchases of grain were made by the Soviet Union without any public announcements.

The first general announcement that the Russians were even in the country and presumably interested in buying grain was not made until July 8, 1972, ten days after their arrival. Then President Nixon in San Clemente and Secretary of Agriculture Butz and Secretary of Commerce Peterson in Washington announced the signing of a major credit pact with the Soviet Union. Under the agreement, the Commodity Credit Corporation of the Department of Agriculture agreed to make available to the Soviet Union a credit of $750 million for the purchase of grain at the usual 6⅛ percent for three years. This was good news, especially in a political year. Not only had the Russian negotiating team been forced to accept the higher interest rate, but the agreement would help to reduce our grain surpluses, particularly of feed grains such as corn. At the press conference Secretary Butz went out of his way to stress (incorrectly) that it was feed grains that the Russians were primarily interested in under the just-signed agreement.[14]

As it turned out, the government's announcement told only part of the story. There was not a word about the presence of the purchasing half of the Soviet mission, which had already agreed to a *cash* purchase of 8.5 million tons of grain. As we shall see, there is ample reason to believe that some senior officials in the Department of Agriculture knew what N. A. Belousov of Exportkhelb and his purchasing group were up to. They also knew that before July 8 the Russians had already approached two companies and were negotiating with at least a third one to buy "large" quantities of grain. Those who had access to this inside information were in a position to make substantial profits. If it had this information, the Department of Agriculture had an obligation to make it available to the public at large. If it did not have it, the department, which certainly knew that something out of the ordinary was happening, should have made some effort to find out just what it was.

THE MARKET PRICE AND SUBSIDIES

There were several ways that insiders could profit from their information. First, those who knew that the Russian grain buyers were in the country had the first chance to sell them American grain. Thus Continental Grain had already sold 4 million tons of wheat and 4.5 million tons of corn for cash before companies like Dreyfus even learned the Russians were in New York or were able to reach them.[15] And of course, those who made the deals were then in the best position to go to the American market and buy up grain or grain futures before prices started to rise.

Grain dealers with good connections in the Department of Agriculture had a second chance for profit. If they knew what was happening in the Department of Agriculture, they could hold off registering their grain export sales with the department for payment of export subsidies until they felt it was most advantageous, that is, when the export subsidies were the highest. To understand what was involved, it is necessary to understand the function of the subsidies. In an effort to improve the income of American farmers, until 1972 the American domestic price of grain was almost always pegged somewhat higher than the prevailing world market price. Therefore, to make it possible for American exporters to sell American grain overseas, the Department of Agriculture offered to make up the difference between the domestic and foreign price. For years the Department of Agriculture had decided that the proper world price of wheat should be about $1.63 to $1.65 a bushel. Whenever the American domestic price plus storage and the cost of moving the grain to an ocean port exceeded $1.63–$1.65, the Department of Agriculture stood ready to pay the exporter a subsidy for the difference. But there was a peculiar quirk in this procedure. Exporters were not required to register with the Department of Agriculture for their subsidies when they signed the initial export contract. If they wanted, they could hold off until the goods were actually shipped.

Normally, because of the massive overhang of grain in storage and the relatively modest size of the average grain purchase, there were almost no fluctuations in price. But orders of the size sought by the Russians were something else. For those who could see what was coming, the best strategy was to buy grain for export when no one else knew the Russians were in the market and the price was low. Then the seller could wait until the news broke about the completion and size of the purchase before registering for grain export subsidies. The news would make the domestic price rise, which in turn would also increase the export subsidy. The alert, well-connected company could thus make money on both deals. Some estimates suggest that the Continental Grain Company, the first to sell to the Russians, bought some of its domestic wheat at about $.10 above the price it sold it to the Russians. But by waiting to the last minute to register the bulk of it, Continental was also in a position to collect a subsidy of $.47 a bushel, a profit of about $.37 a bushel.[16]

CONFLICTS OF INTEREST

While almost all grain-exporting corporations seem implicated in one way or another, two individuals and two firms played the most prominent roles. Clarence Palmby, who served as assistant secretary of agriculture until June 7, 1972, was approached by Continental Grain in January, February, and again in March 1972, about switching jobs and going to work for Continental.[17] He formally joined Continental on June 8, 1972, the day after his resignation from the Department of Agriculture. Although he later acknowledged that as early as March 1972 he and his wife went to New York to buy a condominium with the Continental Grain offer in mind, Mr. Palmby still insists that this did not necessarily mean that he would go to work for Continental. In any case, it has to be regarded as a logical presumption or a bit of extraordinarily good luck for both Mr. Palmby and Continental Grain that Mr. Palmby should subsequently be among those selected to accompany Secretary Butz to Moscow in April to see Soviet crops and meet and negotiate with Soviet officials in the Ministry of Agriculture about Soviet credit and import needs. Perhaps it is also more than coincidence that Continental Grain turned out to be the first company to sign a large contract for the sale of wheat to the Soviet Union in July 1972. Although he keeps changing his mind, even Secretary Butz at one time indicated that he thought Mr. Palmby's dual role was a bit indiscreet. Secretary Butz acknowledged that it created the appearance of impropriety. He agreed that he would advise against such job switching in the future.[18]

Mr. Palmby claims that even though he showed some of the Russians around Washington on July 2 and sat in briefly on the negotiations on July 3, 4, and 5, he had nothing to do with the actual negotiating. In fairness to Mr. Palmby, it should be noted that his boss, the president of Continental Grain, Michael Fribourg, who was very much involved in the negotiations, is also a close friend of the Russian negotiator, Mr. Belousov. In fact, they almost drowned together on a yacht in a gale off Corsica in 1971. One way or the other, through foresight, accident, or friendship, Continental ended up selling the Soviet Union more than 60 percent of what it purchased in its July–August 1972 shopping spree.

Although the timing was not as fortuitous, another former official of the Department of Agriculture, Clifford G. Pulvermacher, has also had to face accusations similar to those made against Mr. Palmby. Like Mr. Palmby, Mr. Pulvermacher made the trip to Moscow with Secretary Butz and then similarly crossed over from the Department of Agriculture to private business, in this case the Bunge Corporation, another of the grain-exporting giants. According to his statement to a House Subcommittee on Livestock and Grain, Mr. Pulvermacher decided on his retirement from the Department of Agriculture as early as March 19, 1972, and had arranged for it to become effective June 30, 1972, in order to take advantage of his retirement benefits. He was only offered a job by Bunge on July 18, 1972, accepted it on July 24, and reported for duty on August 1.[19] He reports that he had no part in the sale of grain that Bunge had been negotiating with the Russians since July 10. Nevertheless, the fact remains that despite almost a month of trying, no deal was consummated by Bunge until August 2. That was one day after Mr. Pulvermacher's arrival, but a week after he decided to take the job.

Whether or not Mr. Pulvermacher or Mr. Palmby were guilty of illegal or at best unethical procedures may ultimately be up to the courts to decide. Assistant Attorney General Henry Petersen (who was also involved in some unusual discussions and determinations during the Watergate investigations) concluded as of March 1974 that no conflict of interest existed. In any case, the catalogue of coincidences involving the Department of Agriculture extends far beyond the activities of these two individuals. Several Congressional committees have demanded to know why the Department of Agriculture and Secretary Butz seemed to be doing all they could to disguise what the Russians were doing. As late as July 31 the Department of Agriculture was advising wheat farmers that the average price they would receive for wheat for the year was likely to be no more than $1.31 a bushel. Indeed, farmers further south who had already sold their crop in July were receiving as little as $1.35 per bushel. In the vast majority of cases, this was less than they had received the preceding year![20] Yet by mid-August, those who had not already sold were receiving $1.51 a bushel, and by the end of the month the price was $1.70. Those who sold early were naturally a bit grumpy about not having been let in on the secret.

While many farmers were losing out, most of the grain exporters were benefiting, especially those who bought their wheat on the market in July or early August. Not only were they able to purchase their grain cheaply, but in many instances they were able to benefit doubly by postponing their requests for export subsidies with the Department of Agriculture.

As of July 3, while the first negotiations were taking place, it cost about $1.68 a bushel for an exporter to buy, store, and ship grain to a U.S. port for export. (This means that storage and shipping added to export costs as much as $.30 above what the farmer received.[21]) Thus, as of July 3, in order to make it possible to export at $1.63¼ per bushel, the Department of Agriculture provided an export subsidy of $.05. As domestic prices rose, the export subsidy rate shot up sharply to $.47 in late August. Obviously, those firms that bought early and registered late stood to make $.42 a bushel on subsidy payments alone. Most estimates are that this action cost the United States Treasury about $316 million, $160 million of which was specifically spent on Soviet purchases.[22] At the same time, continuation of the subsidy made it possible for the Russians to buy wheat at prices far under what should have been the going rate, especially that portion of their purchase arranged for during their second buying trip in late July and early August.

Several accusations have been made that officials of the Department of Agriculture went out of their way to help the grain exporters. If nothing else, the return visit by the Russians in late July and the start of their second purchasing spree should have alerted the department that the Russian purchases would fundamentally affect world prices. While Assistant Secretary of Agriculture Brunthaver claims ignorance on this as on so many other events, the Foreign Agriculture Service of the Department of Agriculture was officially notified by the State Department that the Moscow Embassy had again issued visas to Mr. Belousov of Exportkhleb and his companions, who were returning to the United States in order to "negotiate with Continental Grain." [23] Apparently, as news of the crop disaster kept coming in, the Russians realized they had not bought enough during their early July visit. Certainly, when they had to come back for seconds, the Russians were potentially in a considerably more difficult trading position than they had been earlier in the month, when there were fewer rumors about the extent of their plight. At this point, therefore, they were obviously prepared to pay considerably more than they had during the first round of purchasing.

The Department of Agriculture remained steadfast; no one could ever accuse it of being greedy. Despite the Soviet need and its lack of alternative sources, the Department of Agriculture continued to maintain American export subsidies until the Russians had completed all their purchases. Only in late August, more than two weeks after the Russians had made their last purchase, did Secretary of Agriculture Butz finally come to realize that he could not single-handedly stem the rising price of wheat on the world market, and that perhaps the Department of Agriculture should let the price of wheat rise to its natural level. Belatedly he did away with the export subsidy. Even then the decision was largely forced on the Department of Agriculture by the Office of Management and Budget in order to stop the surge of subsidy payments from the federal budget.

Nor did the Department of Agriculture limit its largess to the Russians. To cushion the impact of "subsidylessness," officials in the Department of Agriculture apparently did their best to warn the grain exporters and their former colleagues now employed by the exporters about the coming revocation of the subsidy. This made it possible for the companies to complete their purchases on the domestic market and obtain their export subsidies before the revocation. Thus on August 24, 1972, officials in the Department of Agriculture made telephone calls to inform ten of the largest exporters that as of August 23 the department export payment policy on wheat would no longer attempt to hold down world wheat prices. This gave these exporters a chance to make their final purchases on the domestic market before the public was notified. The next day, August 25, the changed policy was announced publicly. The Department of Agriculture also revealed that exporters would have five more days, until September 1, to register for the $.47 per bushel subsidies on export sales made on or before August 24.

Between August 24 and September 1, 282 million bushels of

wheat were registered in order to take advantage of this last boun-
tiful opportunity.[24] Of that amount, 167 million bushels were destined for the U.S.S.R., about 40 percent of the total Soviet order.
Thereafter, the export subsidy rate was cut gradually until it was
abolished completely on September 22, 1972.[25] By that time the
American domestic, and by extension the world, price (since there
was no other country with wheat available for sale at the point)
had reached $2.43 a bushel. However, the Russians had long since
withdrawn from the market, having made their purchases at
$1.61–$1.63 a bushel. The American taxpayer was left to shell
out over $300 million in export subsidies.

OTHER "COINCIDENCES"

Mr. Palmby and Mr. Pulvermacher are not the only Department
of Agriculture officials mired in controversy. Another controversial
figure is Assistant Secretary of Agriculture Carroll Brunthaver,
who succeeded to the post left by Mr. Palmby. (Making it even
more like musical chairs, before replacing Mr. Palmby at the
Department of Agriculture, Mr. Brunthaver had been an executive
for Cook Industries, another of the six companies exporting grain
to the Soviet Union.) Mr. Brunthaver is now blamed for the Agriculture Department's decision to notify everyone but the farmers
and general public about what was happening. In rebuttal, Mr.
Brunthaver has adhered to the general department line that he had
no precise idea of how much grain was being sold by whom. On
September 14 and 18, 1972, he testified to the House Subcommittee on Livestock and Grain that he did not know yet how
much Continental Grain Company sold, nor how much subsidy
they had sought.[26] Yet senior officials of Continental Grain have
sworn that they kept Department of Agriculture officials, specifically Mr. Brunthaver, closely informed about their dealings with

the Russians. Bernard Steinweg, a senior vice president of Continental Grain, reported that he visited Mr. Brunthaver on July 3, 1972, told him of the ongoing negotiations, and indicated that he thought the Russians wanted at least 4 million tons of wheat and about 3 million tons of corn. He is supported in his assertions by two other vice presidents of Continental who say they accompanied Mr. Steinweg on his visit.

According to Mr. Steinweg, the object of his visit was to insure that the Department of Agriculture would continue its export price support program. Continental needed this assurance in order to make a deal with the Russians to export wheat at \$1.61–1.63 a bushel. It obviously occurred to the people at Continental, if to no one else at this juncture, that a sale of this magnitude would affect the existing price structure of the market and cause a sharp increase in price. The deal would therefore become unprofitable for Continental unless the company could be assured of a stable export price. The Continental executives sought and received such assurance. Mr. Steinweg has testified that Mr. Brunthaver called him on July 3, 1972, after Mr. Steinweg's Washington visit, to reassure him that the subsidy would be provided. Mr. Steinweg also reports that he called Mr. Brunthaver again on July 6, two days before the announcement of the \$750 million grain credit agreement, to say that Continental Grain's deal with the Russians had been completed. Since Continental's sale was the largest made to the Russians, Mr. Brunthaver should have had a good idea by that time how much grain was involved and what effect this would have on the market. Officials of Cargill, Bunge, and Louis Dreyfus have also sworn that they made similar calls for similar reasons to Mr. Brunthaver a few days later.[27] Though Mr. Brunthaver acknowledges that he participated in some of the meetings and phone calls, he continues to deny that he knew how much was being sold.

There were other unusual coincidences. On September 18, the very same day on which Mr. Brunthaver had testified before the House Subcommittee on Livestock and Grain that he did not know how much Continental Grain had sold to the Russians, he warned one of his subordinates in the Commodity Exchange Authority that Continental had understated the size of the sales reports it was filing with the authority.[28] This does not say much for Mr. Brunthaver's consistency, but it also speaks rather poorly of Continental Grain. Its officials justified their faulty records by claiming it was merely a communication and bookkeeping snafu. By what seems to be more than a coincidence, at least two other major grain companies, Dreyfus and Garnac, have also been accused of filing false reports. All of their faulty reports occurred at the time of their sales to the Russians.[29] The clear implication is that all three companies tried to keep the size of the Russian purchase secret.

Apparently the grain companies did not limit themselves to filing false documents. The Commodity Exchange Authority charged that some grain firms purposely bunched their buying orders toward the close of the trading day on the Kansas City Board of Trade. This had the effect of forcing up the final quotations for the day. Even though the quotations may have fallen the next morning, it was the closing quotation that was used by the Export Marketing Service of the Department of Agriculture to set the export subsidy rate. The period from July 16 to July 19 seems particularly suspect. One company allegedly ordered 4 million bushels of wheat in the last five minutes of July 13. Once the price had been bid up, the companies would then register for export subsidies whenever they found the rate most favorable.

As we have come to learn as a result of the Watergate Hearings, everyone has his own particular set of "recollections," and certainly the truth does seem particularly elusive these days. Thus Secretary of Agriculture Butz insists adamantly that all the charges were politically inspired to embarrass President Nixon during his 1972 Presidential campaign. Indeed the first set of hearings on the grain sale was called in September 1972 right before the election, and the charges were loudly echoed by Senator McGovern.

In his defense, Secretary Butz has pointed to all kinds of evidence to show that the Department of Agriculture did not know how poor the Russian harvest was. He concedes, however, that Department of Agriculture reports suggesting the true dimensions of the Soviet crop failure were received on July 14 and August 18 and that both were withheld from the public.[30] For that matter when the Department of Agriculture learned that the Russians were sending over their first purchasing delegation in late June, the Department sent an emergency request to their special representative in Moscow on June 28 asking him for a special grain situation report. The report which was received on July 5 by senior Department officials predicted accurately that the Soviet harvest would fall short by about 20 million tons.[31] Despite such embarrassing events, however, Secretary Butz can and has pointed to an FBI investigation that concludes there was no misconduct. Moreover Secretary Butz's own analysis of the buying and selling transactions of the grain exporters showed that on July 6, 1972, in the middle of the Russian purchasing activity, some of the grain companies were trying to <u>sell</u> grain for use in the government's grain donation program, which goes to the developing countries.[32] Furthermore, it also turns out that most of the grain companies had <u>sold short</u> prior to the arrival of the Russians in late June. Surely, Secretary Butz argues, the grain companies would have tried to hold on to their grain rather than sell it if they had expected to make large sales to the Russians. Indeed, the General Accounting Office has reported that as late as August 7, 1972, the grain "exporters still had not purchased sufficient quantities . . . to cover their sales commitments."[33] Yet subsequently, in August 1974, both Dreyfus and Continental Grain conceded in a "cease and desist" order that they had filed inaccurate documents with the Department of Agriculture which misrepresented their position in the market. Not only did they understate their sales reports, as we saw earlier, but they also understated their purchase and future positions. Dreyfus understated its position by as much as 25 million bushels of wheat, almost one-third of its ultimate sale to the Soviet Union.

As we begin to learn more about what really happened at the time, it begins to look as if the grain companies were not as ignorant of what was taking place as Secretary Butz would have liked to portray. Certainly the grain companies found out what was happening before the general public and therefore they had a chance to act even if they did not. If anything, some of what they did or did not do was probably due as much to incompetence as to lack of opportunity. Thus Continental Grain claims that it made only $1 million on its share of the wheat deal—a much lower than normal figure. Incredibly, at least one firm, Cargill, has publicly claimed that it lost over $600,000 on the deal because it sold early but bought late.[34] Supporting this contention is the investigation by the General Accounting Office, which reveals that of the five exporters canvassed, three sustained losses of .9 cents (probably Cargill), 1.5 cents, and 1.9 cents per bushel, while two others showed profits of .3 cents (probably Continental) and 2 cents per bushel on their hard winter wheat sales.[35] A normal profit would have been 1.6 cents per bushel.

ADVANTAGES OF THE DEAL

Having spent so much time on the mistakes and shortcomings of the transaction, it should be noted that the U.S. did obtain some advantage from what happened. After all, as cheap as it turned out to be for them, the Russians did end up buying over $1 billion worth of American goods, providing a much-needed boost for our balance of trade. There is also agreement that the wheat deal provided a big boost to the shipping and farm equipment industries. Farm income rose significantly, which in turn created new jobs and opportunities that otherwise would not have come into being.

The sale of so much grain also helped to empty out our grain storage warehouses. The Department of Agriculture estimates this alone saved the taxpayer $73 million.[36] Similarly, higher market prices have meant reduced subsidy payments to farmers for the wheat they grow. At the same time, the government no longer has to make payments to farmers who agree to set aside land for wheat cultivation. As of 1973, all land withdrawal payments were abolished. The Department of Agriculture calculates that the total of such savings amounted to almost $800 million. This, they feel, should more than offset the export subsidy costs of $316 million.

If we pay heed, the wheat deal may also have provided us with a useful lesson in that it showed us that if their needs are great enough, the Russians will make concessions. In the case of the grain deal the Russian need was so great that they did back down on several occasions and probably would have yielded even more if pushed. As we saw, they first wanted to pay no more than 2 percent interest, yet ultimately they agreed to pay the going rate of 6⅛ percent and accepted loans of three years duration rather than the ten years they initially demanded. (As of August 22, 1973, the Russians had even agreed to a rate of 9.5 percent). Conceivably there were those in the Department of Agriculture who felt that the United States should agree to the Russian demands for fear the United States would lose the entire deal. If so, these officials were probably deterred as much as anything else by the realization that it would have been awkward to extend the Russians more favorable terms than those offered the Japanese. However, since we have treated the Japanese so shabbily on other matters, as in the summer of 1973 when we embargoed their purchase of soybeans, it may have been luck more than equity that resulted in equal demands being placed on the Russians.

The Russians also agreed to pay a higher transportation rate than they originally planned to pay. Indicative of the Department of Agriculture's poor economic analysis when dealing with the Russians was the fact that no one thought to anticipate the surge in demand for ocean freighters and higher prices that would result. This was important to the U.S., since the revised U.S.-U.S.S.R.

maritime agreement of October 14, 1972, called for American ships to carry one-third of the American grain sent to the U.S.S.R. However, as we saw, every shipment on an American carrier necessitates a government subsidy. Thus the more we ship, the more expensive it becomes to our government.

In recognition of this problem, the U.S. insisted that the Soviet Union pay part of the extra freight cost for sending one-third of the wheat on American ships. Initially in September 1972, the Department of Commerce thought it would be sufficient for the Russians to pay $8.05 a ton to American shippers. This would have amounted to $1 more than the going world rate of about $7.00. Since the actual charge demanded by the U.S. shipping lines by the end of the year was $21 a ton, that meant the American government would have to pay the $13 difference. Thus, in addition to paying American farmers and the grain exporters for each ton of grain, the U.S. taxpayer would also have had to pay the shipper for each ton of grain shipped to the U.S.S.R. on an American ship.

As political heat rose over the size of the wheat export subsidy and the low price charged the Russians, the American government negotiators began to fear additional criticism for unduly subsidizing the shipment of grain for the Russians. The problem became even more acute as the price of world shipping rose rapidly from $7 a ton in July to $9 and $10 in October. However, according to the original agreement, the Russians were required to pay only $8.05, already $1 to $2 below the then-existing world rate. Consequently, in what was probably regarded as a bold move for the U.S., our negotiators reneged on their earlier agreement and insisted the Russians pay "the world rate." To the surprise of some, the Russians agreed to increase their shipping supplement and pay either $8.05 a ton as a minimum or 110 percent of the world market rate, whichever was higher.

Unfortunately, the Russian concession was not as generous as it first appeared. A dispute arose immediately as to what the world rate was. The Russians claimed they could find ships on the world market at prices $3 a ton cheaper than the U.S. could find. After several days of conflict and after tons of grain destined for the Soviet Union began to clog up American ports, the Russians acceded to the new American terms. Belatedly the Russians agreed to pay a rate of $10.34 per ton between November 11, 1972, and December 15, 1972; $10.12 between December 16 and December 25, 1972; and $9.90 between December 26, 1972, and January 27, 1973. Subsequently, the Russians agreed to pay even more. They would pay $10.34 between January 26, 1972, and July 1, 1973, and $16.94 thereafter to December 31, 1973. Yet it appears as if the Russians still came out ahead. As of late September 1973, the United States government still had to pay out $40 million in shipping subsidies to move the Russian grain.

CONCLUSION

Although the lessons of the wheat deal are not hard to find, there is no guarantee that a similar occurrence could not happen again. The Russians can move adroitly in capitalist markets. Obviously, if given the proper opportunity, they can sometimes run rings around their bargaining counterparts. Nor are we in the United States the only ones susceptible to this kind of maneuvering. Largely under French pressure, the Common Market countries agreed in August 1972 to subsidize the sale of wheat and barley to the Soviet Union at a cost to the Common Market taxpayer of $42 million. In April 1973 the Russians also managed to buy 200,000 tons of stockpiled butter at $420 a ton, about $.20 a pound, from the Common Market. The price to the French housewife at that time was about $.60 a pound. The total subsidy on such a sale amounted to about $250 million for all the Common Market countries. Moreover, there was fear that the Russians would turn around and reexport the butter at a profit.

To avoid further raids by the Soviet Union, the United States government should seek to provide some coordination for American companies whenever they are approached by Exportkhleb of the Soviet Union. As a minimum, we should try to improve the flow of agricultural intelligence. It is incredible that the United States government should spend $6 billion on gathering intelligence about the Soviet Union and yet have the Secretary and Assistant Secretary of Agriculture say they had no precise idea of what was going on inside either the Soviet Union or the offices of the American grain exporters.[37] Similarly, we should look to see how Canada and Australia have handled their negotiations with the Russians. The Canadians and Australians have set up grain marketing boards which handle all such country to country deals.

When huge purchases are made by one buyer, as was the case in the wheat deal, the private market system, with its multitude of sellers, is at a disadvantage. The monopsonist (the buyer counterpart of the monopolist) can move fast; if he can do so in secret, he does not even have to be especially adroit. Our grain dealers are accustomed to negotiating with many grain purchasers, none of whom heretofore could ever single-handedly buy up one-quarter of our total crop in one purchasing sweep. When a buyer is able to purchase that much, inevitably he must have a significant impact on the market. Under these circumstances, the United States government should not only be expected to provide more effective coordination for the sellers, but it should be prepared to engage actively in the transaction as well.

Short of establishing a wheat marketing board to handle country-to-country deals on the pattern of Canada and Australia, there are still some other steps that can and fortunately have been taken to facilitate the government's efforts at coordination and participation. Thus grain exporters are now required to report their export sales and the destination of their wheat, feed grains, and other food products on a daily and weekly basis.[38] It was presumed that this would provide the Department of Agriculture with more current intelligence about any large purchases.

Furthermore, in June 1973 Soviet agricultural officials agreed with our Department of Agriculture that the U.S.S.R. would provide our planners with estimates of Soviet crop, harvest, and consumption needs. The Soviet Union agreed to open up Soviet crop areas for on-site inspection by our Department of Agriculture representatives. At the time the agreement was announced, some skeptics questioned how meaningful such cooperation would be. Indeed, one year later, the American team visiting the Soviet Union for that purpose was denied access to the virgin lands of Western Siberia and Kazakhstan, an area reportedly affected adversely by drought. As we should have suspected, this was an ominous sign. It was followed by the completely unexpected October order for 2.4 million tons of corn and 1 million tons of wheat from Continental Grain and Cook Industries. Even though this was less than 20 percent of the 1972 purchase, it was larger than the 1964 sale. More important, given the taut state of the grain market at that time and the strong possibility that this initial purchase would be followed up by additional purchases, the impact on world grain supplies and prices threatened to be extremely serious. Until strong-arm pressure from President Ford induced Continental Grain and Cook Industries to break their contracts with the Russians and reduce by almost half the size of their ultimate purchase, it looked as though the Soviet Union was about to repeat its 1972 coup.

The reason for the Soviet failure to live up to the agreement about shared information was obvious. By moving fast and without prior warning, it hoped to benefit from a more favorable set of prices than it would have had to pay if the early warning system had worked. Nonetheless, the new export reporting requirements imposed on American grain companies did mean that the Department of Agriculture and President Ford were provided with information much sooner than would have been the case in the past. The Continental and Cook contracts were signed on Thursday and Friday and the Department of Agriculture was notified immediately after each deal. Yet this early notice was still not enough to insure that a large buyer like the Soviet Union would not disrupt the market and would pay a fair price (however that would be defined in the market conditions of 1974). By the time the Department of Agriculture found out about the order on October 4, 1974, the contracts had already been signed and a price agreed to.[39]

Even if such measures could be reworked to make them more effective, it is impossible to insure that some officials might not secretly make an unnecessary concession to a large buyer like the U.S.S.R., particularly in an election year. One legacy of the whole Watergate episode has been to expose the Nixon administration's sense of secrecy and paranoia which seemed to afflict Secretary Butz and which he transmitted to his subordinates. Presumably there will be less secrecy in the future. In addition, American officials may now be a bit more leery when they are asked to forgo established American practices and adopt typically Soviet customs for the sake of a "particularly important contract" or for the creation of a certain "political atmosphere."

Without denying the benefits of the 1972 transaction to the United States, it is unfortunate that such large subsidies had to be paid to sell grain to the Soviet Union and that the deal contributed so heavily to the disruption of the domestic American economy. The Soviet wheat deal was a prime cause for the rise of American bread and livestock prices, which in turn helped set off a general inflationary spiral. The jam-up on the railroad and at our ports because of the backlogged wheat shipments further hurt the economy, as did the extra stress placed on American banks which provided the financing.

In all fairness, however, it is necessary to point out that once the Russians set out into the world market in 1972 to buy their 27 million tons of grain, or in 1974 to buy their 3.4 million tons, there was no way to escape an increase in world grain prices. Even if the errant anchovies had returned to Peru, and even if we had decided to restrict our shipments to the Soviet Union directly, there would still have been an impact on world prices. If all else failed, the Russians would have tried to go to countries like Canada and Australia, which then would have tried to come to the United States to replenish their own wheat, which they would have then sent on to the Soviet Union. An American wheat embargo to all countries might have provided some protection, but no matter what action we might ultimately have taken, there was no escaping the fact that the effect of the poor Russian harvest was to increase the world demand for wheat. As all beginning students of economics know, when the demand for a product is increased by 25 percent and there is no change in the available supply, the price is bound to go up. What has been resented more than anything else, however, is that the Soviet government did not have to bear any of that increased price. Instead, because of incredible incompetence on the part of the senior officials in the Department of Agriculture, the full burden fell on the American taxpayer (who had to pay the export subsidies which were made available more than a month after they should have been) and the American and world consumers who alone had to pay the higher prices.

It may well be that if the price of grain had risen earlier, the Russians would have been forced to buy less. Given the resentment that has followed this transaction, that was probably a chance worth taking. If our government could have shown that the Russians had also borne some of the additional cost of the inflationary situation they had been largely responsible for creating, not only would there have been less bitterness over the deal, but the cause of détente would probably have been furthered rather than hurt. As it is, the feeling is now widespread that the Soviet Union took advantage of us in 1972 and tried to repeat the performance in 1974.

But the Russians have not had to bear any of the cost, and as a result there have been all kinds of awkward situations. For instance, once their own 1973 harvest had started to come in, the Russians decided in September 1973 to present the grain-short government of India with a "loan" of 2 million tons of grain. Technically the grain may, as advertised, have come from the Soviet Union. Nonetheless, the United States has found it somewhat difficult to provide a similar "loan" partly because, at the time of the announcement, it was still delivering grain to the Soviet Union under the low prices agreed to in 1972. Nor was it any less embarrassing when Deputy Minister of Foreign Trade Vladimir S. Alkhimov was heard to say in January 1974 that, in order to replenish American stock, the Soviet Union would be happy to resell some of the wheat it had purchased back to the United States at current market prices, i.e., three times what the Russians had paid in 1972. "After all," said Alkhimov, "we bought the wheat at market prices. They may have been low, but look at Alaska, which we sold you for $7 million back in 1867. That was cheap too, but you don't hear us complaining." [40] The Russians did agree to a delay in the delivery of some of their American wheat purchase, which in effect was a form of resale. Yet their sudden and in some ways secret return to the market in October 1974 more than offset their apparent cooperation in the earlier part of the year.

But of all the ironies, none exceeded the fact that as late as two years after the transaction took place, no official notices were provided the Soviet populace that anything out of the ordinary had happened. Until June 1974, the Soviet people were virtually the only ones in the world who did not know about the 1972 wheat purchase. Then again, the Soviet Union is the only place in the world where the price of bread has remained constant. Who says there is a price to pay for ignorance?

CHAPTER

8

Selling High Technology

to the Soviets:

The Raytheon Corporation

A S the wheat deal shows, even simple negotiations with the Russians can be complex. In this chapter and the next, we shall see that negotiations concerning manufactured goods can be even more complicated, time consuming, and expensive. This is largely due to the fact that doing business with the Soviet government frequently involves new and unique practices. Because it is virtually impossible to walk in uninvited on Soviet factory purchasing agents, one of the biggest difficulties American salesmen face is how to make the initial contact. It is here that creative use can be made of institutions not normally involved in commercial negotiations. That such new and innovative approaches sometimes work is due often to chance, almost always to alertness, and invariably to the recognition by either the buyer or the seller that a basic need exists. The Raytheon Corporation's efforts to sell the

Soviet government an air traffic control (ATC) system involved a combination of all these factors.

While there is some disagreement as to who took the initiative, everyone agrees that the professional society, the American Institute of Aeronautics and Astronautics (AIAA), played a vital role in interesting Soviet aviation authorities in the American ATC system. The AIAA in turn had become interested after the American press, particularly the magazine *Aviation Week and Space Technology,* ran several articles describing a series of serious airplane crashes in the U.S.S.R. After these articles, American specialists in ATC systems became aware that the Soviet Ministry of Civil Aviation had been ordered to plan a ten-year program to rebuild the Soviet ATC system and to improve air traffic safety. This seemed to be a unique opportunity for American firms. The news that several European companies also sought to take advantage of this situation caused the Americans to take immediate action.

The approach adopted by the American corporations was unusual. Conceivably, individual corporations could have set off by themselves to solicit ATC contracts. Soviet air authorities should have been open to solicitation by the American corporations because of the seriousness of their problem. Indeed, under normal circumstances, one would have thought that since the Americans were the ones with the most advanced ATC technology in the world, the Russians would have taken the initiative and beaten a path to the American producers' doors. But the Soviets did not beat any such paths, nor did any American firms set off for Moscow. The explanation for the reticence by both parties reveals much about the unusual nature of American-Soviet trade, particularly when it comes to selling goods that could have a military use.

The American manufacturers of the ATC components perceived that the sale of an entire ATC system to the Russians would not be an ordinary type of transaction. Of all the acquisitions the Soviet Union might make for its civilian sector, probably few would have as much military significance as the purchase of an American ATC system, which involves some of the most advanced radar and computer hardware and software that have been designed in the United States. Without too much effort, skilled engineers and planners can transform a civilian ATC system into a military system that will provide for missile and antiaircraft defense. It was anticipated, therefore, that the Defense Department would react with something less than enthusiasm to the spectacle of an American corporation trying to sell such a system to the Soviet Ministry of Civil Aviation. Some corporate executives feared that any single American firm which attempted to sell the Soviet Union such a system would risk the private as well as public wrath of the Department of Defense. However, if a group of corporations made a joint effort, there might be less chance that any one corporation would be singled out for specific attack.

It was not just the desire to disarm resistance by the Department of Defense that prompted individual American corporations to band together. The Russians also seemed to prefer it that way.[1] From the beginning Soviet authorities indicated that any purchases made by the Soviet government would probably be made through a counterpart government organization in the United States. From all appearances, they were not prepared to deal with individual American corporations. Soviet officials assumed for some reason that the Federal Aviation Administration (FAA) would be able to serve as the prime contractor. If the FAA were to refuse, the next likely candidate seemed to be the AIAA. The Russians seemed to feel the AIAA operated in much the same way as did the foreign trade organizations (FTO) in the U.S.S.R. They failed completely to understand that the AIAA was nothing more than a professional society—it was not even a trade association—and could not undertake to organize the sale of millions of dollars' worth of equipment. Nonetheless, the Russians have always preferred to deal with a single entity when contemplating a massive contract. Since the AIAA appeared to be such an entity and did represent all the major American producers of ATC equipment, the Russians were quick to respond when the AIAA offered to show civil aviation authorities in the U.S.S.R. what American industry had to offer.

The AIAA moved on several fronts. Soviet authorities in the Ministry of Civil Aviation were invited to send a delegation to the AIAA annual meetings and trade exhibition in Washington in January 1973. The AIAA synchronized its invitations with a similar one from the FAA. The FAA offered to discuss its operating methods with Soviet air traffic authorities on a semiofficial basis. This invitation was issued in the wake of the 1972 summit meeting between Party Secretary Brezhnev and President Nixon. Such an exchange concerning safety for civilian air traffic seemed to fit appropriately with the spirit of détente. Acknowledging the importance of the exchange, the Russians sent some of their leading aviation officials, including a senior air force officer, General Aleksei Semenkov, and Tatiana Anodina, deputy director of the Science and Technology Department of the Ministry of Civil Aviation.

The linkage of the FAA invitation with the AIAA annual meeting and exhibition was an intentional signal to the Russians that the U.S. government viewed the AIAA endeavor with favor. This spared the Soviet Ministry of Civil Aviation any embarrassment it might have incurred as the guest of a single corporation. Similarly, it spared individual corporations charges of disloyalty from the U.S. Defense Department and other groups opposed to commercial dealings with the Russians. (The strategy was threatened by the arrival of the Soviet air force general as leader of the Soviet delegation. Fortunately, the Russian general left before the end of the tour.)

Following the annual AIAA meeting and discussions between the FAA and the Soviet Ministry of Civil Aviation officials in Washington, the AIAA arranged for the Russians to visit several ATC installations scattered across the country. Included in the itinerary were O'Hare Airport in Chicago, the FAA Air Route Traffic Control Center at Islip, New York, and the FAA Air Traffic Control Training and Aeronautical Center at Oklahoma City, as well as various factory facilities where ATC equipment is manufactured. One purpose of the visits was to show the Russians how our systems operate so they would have a better idea of what they should buy to bring their operations up to our standards.

Originally the Soviet mission had established the following order of priorities: 1) build up Soviet terminal control capabilities in order to control aircraft within 36 miles (60 kilometers) of the airport; 2) update Soviet navigational aids such as beacons and radio equipment; 3) obtain ATC simulators; 4) learn more about American air traffic controller training systems; and 5) consider "en route control automation equipment."

From Raytheon's point of view, Soviet priorities were inverted.[2] While the Russians seemed to feel they could solve their safety problem by buying a set of "terminal systems," Raytheon felt that the "en route system" was more important than the "terminal system." Coincidentally, the "en route system" happened to be the area in which Raytheon equipment excelled. The trick was to convince the Russians of their misconceptions.

The first doubts about the wisdom of the original Soviet priorities were planted at the Washington meeting. The Russians were apparently impressed with Raytheon's exhibition at the Sheraton Park Hotel, which included a model of the "en route system." These feelings were reinforced during the tour of actual FAA installations such as the one at Islip, where the Russians could see Raytheon's equipment in operation. Gradually, Tatiana Anodina, who Raytheon officials soon came to realize was the key member of the delegation, became responsive to what Raytheon was doing. This was a crucial breakthrough. Now that someone of importance understood the basic workings of the system, Raytheon officials knew they had a good chance to sign a major contract with the U.S.S.R. To do this, however, they would have to find some way to make further contact with Deputy Director Anodina and her staff.

Raytheon was not alone in its desire for additional contacts with officials in the Ministry of Civil Aviation. Other American corporations in the aerospace industry sensed the same opportunity. What about setting up an exhibition in Moscow? The question was raised at the Washington meeting. Why not have an exhibition and a symposium with technical papers presented by specialists from both countries? The AIAA offered to serve as a sponsor, the first time a professional society had ever assumed such an undertaking. Success was by no means assured.

As it turned out, arranging for the exhibition was not a simple matter. AIAA's proposal fitted in with Soviet wishes because authorities in the Ministry of Civil Aviation, particularly Mrs. Anodina, wanted to have another look at American technology. Presumably it would have been a simple matter for her to arrange for the Ministry of Civil Aviation itself to sponsor an exhibition of American firms in Moscow. Such sponsorship, however, might have caused political repercussions, because it might appear that the ministry was favoring American firms. Consequently, some other Soviet organization had to be found to serve as host in Moscow.

This was not easily arranged. If the AIAA were to put on the show itself without an official Soviet cosponsor, it would be awkward for the FAA to participate. But without FAA participation, the Russians in turn would feel that the American government was not supporting the venture. In fact, the Russians wanted the FAA not only to participate, but to sponsor the exhibition. More than that, as we have seen, it turned out that the Russians wanted the FAA to serve as the prime contractor in any sale of American ATC equipment to the U.S.S.R. Mrs. Anodina told the FAA that she would like to buy an exact duplicate of the FAA system if the FAA would put it together. The FAA refused because it did not consider this a proper type of activity for a U.S. regulatory agency. The Russians could not understand this reasoning. For them, the Soviet government is normally involved in all economic or trade activity, just as in the United States the government is normally excluded as an active participant in such transactions. Here is another instance of institutional procedures of the United States and the Soviet Union differing significantly. For American-Soviet trade to grow, there must be either greater tolerance for such differences in form and style between the two countries, or ways must be found to bridge some of these institutional gaps.

The question of Soviet sponsorship was eventually resolved in a way that assured FAA participation. After some prompting from Mrs. Anodina, the Soviet Chamber of Commerce agreed to serve as sponsor. But at this point the (Soviet) State Committee for Science and Technology (SCST), which had not responded to an earlier offer to act as sponsor, suddenly decided it should be the sponsor instead. From the American point of view this was preferable, since the involvement of the SCST made it an official governmental affair and thus opened the way for FAA attendance. In the end, both the Chamber of Commerce and the SCST shared the sponsorship.

Having finally solved the question of sponsorship, the AIAA next turned its attention to the exhibition itself. It was agreed that in late July 1973 there would be a ten-day display of equipment and technology and a five-day symposium covering the whole field of commercial aviation.[3] Not only had the AIAA never sponsored such an event outside the United States, but it had no experience in mounting anything of the scope of this proposed exhibition with such little warning. For that matter, by May 1973 the AIAA had not even lined up all the potential exhibitors. The fact that the whole thing was to take place in a country like the Soviet Union, where procedures were so different, did nothing to simplify matters for the organizers.

Despite the difficulties or maybe because of them, the participants responded rapidly and positively. Against almost impossible odds, the whole affair was put together on time and with considerable skill. This alone made an enormous impression on Soviet officials.

While the Americans tried to move rapidly, the Russians did not seem particularly anxious to help them. Because of bureaucracy and red tape, decisions by the Soviet hosts were slow in coming. A site was set aside in the Chemical Pavilion at the Exhibition Site for National Achievement in Moscow, but the Russians provided little information about costs, rental space, and other necessary data.[4] Expecting it would be expensive, the AIAA set exhibition space rentals at $10 a square foot for the 24 American exhibitors who took space. That was higher than the rent charged at the New York City Coliseum. Nonetheless it proved to be too low, despite the fact that SCST officials reported that as a courtesy the Americans were being charged special low rates. The Russians had no intention of letting any profit opportunity pass them by.

For Raytheon the exhibition was their big opportunity, providing them with a chance to deal directly with the ultimate consumer—senior officials in the Ministry of Civil Aviation. This was an unusual arrangement, since most American exporters are shielded from the ultimate consumer by the FTO of the Ministry of Foreign Trade. The exception for this exhibition was probably due to the urgency of the Soviet air safety problem as well as the extremely specialized nature of the technology involved. In any case, if a sale were to be made, it was of utmost importance for Raytheon officials that Mrs. Anodina and her staff agree to include a visit to Raytheon's exhibit on her schedule. Until the arrival of some senior Raytheon officials midway in the show, no one had managed to tie her down. Fortunately, soon after their arrival, contact was made and she agreed to return the next day with her staff.

Having arranged for an audience, the next job was to find a conference room in which to put on their briefings and technical discussions. There were none available. In a display of organizational efficiency that again left the Russians expressing astonishment, Raytheon managed to find some unused space in the Pavilion and transformed it overnight into a conference hall. As part of its planning, Raytheon had arranged to bring to Moscow a West German company which specialized in setting up exhibition displays. Having had some previous experience with improvisation in the U.S.S.R., the Germans managed to finish the construction of a conference room a few minutes before the presentation was to start. Though Raytheon had to spend $5,000 to $10,000 in overtime pay, the expenditure helped to build Raytheon's image of a well-organized and innovative company. Moreover, the cost was offset when other companies, such as IBM and Univac, subsequently rented the facility from Raytheon to put on their shows.

Raytheon was able to demonstrate what its system was capable of doing and what it did in the United States. Soviet officials wanted to know, however, how the Raytheon approach could be adapted to Soviet needs. Since Raytheon had no precise idea of what Soviet needs were, this was not easy. Initially Raytheon drew up a set of logical assumptions. As one executive told the Russians, "This is what we assume your requirements are, and based on these assumptions, this is what our system will do for you. But," he told them, "to be effective you will have to tell us what your requirements are."

The Russians were unresponsive. Even though the Americans had been forthcoming about American needs and procedures, the Russians appeared fearful that similar disclosures on their part would reveal military information. While that may have been part of the explanation, several Raytheon officials suspected that a more important reason for their secrecy was that the Russians actually did not know what their requirements were. This was one of the reasons for their many accidents. Ultimately Raytheon officials persuaded the Russians to set forth their needs and confide them to Raytheon. In the meantime, however, the company had to guess what they thought Soviet needs were from the equipment they were shown and the questions they were asked. Fortunately, unlike most of the other exhibitors, Raytheon brought with it a full team of technicians who could respond on the spot to Soviet needs. Thus Raytheon was able to design a custom-made program for ATC in the U.S.S.R.

Once they had some idea of Soviet needs, vague as they were, the Raytheon people assumed they had overcome their biggest hurdle. But, as they soon discovered, this was not the case. What should have been the simplest of all problems to resolve almost stumped them. How were the preliminary plans to be presented to the Russians? The usual presentation in such situations consists of a chart show—but there was no poster-sized paper available in Moscow. Since no one in Gosplan had anticipated Raytheon's needs (or even that Raytheon would be in Moscow) when the yearly Soviet plan had been drawn up the preceding year, the planning authorities had not allocated Raytheon or the Ministry of Civil Aviation the large-sized sheets of paper it needed to sketch its plans for the Soviet ATC system. There is no office supply store in Moscow where such things are readily available for sale. Once again, however, their resourceful German assistants came to the rescue, and the ATC system was sketched out on the back of a roll of wallpaper.

Nor did Raytheon's problems end once they found their paper. Because the language used by air traffic controllers is so colloquial, it is extremely difficult to translate into Russian. Raytheon had brought two translators with them and they worked long and hard to find the Russian equivalents of what they wanted to say, but it is hard to find the Russian for such words as software, computer interface, IFR (instrumental flight rules), flight plan, and a hand-off (transferring the plane from one traffic controller to another). On occasion even simple terms were garbled. In one instance, when Raytheon asked its translators for a sign depicting a display of "secondary radar," they ended up with "second-rate radar."

Overall, despite such shortcomings, both sides considered the show a success. Between 15,000 and 25,000 Russians, including most of the senior air traffic personnel in the U.S.S.R. and their counterparts from the East European countries, visited the site and asked questions. Soviet authorities even allowed in a number of ordinary citizens.

Nonetheless, during the seminar and visits to airports, research laboratories, and factories that followed, many Americans came to feel that they were being more forthcoming than the Russians, that while their side offered facts the Russians offered abstractions. Except on the factory and institute visits, most efforts to communicate in the symposia or to learn the identities of the visitors to their exhibits met with failure.[5] The Americans generally were not allowed to pass out inquiry cards to those visiting the exhibition. Just as they had done with the address cards the Singer Company attempted to bring in (see Chapter 6), the Soviet customs authorities confiscated a similar set of cards from one of the exhibiting aerospace companies. The publishers of *Aviation Week and Space Technology* could not even distribute free copies of their magazine until all subscription blanks had been removed.[6]

Compared with the relative freedom the Russians had enjoyed on their visits to American installations in January 1973, the Americans were strictly limited in what they could see. Sometimes, of course, Soviet efforts to limit the visitors were to no avail. Initially denied a visit to the heat treating facility of the aircraft engine works in Zaporozhe, the group inadvertently got to see what it wanted only when it was realized that the nearest toilets were in the heat treating building.

Still, by Russian standards, the Americans received a more cordial reception than was accorded most visiting foreign groups. It was also clear that the Russians were impressed by what they saw and heard at the fair. So much so that the Russians decided to seek bids on an ATC system that was to provide for an "en route" traffic control center in Moscow and terminal systems for Moscow, Kiev, and Mineralynye Vody, a resort area in the Caucasus. The Ministry of Civil Aviation asked five companies, Raytheon, IBM, Univac, Texas Instruments, and Lockheed Electronics, to submit proposals by October 1, 1973.

That the Russians wanted a concrete proposal was both good and bad news. The good news was that all the time, effort, and money expended might pay for itself. For Raytheon, mounting and presenting the show had already cost about $150,000. That was above and beyond the salaries and travel expenses of the Raytheon people involved with the project, which added another $60,000 to $70,000 to the total. The cost would have been even higher if Raytheon had had to build a special exhibition for Moscow. As it was, a few weeks before the Moscow exhibition, Raytheon had put together a display for the Paris Air Show. After the conclusion of the Paris Show, Raytheon simply picked up its exhibit, substituted Russian for the French translation, and flew it to Moscow, thereby saving another $150,000 that would have been required if the display had been designed from scratch.

The bad news was that a finished project proposal would necessitate expenditure of additional funds. Moreover, there was still no guarantee that the Russians were really serious. They might just be seeking as much information as possible to enable them to pirate the basic plans, fit them out with as much of their own equipment as they could, and buy the rest from European sources. Certainly the Russians understood the theory of ATC and had the expertise necessary to build and operate such a system. It was concluded, however, that it would take the Russians a long time to build such a project on their own since, among other things, they did not have the reservoir of standard parts to draw upon. Thus, it was decided to move ahead.

Raytheon officials had to decide on a strategy in presenting their bid. Should they draw up their own proposal or enter as a subcontractor for IBM? Presumably the profit potential and prestige would be greater if Raytheon were its own contractor, but the more bidders there were, the greater the chance that the Russians would play off one bidder against another. Yet almost all the Americans had the impression that the Soviet Union wanted only one overall bid submitted. This impression stemmed from the persistent request by the Russians that the FAA submit a bid on behalf of the whole ATC industry. However, if Raytheon joined with IBM, the U.S. Department of Justice might raise some antitrust issues on the assumption that there had been collusion between the two corporations to reduce competition. (This is ironic, since the major beneficiary of unrestrained competition and the resultant lower prices would undoubtedly be the Soviet Union.)

There were other considerations. Because IBM had been a major contributor to the ATC system that presently exists in the United States, and because Soviet authorities had already expressed their desire to buy a duplicate of the American system, there was good reason to believe that IBM had the inside track. Besides, IBM was the epitome of American technology as far as most Soviet technicians were concerned. No matter what other bids would be submitted, IBM seemed favored. Adding weight to that assumption was a sudden and unexplained switch within the Ministry of Foreign Trade. Raytheon had been told in May by officials in the Ministry of Civil Aviation that if and when a firm contract was to be discussed, the FTO, Aviaeksport, would do the negotiating. But subsequently, to the evident concern of the Soviet Ministry of Civil Aviation, which after all was to operate the system, Aviaeksport, which had the capability for evaluating such a contract, was pushed aside in favor of a newer and smaller FTO, Elektronorgteknh. Since the latter's main competence lay with computers, this was taken as a favorable sign for IBM.

Despite all these negative signs, there were some in Raytheon who continued to insist that it was Raytheon, not IBM, that produced the crucial components of the system. In addition, some feared that IBM would request too high a price. While this might bring greater profits for everyone, it might also put the whole project out of the reach of the Russians, or push them toward proposals being submitted by French and Italian-Swedish companies. Finally it was questioned whether any bid by Raytheon, either as the prime contractor or as subcontractor, would be worth the effort, since there was no guarantee that the American government would license the sale of such a system. The IBM system involved the use of IBM's 9020 unit. Not only was this probably a more expensive piece of hardware than was necessary, but the U.S. government had discouraged all past efforts to sell the Soviet Union such equipment. Even if a substitute could be found for the IBM 9020, the government was unlikely to be particularly enthusiastic about the sale of Raytheon's radar and computer programs.

After a good deal of debate, Raytheon decided to subcontract to IBM—only to receive a cable from the Russians shortly after the bids were submitted on October 1, 1973, asking it to submit its own bid as the prime contractor. Told specifically to base its proposals on the "wallpaper" scheme prepared for the Russians at the Moscow show that past July, Raytheon submitted a second set of estimates to the Ministry of Civil Aviation in December 1973.

This proposal in some ways was an uncertain venture. Russian specifications had called for the use of IBM's 9020 system. In its place, Raytheon substituted minicomputers which it argued would do the job nearly as well. The great unknown was whether or not the Russians would accept that arrangement.

At the time of this writing, no final decision had been reached. For that matter, there was some question as to whether the Russians would allocate enough foreign currency for such a project. Given their windfall in the sale of oil and other raw materials, the Russians were certainly in a more liquid position in the spring of 1974 than when they first began to talk about the need for such a system in early 1973. There were hints that a decision as to the availability of the currency would be made in April 1974. Conceivably the Soviet officials were waiting until April so they could have a chance to evaluate their grain import needs. By April the government would know about the prospects for its winter wheat harvest and whether or not foreign currency would have to be diverted to the purchase of food, as it was in 1972. There was also a report that the FAA had told its Soviet counterpart that the FAA wanted a decision no later than April. The FAA was worried about the investment already made by the American corporations in preparing their proposals, and wanted to protect them from further needless expenditures. Despite the hints, April 1974 came and passed, and as of February 1975, the Soviet government had not yet announced their decision.

Involvement by the FAA was a unique but welcome step by an organ of the U.S. government to offset to some extent the immense bargaining power of the Soviet Union acting as one buyer playing off several competitive sellers. In an effort to reduce the cutthroat bidding the Russians were attempting to stimulate, the FAA told the Russians it wanted an early decision and wanted them to pick one American bidder. Only in this way could the Russians obtain full advantage of the FAA system's training and software. This did not prevent the Russians from seeking several bids, but the FAA's hope was that a quick decision would prevent the bidders from offering ever-increasing bargains. In addition to the bids by IBM and Raytheon and a possible last-minute entry by Univac, the Russians had also solicited bids from Thomson CSF, a private company heavily involved with the French government, and from an Italian-Swedish consortium, a partnership made up of Selenis and Stan Saab. According to the Russians, the Italian-Swedish bid was one-half the French bid, which was one-half the Raytheon bid, which was about $80 million. In turn, the Raytheon bid, because it utilized minicomputers, was considerably under the IBM bid of $250 million.

By letting each bidder know that his bid was higher than that of a potential competitor, the Russians were trying to obtain better prices. Reportedly IBM had been told that it should lower its bid to the $80 million range if it wanted to compete. At the same time, Raytheon was told that it was not competitive with the French. Raytheon officials responded by saying that "if you want a less far-reaching proposal, tell us and we will draw up a cheaper one."

Considering that Raytheon had already expended between $300,000 and $400,000 on mounting its exhibition in Moscow and preparing its proposal, it had a keen interest in recovering as much of its investment as possible. Presumably IBM spent a comparable sum. One or the other and possibly both will have to write off the whole expenditure.

To some extent, these are normal hazards that prospective bidders must be prepared to risk. Yet the scale of the bids, the uniqueness of dealing with a monopsonist like the Soviet Union, the possibility that the Russians may simply take the proposals and use them for their own purposes, and finally the uncertainty as to whether the United States government will even license the sale of such a system—all these factors highlight the need for some new institutional approach for dealing with the U.S.S.R. on this kind of venture. With something as technologically advanced and sophisticated as an ATC system, the American manufacturer cannot even be certain that he can obtain a government license to exhibit his equipment in the U.S.S.R. Simply sending a prototype to the Soviet Union for exhibition is regarded as the export of technical information. Such permission was granted before the AIAA exhibition was held in July 1973. However, whether or not the American government would issue export licenses for the actual equipment was not known until March 1974, when the government finally gave its assent.

On smaller and less technologically complex transactions, it may well be that the traditional system of competition between American corporations and the rest of the world is better than a system that encourages the kind of abuses that invariably arise when there is collusion and market sharing. But on projects the size of the ATC deal, the Russians seem to be the major beneficiary of any price cutting, while at least one competitor is sure to be a substantial loser. Even the American winner may be a loser if the final bid is pushed down so low that a reasonable profit margin is eliminated.

On top of everything else, the Russians try to push the price even lower by insisting at first that they will pay cash for their purchase, and asking for price quotations for a cash deal. There is the constant fear that if and when the decision to buy is finally made, the Russians will suddenly announce they need financing after all; at the same time, they will insist on paying no more than the original price quoted when the assumption was that there would have to be no allowance for financing.

If our institutional patterns of trade are changed in an effort to cope more effectively with Soviet patterns of bargaining, it is unlikely that one pattern will be suitable for all industries or all projects. At the least, however, the Bureau of East-West Trade should exercise more of a coordinating role. The Raytheon people acknowledge their gratitude to the Bureau of East-West Trade for its assistance in obtaining the necessary clearance so that Raytheon could take its materials to the Soviet Union for the July 1973 exhibition. A few years ago, before expansion of the Bureau of East-West Trade, such permission would have taken months or may not have been forthcoming. But the Bureau of East-West Trade should not only be equipped to deal with the United States bureaucracy; it should also be authorized to coordinate the efforts of competing American corporations. It might be helpful, for example, if the various bids submitted by American corporations to the Russians were also reported to the Bureau of East-West Trade and then made public. As it is now, the Russians are the only ones who know what the various bids are, and they tend to use this information to force lower bids from other manufacturers. Unfortunately, the bidders never know if the Russians are reporting correctly what the others are bidding. Senior officials in the Bureau of East-West Trade have indicated that they have been attempting to provide such a coordinated function among those engaged in trying to sell the Russians the ATC equipment. However, officials of some of the bidding corporations involved have generally been unaware of any such help.

Corporate officials involved in the sales effort have also acknowledged with appreciation the assistance of the FAA. Not only did the FAA take an official role at the 1973 Moscow aerospace show, but it used considerably more pressure than most federal civilian agencies exert on behalf of the foreign trade dealings of American corporations. In contrast, the French government is openly lobbying for Thomson CSF. It is possible that Thomson CSF's low bid is predicated on the receipt by the French government or some other sector of French industry of some service in kind from the Russians to compensate for the lower bid.

Bringing in extraneous matters is another common tactic of Soviet negotiators. For example, some American companies have been told that their bids would receive more favorable consideration if they were to agree to an offset sale by the U.S.S.R. Thus the Russians have tried to pay for their proposed purchases of ATC equipment by means of an exchange for the YAK 40 jet aircraft made in the U.S.S.R. There were also rumors that the Russians would probably "be forced" to award the contract for an ATC system to corporations in other countries unless the United States granted Aeroflot additional landing rights, particularly on the West Coast.[7] This was written off by most Americans as a political bargaining bluff, but it is typical of the leverage the Soviet Union will try to exert, not only on individual American firms, but on the American government as well. Needless to say, when other governments attempt to use somewhat similar tactics on the Soviet Union, as for example when the United States attempted to balance off most favored nation treatment with freer emigration from the U.S.S.R., the Russians were quite indignant.

Here the FAA has proved helpful. During early discussions between the FAA and the Ministry of Civil Aviation, and before there were any discussions about buying American equipment, ministry officials proposed that as part of the general détente the Soviet Union should have "free" access to the computer program being used in the United States. This would not only improve understanding, they argued, but would provide air traffic safety for American flights going to Moscow. If the Russian request had been met, they would have been presented, at no cost, with what it took the FAA and American corporations many years and millions of dollars to develop. The FAA ultimately agreed to supply such a program to the Soviet Union, but only if and when the Russians sign a contract with one of the major American corporations. That perhaps is the best kind of support the American bidders can expect at the present time.

Certainly I do not mean to suggest that dropping antitrust restraints would be an unmixed blessing. As we discovered in the aftermath of Watergate, whenever the government and industry become too cozy, there is always the danger that political and personal rather than economic considerations will influence the government's actions. Moreover, in the present instance, absence of competition might have meant that Raytheon would not have gone to the trouble of designing the more technologically advanced system they eventually presented. Without competition, it is likely that Raytheon would have settled to subcontract for the significantly more expensive and less advanced proposal put out by IBM. In either case, the state of ATC technology would have been the loser.

The Russians cannot be faulted if the competitive situation makes it possible for them to have access to an ATC system that is more advanced than the one presently in operation in the United States. The development work done by Raytheon in the process of preparing their bid might not have been forthcoming otherwise, and will probably be incorporated in the American system before too long. It would be unfortunate if such innovations were discouraged.

Yet Raytheon's experience illustrates how corporations which hope to sell high technology equipment to the Soviet Union can commit themselves to speculative outlays of hundreds of thousands of dollars with no assurance that there will be any return. And like Raytheon, there were others who, once they had decided to go after the contract, succumbed to the temptation to throw in new money in the hope they might recover at least a portion of their old money. This serious dilemma becomes particularly acute when, as is frequently the case when the sale of high technology is involved, there is little likelihood of repeat sales and there are several producers who can be played off against one another.

Of course, companies like Raytheon must take some such risks whenever they decide to compete for a contract in any country. Yet in dealing with the Soviet Union, the possible losses are usually much higher. To begin with, the size of the contract tends to be larger—the Russians want to do everything in a grandiose way. Moreover, it usually takes the Russians longer to make up their minds, so that bids must be kept open longer, thus increasing expenses for the bidder.

If private corporations were the only ones affected, it would be enough to point out the advantages and disadvantages of such transactions and let the corporations and their stockholders worry about it. But the national interest may also be involved, particularly when the research and development costs for the technology being offered were financed in large part with public funds and when the product has military potential. Presumably the Pentagon will continue its monitoring of the sale of military technology, but so far there is no agency assigned to guard against the underbidding and price cutting which often take place when American manufacturers are maneuvered into competing with themselves to sell the Soviets highly technical equipment at little more than the marginal cost of production. When, for example, the United States, as reported, sells the Soviet Union space suits that cost the United States approximately $20 million apiece to develop for $150,000 apiece, the United States is being unduly generous. When such advanced technology is about to be transferred, the Bureau of East-West Trade or some comparable agency should be authorized to establish an upset price that reflects not only the marginal costs, but much, if not all, of the average costs. This should be done particularly when there is no other country with manufacturers that can supply such equipment. Certainly the opportunity cost the Soviets would have to bear to develop the suits themselves would be much higher than $150,000. When they can make comparable goods, the threat of competition from Western Europe and Japan should be sufficient to keep the prices of American manufacturers in line. What the Raytheon experience shows is that we should avoid the present situation, in which the Soviets are free to play off one American firm against another and then use the resulting price concessions to force foreign competitors to lower their prices as well. When this happens, the only apparent beneficiary is the U.S.S.R.[8]

CHAPTER

9

Success Stories:

Armand Hammer and

the Pullman Corporation

I T certainly is not a rigid rule, but the Soviets seem to have gone out of their way to recultivate commercial relations with companies that originally had dealings with the Russians in the 1930s or even before the revolution. That as much as anything seems to explain their warmth for Armand Hammer, Ford, General Electric, Holcroft, International Harvester, Singer, and the Chase Manhattan Bank. In some instances this may indicate appreciation for help during the revolution; in other cases it may just reflect the Soviet tendency to stick with the tried and tested.

DR. ARMAND HAMMER

The individual who has received the most notoriety about his dealings with the Soviet Union is Dr. Armand Hammer, the chairman, president, and largest stockholder of the Occidental Petroleum Company. We have already discussed in detail Dr. Hammer's proposed 20-year agreement with the Russians for the exchange of American super-phosphoric acid for Soviet ammonia, potash, and urea.

Originally the Soviet fertilizer factories which will produce the ammonia and urea were also to have been built by Occidental and Bechtel, but, as we saw, the contract was finally awarded to the Chemical Construction Corporation. The ammonia factories will be built near Kuibyshev, which is located at an important junction of a Soviet pipeline for natural gas—the major nonair ingredient for ammonia. By the time construction is completed, these plants will provide the Russians with an annual output capacity of about 4 million tons of liquid ammonia and 1 million tons of urea. Occidental will then supply about 1 million tons of super-phosphoric acid in exchange for an equivalent value of ammonia, urea, and potash from the Soviet factories.

After Occidental lost the contract to build the fertilizer plants, there were some who reasoned that Dr. Hammer had been outmaneuvered. If that was actually the case, he and Occidental still emerged with what looks like a profitable deal. From the American side, the barter of the fertilizer will be handled by Hooker Chemical Corporation, an Occidental subsidiary. But it is more than a barter arrangement. Occidental is guaranteed a commission of 2.5 to 3 percent on the Soviet products that it receives for sale in the United States. This reduces the risk considerably and should be worth about $15 million a year, based on 1974 prices.

The fertilizer exchange was broadly hinted at in the general "technology exchange" agreement announced on July 18, 1972, between the State Committee for Science and Technology of the Soviet Council of Ministers and Occidental Petroleum. As we saw in Chapter 6, the exact meaning of such "technology exchange" agreements has always been unclear, but in the case of Occidental, at least, some of the generalities have been followed up with specifics. Thus the July 1972 general agreement also makes provision for the large-scale purchase of natural gas, construction of the hotel and commercial office center to be used by foreign businessmen, and a system to improve utilization of solid wastes in the U.S.S.R. On December 14, 1972, Occidental announced a firm contract for the sale of $80 million of finishing equipment to the Soviet Union. This was another barter arrangement, with the Russians paying for their purchases by providing Occidental with nickel. An Occidental subsidiary, the Barrett Research and Development Company of La Verne, California, has been working with Russian technicians on the solid waste disposal plant. Similarly, Occidental and Bechtel engineers are consulting with Holiday Inns and Intercontinental Hotels about construction of the offices and hotel complex in Moscow. On a smaller scale, another subsidiary, the Oxy Metal Finishing Corporation of Warren, Michigan, is supplying a $3.6 million order for metal finishing equipment and effluent control systems for two Soviet plants that will produce hollowware and flatware.

Almost all these arrangements, except for the hollowware and flatware factories, involve considerable risks because of the long payback period. Most of these deals, moreover, are to be paid for by the Russians through barter or delivery in kind from the factory that is to be built. Dr. Hammer is one of the last of the big time barterers. Since this is the Russians' preferred way of trading, his practices obviously attract them.

Dr. Hammer is clearly one of the Soviet Union's favorite businessmen. To some it seems that he is held in higher regard on Moscow's Gorky Street than on New York's Wall Street. Wall Streeters tend to snicker at some of his proposals and to write off his talk of big Soviet deals as an effort to promote Occidental Petroleum stock, once one of the wonder stocks of the 1960s (but forced to suspend dividends temporarily in 1972). When Dr. Hammer announced his general technological agreement with the Russians on July 18, 1972, the stock immediately rose by 2.75 points to 15.5. Subsequently it fell again. Then in December, 1973 the Securities and Exchange Commission charged Occidental

Petroleum and Dr. Hammer with defrauding the public when they sold some securities in 1971. Finally in March 1974 the Internal Revenue Service announced that it was trying to collect $800,000 in back taxes from Dr. Hammer because of a dispute over some of his charitable deductions.

While Wall Street may write off Dr. Hammer, senior Russian officials either are unaware of Wall Street's skepticism or do not care. In 1972–1973, Dr. Hammer had greater access to senior Soviet officials, including Kosygin and Brezhnev, than almost any other American and seemingly any other foreigner. Because of Dr. Hammer's personal initiative, the Russians announced a loan of 41 major paintings for display at the National Gallery in Washington and his own Knoedler Gallery in New York. Dr. Hammer certainly must be the only American in recent years who has donated a $1 million painting to the Soviet Union. He gave a Goya to the Hermitage, an act that undoubtedly did much to spur the Russians into sending their 41 pictures to the United States. In another such gesture, Dr. Hammer offered to give Moscow its first golf course. No wonder the Soviet Ambassador to the United States, Anatolyi Dobrynin, has jokingly suggested that Dr. Hammer be made American Ambassador to the Soviet Union.

But the Soviet affection for Dr. Hammer is not due solely to the ingenuity of the deals he proposes or the remarkable risks this 75-year-old man is willing to take. It also happens that Dr. Hammer is one of the few people alive today, foreign or Russian, who can boast that he had a close working relationship with Lenin.

Dr. Hammer's association with the U.S.S.R. goes back to 1921. Fresh out of Columbia Medical School, he set off for the U.S.S.R. to do what he could in the wake of the chaos which followed the Russian revolution.[1] With an army surplus mobile hospital he had purchased, he planned to help care for those stricken with typhus and cholera in the Urals. But when he reached Sverdlovsk (then called Ekaternburg) he was so shaken by the hunger and starvation that he saw that on his own he financed the purchase of 1 million tons of American grain. He offered to take repayment in Russian commodities that he could resell in the U.S. Lenin soon found out about his efforts and suggested that he could be more helpful to the new government if he switched to helping it with its business dealings rather than with its medical problems. It was unclear at that point if this implied more about Dr. Hammer's medical or his commercial skills.

In effect Lenin gave Dr. Hammer a free hand to arrange almost any kind of deal he could devise, using Russian raw materials such as asbestos, hides, caviar, and even confiscated Czarist art.[2] Dr. Hammer was given the first concession awarded by the Soviet state when Lenin allowed him to take over the Alapievsky asbestos mine. Ultimately Dr. Hammer sold it back to the Soviet Union in 1929. (It was one of the few foreign concessions not confiscated.) He was also allowed to open up his own factory, another unusual favor. Since none existed at the time, Dr. Hammer decided to open a pencil factory. Now called the Sacco and Vanzetti Pencil Factory of Moscow, it too was sold to the Soviet government in 1930. In each instance the Russians paid Dr. Hammer in cash.

During his nine-year stay in the U.S.S.R., Dr. Hammer ultimately came to represent about 40 American companies, including Ford, U.S. Rubber, Allis-Chalmers, and Parker Pen. By the time he left in 1932 he had accumulated a fortune in hard currency and Czarist era art treasures. Yet he left on good terms and apparently did manage to obtain items sorely needed by the U.S.S.R. at a time of dire emergency. If nothing else, his cordial relationship with Lenin has been worth millions of dollars in good will.[3]

THE PULLMAN CORPORATION

While Dr. Hammer and his Occidental Petroleum have received most of the publicity, his is not the only company that has had impressive dealings with the Soviet Union. The considerably more sedate Pullman Corporation has also been warmly received by the Russians. For example, Pullman was authorized to open an office in Moscow in July 1972, ahead of Occidental Petroleum. Indeed, although American Express and Pan American Airlines had opened offices several years earlier, Pullman became the first United States manufacturing company to do so.

Pullman, too, has old historical ties with Russia. As pointed out in an article in *Fortune* by Herbert Meyer, the word "pullman" has even become a part of the Russian language.[4] Pullman sleeping cars were bought for use on Russian railways prior to the revolution and were called *pullmanovskye spalnye vagony.* In one of the strangest twists of all, the Soviet Embassy in Washington is located in what was once George M. Pullman's mansion.

Sentiment aside, Pullman's initial involvement with the Soviet Union seems more like a fortuitous happening than any grand strategy. According to Samuel B. Casey, Jr., the president of Pullman, the first contact with the Russians occurred at the International Foundry Congress in Brighton, England, in September 1970. A representative from Swindell Dressler, a major division of Pullman, was casually introduced to two Russians at one of the congress' cocktail parties. Unexpectedly, the Russians called the next morning at 7:30 and asked to meet again. It turned out that the Russians were members of that all-important State Committee for Science and Technology. Their main interest was the foundry Swindell Dressler helped to build at the Ford Motor Company's plant at Flat Rock, Michigan, then the newest, most automated casting plant in the world.

It is not difficult to account for Soviet enthusiasm for Ford's foundry at the Flat Rock plant. But since the Soviet interest in Swindell Dressler stems from its involvement in the Ford project, we will have to digress for a few paragraphs to talk about how the Soviet Union tried to enlist Ford's help in building a new truck plant. After deciding they needed such a plant, one of the first things the Russians did was to seek out Henry Ford II, whose grandfather had helped them build one of their early auto plants at Gorky in the early 1930s. Invited to the Soviet Union by Dzherman Gvishiani of the State Committee for Science and Technology in April 1970, Mr. Ford was asked if his company would be interested in building a massive truck facility for the Soviet Union. The Russians were well acquainted with Ford's new plant at Flat Rock, particularly the foundry. Since this plant was the most advanced one in existence, they were determined to build a similar one.

(Rumors of the Soviet interest in such a plant had circulated for at least a year before that. On April 16, 1969, another American businessman had been approached to see if he could arrange for an American firm to build a truck factory for the Russians. It was to have a capacity of 150,000 trucks a year and indeed had all the characteristics of the plant presently being built. After a visit with Henry Kissinger's staff in the White House in 1969, however, he and I soon discovered that the Nixon administration was then not ready for such a contract.)

The truck plant that the Russians were seeking to build was to be located on the Kama River at Naberezhniye Chelny, about 600 miles east of Moscow. In addition to the 150,000 heavy diesel trucks that plant was to produce, it was also to have the capacity of producing another 100,000 diesel engines a year. The trucks would come in three models. One would be a tractor with a 260-horsepower engine for use with a 20-ton semitrailer. Output would be 55,000 units a year. The second, also to be produced at a rate of 55,000 a year, would have a 210-horsepower engine and a carrying capacity of 16 tons. The third model would be a dump truck with 160 horsepower and 70-ton capacity, of which 40,000 units would be produced. The Russians were particularly interested in American help with the foundry that was to go with the plant, but they were prepared to turn over the whole operation to Ford, at a potential cost of from $1.5 billion to $2 billion.

Before Ford had too much time to worry about the profit margins in such a venture, the project came to an abrupt halt.

Only a month after Henry Ford's return from the Soviet Union, Melvin Laird, then Secretary of Defense, attacked the whole concept. In a direct reference to the Ford situation, Laird insisted, "I am against exporting American technology to the Soviet Union while they are sending trucks to North Vietnam." The sharpness of the attack was in part unexpected because Ford officials had taken initial soundings elsewhere in Washington and had been told the project might be sanctioned. After all, the American government had approved the sending of machinery for use in the Fiat plant at Togliatti. Nevertheless, due to government pressure, Ford was forced to turn down the Russian invitation.

After Ford's withdrawal the Russians began to look elsewhere. Although they stepped up their soundings in France, Germany, and Japan, they again demonstrated their preference for American products and processes by focusing most of their negotiations on another American firm, Mack Truck. On May 18, 1971, virtually a year after Ford's withdrawal from the project, Mack Truck signed a preliminary agreement to design and supply equipment for what was estimated to be a $1.4 billion plant. The deal was contingent, however, on White House approval of the necessary export permits.

What a difference a year makes. While there was still determined opposition in the Department of Defense, the Nixon administration had become more favorably disposed. As mentioned earlier, 1971 was a bad year economically, an ominous situation prior to an election year. A contract of the size proposed by Mack Truck could mean a large number of jobs and a big boost to the balance of trade. The administration had signaled a major change in its stand in early June by authorizing export licenses to the Soviet Union for $50 million worth of machinery intended for the manufacturing of light trucks. As recently as two weeks prior to the issuance of the June licenses for the truck machinery, the Department of Commerce had reported that such licenses would not be issued because of national security considerations. Coincidentally, the issuance of the June license followed another decision to end the embargo on exports to the People's Republic of China, which in turn was linked to Henry Kissinger's arrangements for a secret visit to Peking and similar discussions somewhat later about a visit by Kissinger and Nixon to Moscow.

In any case, the question of whether or not the government would issue export licenses to Mack Truck was never answered directly (or at least publicly). Somewhat unexpectedly, after a few months' time with no answer from the government about the license and the expiration of several deadlines, Mack announced in September 1971 that it was dropping out of the whole project. Reportedly Mack's parent company, Signal Company, was worried because of the immensity of the project. After all, the proposed plant was to produce 150,000 diesel trucks a year, whereas Mack's total American output in 1970 was 22,000. For that matter, total diesel output in the entire United States was 105,000 in 1970. In addition there were troubling reports about difficulties at Russia's Fiat plant and the negative or zero profit margin earned by the Italian firm. Apparently Signal executives believed the Kama River project might overextend the resources of not only Mack Truck, but Signal as well.

There is reason to believe, however, that Mack Truck would ultimately have received its export license if it had persisted. The reason for such speculation is that simultaneously with the discussion being conducted by Mack, another set of license negotiations was being conducted by Swindell Dressler. Despite various feints toward other foundry builders, it seemed clear that the Russians were intent on having Swindell Dressler design its foundry. Among other indications, Soviet negotiations with Mack Truck included the proviso that the foundry be designed by Swindell Dressler. Just before President Nixon announced his August 15, 1971, New Economic Policy, the Department of Commerce authorized the issuance of an export license to Swindell Dressler. The approved license allowed the company to supply the designs and specify the equipment to be used in the foundry. It had taken Swindell Dressler eight months of patient and intensive lobbying.

One part of the process had been accomplished—all that remained was to see whether the Russians wanted to buy Swindell Dressler's foundry.

Tracing the evolution of negotiations for the Kama River truck plant, it appears that sooner or later the Russians would have been forced to deal directly with Swindell Dressler. In all probability, if the Brighton, England, meeting had not taken place in September 1970, the Russians would have sounded out Swindell Dressler in some other way. Not so coincidentally, Mack Truck was apparently contacted about the same time, in August 1970. Abandonment of the project by Henry Ford three months earlier meant that the Russians would probably have to go to the source itself, particularly if they were to get that foundry. Of course there was no guarantee that Swindell Dressler or even Mack would be any more successful than Ford in obtaining export licenses. If anything, there was probably less likelihood, but the Russians persisted.

There was a brief interval after Mack Truck's withdrawal when the whole operation was in jeopardy. The Russians hesitated for a while but then decided to continue with their plan to build a giant truck plant. Too much time had already been lost. Rather than waste time looking for another foreign company that would assume responsibility, they decided to assume overall supervision themselves. As before, this meant that various foreign companies would be asked to subcontract for the construction of various components of the complex, particularly the foundry—and this in turn meant that the Russians were still very much interested in Swindell Dressler.

After the initial meeting in Brighton, a series of meetings took place which eventually spanned a 15-month period and encompassed 28 trips to Moscow and several other European cities. With the American export license in hand, contract talks should presumably have moved swiftly, but the Russians suddenly appeared to be in no hurry to sign the contract after all.

Moreover, it was not always easy for Swindell Dressler to negotiate with the Russians. Whenever the Russians negotiate with an American firm, it is almost never on a one-to-one basis. As one American businessman put it, the Soviets usually insist that American firms negotiate with the Russians in troika style. Thus, in the traditional pattern, Swindell Dressler found itself negotiating with representatives from three different Soviet organizations. First there was the Automobile Ministry, which represents the ultimate user of the equipment; then there was Metallurgimport, the FTO which is the only authorized importer; and finally there was the Ministry of Foreign Trade, which is responsible for seeing that all foreign trade is standardized and no unnecessary concessions are made in the contract. The result was confusion, delay, triplication, and, as a consequence, extra cost for Swindell Dressler.

The Russians seemed unperturbed by the fact that every month, because of inflation, construction costs rose by about .5 percent. Thus not only were delays in negotiating with Swindell Dressler bound to be costly, but the Russians also lost valuable time when their earlier negotiations with other firms, including two years spent with Mercedes-Benz, came to naught. Any price reductions the Russians might have obtained by prolonged bargaining were almost inevitably offset by increases in the bids presented by the American firm to compensate for inflation. Swindell Dressler would pass on all the extra costs created by Soviet bargaining demands or delays, so ultimately the Soviet Union had to pay for its cumbersome ways. As one businessman deeply involved with the Kama negotiations put it, "The Soviet Union is penny wise and pound foolish."

Swindell Dressler also found that its negotiations with the Russians were complicated by their reluctance to allow foreigners free access to their country and people. Swindell Dressler did not insist, but its officials were not invited to see the site of the projected plant. Some officials of the company maintain that such a visit was not necessary. Yet even though they were supplied with test core borings of the site, a drainage scheme, and photographs, it is hard for an outsider to understand how Swindell Dressler engineers could do their best job as long as they were not invited to visit the site. It may be that the Russians decided to close the area to most foreigners because of their obsession for secrecy. The more likely reason is that they simply lacked facilities for housing and feeding foreign visitors in the somewhat remote area where the factory was being built. Eventually, of course, Swindell Dressler personnel were permitted to survey the site, but only in February 1973, two and one-half years after the start of discussions.[5] Moreover, Donald Morfee and Samuel Casey, the two senior officials of Pullman most involved in the transaction, did not make it to the site until the outer buildings were virtually completed in January 1974.

With or without visits to the site, negotiations dragged on in Moscow. There was a major mix-up over the scope of the initial design contracts. Because of some confusion in translation, Swindell Dressler originally thought the Russians wanted the design plan to include specifications for buildings and supplementary equipment as well as for the basic production process itself. This would have had the effect of increasing the price by 50 percent. When Swindell Dressler quoted such a high price, the Russians were naturally upset and the negotiations came to a halt until it was realized that a translation problem was involved. Related to all of this was the fact that because the Russians planned to construct the factory building themselves, Swindell Dressler did not have much chance to help shape the factory they would eventually have to equip. This disjointed procedure is occasionally followed in this country, but it is avoided whenever possible since it complicates the cost estimation procedure, to say nothing of the strain it places on those involved in the negotiations.

Finally, the Russians demanded a low price. Their strategy involved threats to turn the whole contract over to foreign companies and tempting baits of future contracts. Mr. Morfee was told in early December 1971 that if he would agree to a "reasonable" price on the initial design contract, the Russians would accord

Swindell Dressler favorable consideration on future contracts. Mr. Morfee rejected the bait and insisted that he intended to make a profit on the first contract or none at all. With that, according to Mr. Morfee, he told the Russians to forget the whole deal and immediately returned to Pittsburgh to spend the Christmas holidays with his family.

Although the tactic of walking out on a negotiation is frequently used by the Russians, apparently it unsettles them when they are treated the same way. In this case it was particularly upsetting to them because construction had already begun at the factory site. Further delay to search for a new firm to design the foundry would only mean additional costs and shortages for the Russians. Initially they had hoped to have the plant up and operating in 1974, but with the decisions by Ford in spring 1970 and Mack Truck in fall 1971 not to accept responsibility for the whole plant, a walkout on the foundry component by Swindell Dressler would push the timetable beyond 1975.

It is hard to see how a five-year plan can provide for such complications, particularly when they involve the scheduling of supplies and the manufacturing of the countless components required by an operation of the magnitude of the Kama River truck plant. Undoubtedly the original plan, if there was one, had already been disrupted. But whatever the impact of the succession of uncompleted negotiations on the five-year plans, the fact remained that the Russians wanted to start producing trucks as soon as possible. Moreover they still wanted the truck factory to be equipped with a foundry similar to the one that Swindell Dressler had built for Ford. Consequently a hurried call was put in to Mr. Morfee: "Please return immediately to Moscow." He did on December 19, and the $10 million contract for the design of the foundry was signed with N. P. Maximov, president of Metallurgimport, in the early hours of December 22, 1971, just in time for Mr. Morfee to catch another plane home for Christmas.[6]

With the ice broken, conditions improved significantly, at least for several months. Within a short time the Russians sent as many as 60 men to the Pittsburgh headquarters of Swindell Dressler, and simultaneously opened a purchasing office in the GM building in New York. As a reciprocal gesture, they authorized Pullman, the parent company, to open an office in Moscow. More important from Swindell Dressler's point of view, negotiations then began on the sale of the foundry equipment itself. On October 18, 1972, Swindell Dressler signed a second contract. This one called for it to supply 17 electric arc furnaces for the iron foundry at a price of $15–16 million. The second contract was signed one day after the announcement of the trade agreement between the United States and the Soviet Union. According to Mr. Casey, whereas it took the Department of Commerce eight months to issue the license for the initial design contract, the department needed only one day to issue the arc furnace license.

The closer relationship between the two governments and between Swindell Dressler and Metallurgimport did not necessarily mean that the Russians had suddenly become pushovers. Until ten minutes before it was signed, Swindell Dressler did not know whether there would be a contract or not. Moreover, they never knew when the Russians would make major changes in the arrangements. According to Mr. Casey, while the first $10 million contract was negotiated on a cash basis, negotiations for the $15–16 million contract for the furnaces were conducted on the assumption that it would be financed with a seven-year credit. Suddenly the Russians decided they wanted to pay cash and the whole negotiating framework had to be changed. Eventually the Russians switched again. Ultimately, the Export-Import Bank was brought in to finance the transaction.[7] In bargaining with the Russians, Swindell Dressler officials realized early that nothing could be taken for granted. Mr. Morfee advises that other companies should always be sure that as much as possible is spelled out in advance regarding clauses dealing with specifications, penalties, and financing before the Western firm quotes any price. Failure to do so may cause the American contractor to discover suddenly that the Russians believe they have paid for something that by American custom is not included in the contract.

After having been asked for many things not usually involved in contract performance with a Western customer, Mr. Morfee finally adopted the policy that, for a price, he would agree to provide the Russians with special services not normally provided Swindell Dressler's traditional clients. This included the provision that the Russians would not have to pay for the last 5 percent of their purchase until the foundry was up and operating. The rest of the contract provided for 90 percent of the price to be paid by the Russians at the time of shipment from the United States and 5 percent to be paid on arrival. The remaining 5 percent would only be paid after performance had been demonstrated. Since the Russians are notorious for their practice of cannibalizing, collecting that last 5 percent could prove to be very difficult.

No matter how careful a contractor may be, there will undoubtedly be some costs against which he can do nothing to protect himself. In some cases they may be due to concessions made by a competitor for the contract. Mr. Morfee concedes that Swindell Dressler found it necessary to match a competitor's concession on delivery charges at a cost to his firm of close to $1 million in revenue. Overall, however, he insists that Swindell Dressler provided a proper profit margin for itself. This included provision for the approximately $500,000 Swindell Dressler had to spend on translating its technical documentation into Russian, and the $150,000 it had to spend on negotiating expenses prior to the signing of the contract. A similar contract signed in the United States or in Western Europe would have involved an expense of less than one-half as much.

One thing Swindell Dressler did not bargain for was an attack on their work by the Russians in the American press. Being realistic, they expected adverse criticism from some Americans who would accuse them of dealing with the enemy. There were quite a few such protests after the signing of the initial $10 million contract, but the climate had changed so by the signing of the second contract that they received only one new critical note. What they did not anticipate was an article on the front page of the financial section of the *New York Times* and five other major United States newspapers describing Soviet criticism of Swindell Dressler's inability to adhere to its promised timetable.[8] Apparently work at the Kama site was proceeding slower than the Russians had anticipated. In an effort to embarrass Swindell Dressler and Pullman, Lev Vasilyev, head of the Kama River truck plant, invited five American newspaper correspondents to the previously closed region to show them the site and complain about Swindell Dressler. Mr. Vasilyev made the correct assumption that this would be news in the United States and would cause Swindell Dressler to react. It did. Angry and embarrassed, Swindell Dressler insisted that the material for the foundry would be delivered on schedule. They had no comment, however, about the claim they were one-half year late in delivery of the blueprints.

As the Swindell Dressler people explain the incident, apparently Mr. Vasilyev arranged the news conference on his own, without the knowledge of his associates in the Automobile Ministry, the Ministry of Foreign Trade, and Metallurgimport. Indeed, the Ministry of Foreign Trade had just discussed the delay with Swindell Dressler, urging that nothing be said about the delay since the schedule was in the process of being reworked. Some American officials have heard rumors that there was more to the story than Swindell Dressler has officially acknowledged. According to these stories, the delay was largely the fault of the Russians. Reportedly Swindell Dressler had to hold up its work because the Russians were four to five months late in setting out certain specifications. Since the people in the Ministry of Foreign Trade did not want to acquire notoriety for being difficult to work with, they sought to prevent this information from becoming public knowledge. The newspaper articles soon changed that. Although Soviet newspapers subsequently printed articles very favorable to Swindell Dressler and the good working arrangement that had been created, the retraction in the Soviet press did not attract nearly as much attention in the United States as did the initial criticism in the American press.

Swindell Dressler may also have learned what it is like to be caught in an internal feud between Soviet economic organizations. Work at the Kama River plant is befouled by the normal poor coordination that occurs at any Soviet construction site.[9] As we saw in our discussion of internal planning in the Soviet Union, suppliers are frequently late in meeting their targets. It is bad enough when one ministry is responsible for the entire project. At Kama several ministries are involved, and so there is not only confusion within a given ministry but also among the various ministries. Considering that this is one of the largest undertakings ever conducted in the Soviet Union, it is natural to assume that the confusion and slip-ups are in like proportion.

Though there are disadvantages associated with participating in such a project, there are also advantages. Being on the Soviet Union's approved list serves to certify that Pullman and Swindell Dressler are acceptable for doing work in communist countries. Having experienced their baptism under Soviet fire, Pullman has subsequently established what it regards as a very good working relationship with the Russians. No longer must they feel each other out and perform time-wasting rituals. Pullman personnel now believe they have the same rapport with most of their Soviet counterparts as they have with American businessmen. The proof of their success is reflected by yet a third contract to sell material handling equipment for $5 million and a fourth contract to sell heat treating equipment for $8 million and additional machines for $4 million. That made a total of about $43 million in contracts as of September 1973. Overall, they report they expect to make the level of profit anticipated, although the best returns did not start to flow until 1974. Pullman also hopes to sell the Russians various other projects as well, including a series of ammonia fertilizer plants, a direct reduction ferrous metal plant, and a truck trailer assembly operation.

Success in the U.S.S.R. also helped Pullman's operation in other East European countries. Swindell Dressler signed a $42.9 million contract to build an iron foundry near Lodz, Poland. Together with another anticipated contract, that will bring their total work done in Poland to $110 million. They are also negotiating for work in Yugoslavia, Hungary, and Rumania. In 1973 about one-quarter of Pullman's total work on order was for delivery in East Europe. Although to the Chinese being acceptable for work in the U.S.S.R. may be more of a disadvantage than an advantage, another division of Pullman, the M. W. Kellogg Company, is building eight or more ammonia and urea plants in the People's Republic of China worth approximately $300 million, as well as a $20 million ammonia plant in Hungary.

Pullman's experience with its ammonia fertilizer plants suggests the unusual bargaining position with which American negotiators may sometimes find themselves faced. According to officials in the U.S. Department of Commerce, Pullman was unintentionally caught in a tug of war between the Chinese and the Russians—with the Russians doing most of the tugging. It all began in late 1971. At about the same time that Pullman's Swindell Dressler division was signing its first contract for the Kama River truck plant, a group of Chinese trading officials contacted the Japanese offices of Pullman's Kellogg subsidiary to inquire about buying several ammonia and urea fertilizer plants. The Chinese were very much concerned about increasing their agricultural productivity. They realized they would need more fertilizer, and since Kellogg's technology seemed to rank with the best in the world and American-Chinese relations were beginning to improve, the Chinese turned to Kellogg. The Chinese proved to be hard bargainers, but still they paid in cash, and they wanted to buy millions of dollars worth of equipment. Reportedly the Chinese were also easier to deal with than the Russians. As of early 1974, the Chinese had ordered at least eight ammonia urea plants, each capable of producing 1 million metric tons a day. In addition, Kellogg was supplying two additional plants to the Chinese through the Toyo Engineering Corporation of Japan, which was doing the actual building. Their appetite whetted, the Kellogg people hoped to supply ammonia plants to every province in China.

Somewhat later the Russians also approached Kellogg about

building ammonia urea plants for the same reasons—they wanted the fertilizer so they could increase their agricultural productivity. Initially Occidental Petroleum had been approached about building this particular set of plants, but the Russians apparently changed their minds in the fall of 1973, long before any public announcement was made of their change of mind. There is reason to believe that the Russians became concerned about Occidental Petroleum's relative lack of experience in building such facilities. Moreover, by 1974 the Russians had already had experience with five plants using Kellogg processes that had been built by Japanese companies under license from Kellogg. For all these reasons, the Russians decided to turn directly to others, including Kellogg.

To the surprise of the American side, the bargaining now took a strange turn. Even though they wanted to buy Kellogg's equipment, the Russians felt offended that Kellogg's terms seemed to be somewhat complicated. By comparison, the Russians had heard that Kellogg's negotiations with the Chinese had gone very smoothly. As their rivals had done, the Russians expected to sign a simple and set contract with a penalty clause for late delivery. Kellogg refused to do that. What the Russians could not understand was that they and the Chinese were asking for two different things. The Chinese were taking delivery on 1,000-ton-a-day plants which were the standard models. The Russians wanted 1,500-ton-a-day plants, which were not standard. The materials for such a facility would have to be designed specifically for this model. There would also have to be special engineering, which increased the operating risks for the contractor. Under the circumstances, Kellogg would sell only on special terms, which the Russians did not like. Reportedly, "The Russians were livid about the whole experience," and ultimately the contract went to the Chemical Construction Corporation.

PULLMAN'S MOSCOW OFFICE

Despite such difficulties and some awkward and dramatic moments, Pullman has generally done quite well in its trade with the communist countries. Pullman has even found that its Moscow office with its unique (for Moscow) Telex service to the United States may also be a source of income. Located temporarily in three former bedrooms on the fifth floor of the Leningradskaya Hotel in Moscow, the office has proven to be a valuable asset not only for other branches of Pullman, but for other American and foreign companies as well. Based on the contacts he has established in Moscow, Robert Costello, Pullman's branch manager, finds that he has been able to open doors for about ten companies like Armco, Alcoa, PPG Industries, Honeywell, and Mesta Machine, as well as foreign firms like AEG Telefunken of West Germany. (There have been rumors about Russian resentment over such extracurricular activities on Pullman's part.) Such arrangements go at least part of the way toward meeting the $200,000 to $300,000 a year Pullman officials say it costs them to operate their office. (These costs are not out of line with those encountered by other American offices in Moscow.) Pullman hopes, however, that any new ventures its office helps to arrange will also involve the use of Pullman's construction engineering services in the building of the projects.

Running a Moscow office has not been without its anxieties. Robert Costello's first several months in Moscow were spent primarily on the crucial questions of office space, apartment arrangements, and other day-to-day necessities. These matters which should take days take months in the Soviet context. Once the office was able to concern itself with actual business matters, the Russians unilaterally raised the office rent in September 1973. With devaluation, the Russians wanted double the amount originally negotiated. By late 1973, however, Pullman was allowed to move its office from the hotel to a somewhat more normal office arrangement in a special building, with a somewhat more reasonable rent.

CONCLUSION

Not every transaction is likely to be as complicated as those conceived by Armand Hammer or as drawn out as those of Pullman's Swindell Dressler. In any event, almost everyone will find dealing with the Ruusians a unique experience. As Sam Casey of Pullman put it, Pullman has had larger contracts in other countries, but the contracts with the Russians have a special flavor.

No one can fault the way the Russians have handled their grain negotiations, but there is much they could do to improve their operations in other areas of foreign trade. There is no question that their methods of negotiating for industrial purchases may sometimes end up costing them more money than if they used alternative methods. Their long, drawn-out negotiations with Swindell Dressler simply forced Swindell Dressler to jack up its bid prices to cover these costs. In the same way, the Soviet tendency to reject contracts with interest rates above 6 percent causes suppliers to jack up the contract price in order to permit inclusion of the interest cost in the price of the good itself. Perhaps they are learning. Mr. Casey reports that since opening the Kama River Purchasing Office in the GM Building in New York City, the Russians have begun to negotiate more on the basis of one to one rather than the awkward one to three system that they normally use. Equally if not more important, it is much easier and cheaper for Americans to negotiate in New York City than in Moscow.

Each major contract with the Soviet Union provides new challenges and new opportunities. The Swindell Dressler contract at Kama River was a first in several respects. It should open the way to approximately $200–$300 million of additional contracts for other American firms. Already as of September 1973, over 58 American companies had become involved in one way or another. (See Appendix II.)

In many ways the Kama River foundry was an unexpected opportunity. After all, one thing the Russians presumably do well is metallurgical work. Therefore it seemed strange that they should come to the United States for help in building a metallurgical foundry. Moreover, the timing was remarkable from Swindell Dressler's point of view. First, Swindell Dressler was feeling the effects of the 1970–1971 recession and was badly in need of new orders. Second, who could have guessed that Swindell Dressler would succeed where Ford and Mack Truck had failed? From what we can now see, Swindell Dressler's negotiations occurred at the right moment, just when Henry Kissinger and President Nixon were in pursuit of their most sophisticated linkage policy. Consequently, much of Swindell Dressler's success must be attributed to luck and fortuitous timing. Yet Swindell Dressler must also be given credit for its persistence and willingness to commit significant sums and talented manpower to pursuing not only the Soviet buyers but American policy makers. Equally important was Swindell Dressler's excellent reputation in foundry work and the fact that the showpiece of foundries at Flat Rock had been built by them. That guaranteed them a strong bargaining position. Swindell Dressler realized that while the Russians might threaten to go elsewhere for their work, they were in fact prepared to pay a little more in order to contract with what they regarded as the prime builders. Knowing this strengthened Swindell Dressler's resolve to hold out for what they deemed to be a price with a comfortable margin. In other words, those who have the best chance of signing a successful and profitable contract with the Russians are those who have a superior product and confidence in themselves and their product. In the case of Swindell Dressler, the Kama River truck plant contracts have turned out to be not only political successes, but, equally or more important, for them, what they anticipate will be financial successes as well.

CHAPTER

10

The Need for Both
Dollars and Détente

T H E potential for substantial trade between the U.S. and the U.S.S.R. is no longer just a theoretical possibility. It may be an ordeal for both parties, but the market and the mutual needs are there. A few years ago, when U.S. economic power was at its peak and American products and dollars were valued throughout the world, we did not need the Russians. But faster than almost anyone could have predicted, the international economic climate has changed and now in many respects the U.S. needs Soviet business almost as much as the U.S.S.R. needs American grain and technology.

UNIQUENESS

As important as American-Soviet trade may be, it does have a unique character. While the United States exported more to the U.S.S.R. than to any other noncommunist country in 1973, the bulk of our exports, as indicated in Table 10–1, were agricultural

267

products. Without the sale of grain U.S. exports will fall off sharply, as they did in 1974. Furthermore, no other American economic or foreign trade relationship is so political. On occasion it appears as if politics are the only consideration affecting Soviet imports and exports. Of course, like every other country in the world, the Soviet Union has to worry sooner or later about the bottom line of the profit and loss statement. Still, because all industry is owned by the state and because no firm connection need exist between domestic and foreign prices or currency, the Soviet Union is able to worry less about the profit and loss limitations of its foreign trade than most of its trading partners. If the Soviet Union had a small and weak economy, there would be less leeway to include factors other than profit and loss considerations in the calculation. But it is a large country and economy and thus better able to afford "loss leaders." For example, the Soviet Union is likely to have enough slack from the export earnings of its natural gas division to make it possible to subsidize exports from its au-

TABLE 10–1

U.S. Exports to the U.S.S.R., by Major Categories
(in millions of dollars)

	1971	1972	1973	1974
Total Manufactured Products	$118	$101	$264	$294
Chemicals	38	21	16	28
Manufactured materials	10	10	25	27
Nonelectric machinery	54	53	182	
Electric machinery	6	7	14	225
Transport equipment	3	1	8	
Miscellaneous manufacturing	7	9	9	14
Total Agriculture Products	44	440	922	317
Food	17	366	843	292
Crude material	27	71	73	25
Oil and fats	—	2	6	—
Combined total	$162	$542	$1190	$612

Source: Bureau of East West Trade, and *East-West Trade* (Washington, D.C.: U.S. Dept. of Commerce, Fourth Quarter 1973), pp. 59–63; U.S. Trade status, February 24, 1975.

tomobile division. Since the U.S.S.R. is the world's largest foreign trading entity under one management (the Ministry of Foreign Trade), the Soviets have more room for maneuverability than any private corporation.

Because trade contracts are so closely attuned to political frequencies, dealing with the Soviet Union is in some respects like dealing with any local political body, whether it be in Maryland County or the Commonwealth of Massachusetts. Favorites are rewarded with lucrative contracts either to supply or receive governmental goods and services. It does not hurt to have a superior product, but that in itself is not always enough to influence the award of a contract. The one big difference in Soviet trade is that, as far as anyone can tell, monetary kickbacks play virtually no role. It is the political kickbacks which govern.

Certainly all countries and all businesses, even the most apolitical, find it expedient on occasion to temper good business policy with good politics. American foreign economic policy is no exception. When we provide favorable economic treatment to Pakistan while denying it to India, or impose an embargo on soybean exports to Japan while allowing other feed grain exports to the U.S.S.R., politics plays a role.

For that matter, even when no politics are intended and American and Russian firms are doing their best to focus only on the economic and trade issues, political matters may suddenly intrude. Thus, after long negotiations between timber dealers in the state of Washington and Soviet timber officials, the Canadians began to complain sharply that the Russians were being allowed to take over traditional Canadian markets in the United States. Because the Canadians and the Soviet Union tend to sell the same kinds of raw materials to the United States, a growing number of Canadian businessmen began to warn that increased American-Soviet trade might come at Canada's expense. In a similar vein, the Pullman Company, which, as we saw, sold millions of dollars worth of equipment to the Soviet Union, was suddenly told by the Russians, with whom they had dealt so cordially, that the Russians resented the "forked tongue" approach of the American company. By this the Russians meant that they felt themselves deceived by Pullman. Not only had Pullman entered into negotiations with China, the Soviet Union's greatest rival if not enemy, but it had contracted to sell the Chinese the same type of technology the Russians were hoping to buy for themselves. In addition, it appeared to the Russians that Pullman officials were insisting on special terms from the Russians that they did not require of the Chinese. Nor were the Russians much happier when they found out that even the Rumanians were about to buy the same type of technology from Pullman.[1] The Russians reportedly did not mind if Pullman sold to Bulgaria or even East Germany, but Rumania, like China, was considered to be too much of a rival—politically if not economically.

NEW FORMS

Because of the importance of such usually minor considerations, American-Soviet trade calls for new forms and creative responses which so far have been slow in coming. For example, just as the American Institute of Aeronautics and Astronautics (AIAA) arranged the 1973 aerospace show in Moscow, and the National Machine Tool Builders Association (NMTBA) helped sponsor the Stanki-USA machine tool exhibition in 1974, other trade associations should take a more active role in promoting and coordinating American-Soviet trade. This involves not only holding exhibitions and trade shows in the Soviet Union and bringing Soviet technicians to regularly scheduled shows in the United States, but serving as intermediaries with the Justice Department. The trade associations, or some such groups, should seek permission to increase information flow among American firms once they start to compete with one another for Soviet business. Other organizations, such as consulting firms like the Stanford Research Institute

(SRI) and Arthur D. Little, or American banks or organizations like the Economic Commission for Europe (ECE) or the Organization for Economic Cooperation and Development (OECD), might expand their role and more actively promote exhibitions, negotiations, and coordination. By themselves most American corporations do not have the drawing power needed to round up a Soviet decision-making audience, so usually some group effort is necessary.

Not everyone will be happy with the idea of encouraging increased coordination between American industrial competitors or with ordering the government to reduce rather than increase the amount of competition. What we sometimes find hard to acknowledge is that when the Russians make a deal which turns out to be very one-sided in their favor, it may not always be because they have had an unfair bargaining advantage. Just as often it is simply because the American businessman was a poor negotiator. Moreover, whatever the reason, whenever most private corporations find themselves in such a predicament, their conditioned response is to call for more government intervention. That seems to be the universal panacea for everything, particularly cowardice and ineptitude.

In fact, there is always the danger that increasing government intervention may increase the likelihood of mistakes. The government, after all, is made up of human beings, many of whom have surprisingly parochial viewpoints. It should be remembered that the Soviet grain fiasco was due as much as anything to poor judgment and incompetence by officials in the Department of Agriculture. Nor was the way government bureaucrats consorted with executives of the American oil companies to devise schemes to permit transfer of tax payments from the United States to the Arab countries a reassuring precedent of what might happen when powerful corporations and accommodating government officials conspire together. Government bureaucrats have not always been noted for their resistance to improper advances from powerful and persuasive corporate executives.

Undoubtedly there are real dangers in trying to encourage

greater coordination between government and industry. At the same time, of course, there may be many corporations which will resist such moves even if increased government coordination is determined to be in the public interest. As Ray Vernon of the Harvard Business School points out, it is unlikely that many of the more successful American corporations will accept any government effort to divide up markets and reduce competition.[2] As he sees it, firms such as Occidental Petroleum, Mobil, IBM, and Honeywell are simply too aggressive.

GOVERNMENT COORDINATION

Yet, despite such potential dangers, there is still merit in encouraging American governmental agencies to be supportive and active rather than restrictive and passive when it comes to American-Soviet commercial negotiations. At the least, such government intervention may reduce the likelihood of a cutthroat type of price and technology competition from which the Soviet Union is usually the sole or at least the major beneficiary.

U.S. government participation is most needed when the Soviet Union seeks large contracts. For the smaller contracts, those under $10 million or even $20 million, government participation seems less important. Except for increased logistical support and information gathering by the Bureau of East-West Trade, governmental support in the smaller transactions may actually be counterproductive. The government may increase the amount of red tape involved and complicate an already too complex negotiating process. It does seem wise, however, for the Bureau of East-West Trade to make special efforts to include small business in any trade shows or exhibitions sent to Eastern Europe. The Bureau might also encourage the formation of nonprofit or university-supported translation and market research groups for the purpose of servicing the smaller firms that cannot afford the services that larger commercial firms can provide.

As the magnitude of a contract grows, so should the involvement of the American government. Otherwise the odds are that the American trader will be at a disadvantage. While it sometimes does not take full advantage of its bargaining size, the Soviet Union is, after all, a unique kind of monopsonist with enormous bargaining power at its disposal. For that matter, all national governments are monopsonists of a sort in that they command enormous sums of money and often make one-of-a-kind purchases. They have the ability and often the need to place large orders.

But allowing for such similarities, the fact remains that the Ministry of Foreign Trade of the Soviet Union tends to be in an even stronger bargaining position than the state purchasing agents of the capitalist countries. Government purchasers in the United States, for example, are constrained to favor domestic producers, just as their counterparts in England and France also favor local corporations. Thus the purchasing agent for the American government is less able to play foreign manufacturers off against American manufacturers. In contrast, in the Soviet Union, the Ministry of Foreign Trade usually begins negotiations on the assumption that Soviet enterprises lack the productive ability to produce what is being sought. By definition, the purchase is to be made from among foreign manufacturers. The Ministry of Foreign Trade, therefore, has an obligation to seek out manufacturers from all over the world and extract from them the lowest prices available.

Hence, more than any other country, the Soviet Union is well suited for inducing competitive behavior on the part of corporations which, in their domestic markets and even in some international markets, normally behave as monopolists or oligopolists. Certainly it would be inappropriate to worry too much about "defenseless" corporations like IBM, Pullman, General Electric, General Motors, or Raytheon, but the competitive situation is such that even they may sometimes be in need of support when dealing with the Soviet Union. The Soviet Ministry of Foreign

Trade is particularly interested in the advanced technology the large American companies have to offer. The Russians should not be allowed to purchase technology at the cut-rate prices they sometimes have negotiated if these prices are the result of ruthless whipsawing of American competitors, who in turn have often been supported in their research by the American government. While it may be difficult to ascertain precisely what a "full cost price" should be, it seems particularly foolish to allow Soviet buyers to pay no more than the producer's marginal cost. Soviet bargaining pressures are likely to become even more intensive if the Soviet negotiators think their bargaining position has improved because of the recession in the United States. Thus in late 1974 after having agreed to almost all the contractual details for a tire rim factory, the Russians suddenly demanded a 27 per cent reduction in the tentatively agreed-upon price. Given the dramatic slowdown of industrial activity in the United States, the Soviets apparently assumed that the American manufacturer would grab for any business. If need be, antitrust procedures designed to reduce collaboration and prevent price fixing among manufacturers should be waived. Despite the risks involved, perhaps the Bureau of East-West Trade in coordination with the Anti-Trust Department of the Department of Justice might be authorized to determine the appropriateness of such a joint approach on the setting of an upset price below which the equipment could not be sold.

While such intervention might be unusual for the American government, there are ample precedents in the noncommunist world. The Japanese government, for instance, has institutionalized governmental coordination of private corporate activity in areas extending far beyond the realm of Japanese-Soviet trade. The West European governments, particularly the French, often follow the same policy.

With respect to the sale of agricultural products, an agency resembling the Canadian and Australian wheat boards could be created for handling the sale of wheat to communist countries. As we saw in Chapter 7, because the Russians (and the Chinese) have the ability to make such large purchases, they can play off one seller against another. The improved reporting now required by the Department of Agriculture has lessened the likelihood of a repeat performance of the 1972 episode, but the near crisis of 1974 suggests that the government should become more directly involved. Indeed, because government subsidies are so important in the field of agriculture, the government should be forced to accept responsibility when the Soviet Union seeks to buy food from the United States.

There are other ways in which government agencies can improve the American bargaining position in dealing with the Russians without instituting such potentially far-reaching changes. The stance adopted by the Federal Aviation Authority in the negotiations over the sale of an air traffic control system to the Soviet Union can serve as a good model. It refused to provide important information to the Russians until contracts were signed by American manufacturers. Agencies such as the Environmental Protection Agency, the Federal Communications Commission, and the Federal Power Commission should adopt a similar policy whenever the opportunity presents itself.

There is no doubt that it will be difficult to regulate a schizophrenic system which attempts to distinguish between trade with the communist countries and the rest of the world. It will be difficult to insure that the normally "illegal" business tactics which might be authorized for bargaining with the Soviet Union are not carried over into the non-Soviet arena. Yet trade with the Soviet Union can be completely different from anything else with which American businesses will ever have to deal. The types of goods and the types of negotiating tactics the Russians tend to use in purchasing goods from the United States make it possible for the Russians to obtain high technology products for bargain prices that no other buyers could cajole. Moreover, much of the technology and sometimes the products themselves have been heavily subsidized by the American taxpayer. The initial subsidy for development and production, the bargain prices, and the subsidized interest

275

rate of the Export-Import Bank mean that the Russians are often able to obtain a triple subsidy on their American purchases. On top of everything else, political considerations in American-Soviet trade, whether by the United States or the Soviet Union, are normally more important than in other types of American foreign trade. Thus a different approach involving participation by the American government is necessary.

THE NEED FOR TRADE

Despite the cautious and sometimes skeptical tone of this book, its purpose is to encourage increased trade with the U.S.S.R. There can be no denying that there was something unhealthy about the situation prior to 1969, when the mutual exports and imports between the world's two largest economic powers were generally not much more than $100 million. Given the proper circumspection, an increase in trade can be of both domestic and international benefit for both countries.

Soviet purchases from the United States can be advantageous not only for our balance of trade but for individual enterprises and workers. While purchases like the grain deal that are too large can cause serious distortion, it is clear that the $1.19 billion of Soviet purchases in 1973 did help to give the United States a positive balance of trade for the first time in several years. Moreover, as the U.S.-U.S.S.R. Trade and Economic Council continually stresses, every $15,000 worth of exports to the Soviet Union creates one job for an American worker. If the recession in the United States and Western Europe becomes a serious one, exports to the Soviet Union would become particularly attractive.

While we tend to think of American-Soviet trade in terms of what we can sell to the Soviet Union, the United States also stands to benefit because it can buy. For example, the Soviet Union furnishes us with raw materials we would otherwise be hard put to find. Consequently, American-Soviet trade ameliorates not only the shortcomings of the Soviet economic and political system, but of the U.S. system as well. After all, mutual benefit and mutual avoidance of unpleasant alternatives is what foreign trade is all about.

Yet there are those who worry that because of the technological backwardness of the Soviet economy and the economic problems it has had in the past, the Soviet Union will benefit unduly from such trade. More than that, there is a feeling that by being able to rely on crucial agricultural and industrial supplies from the United States, the Soviet government has been able to avoid major political and economic reforms it might otherwise have been forced to make. Certainly the ability to fall back on the United States for large quantities of food in 1964 and 1972 made it possible to keep intact the collective and state farm system of Soviet agriculture. Perhaps we will never know what kind of changes the Russians would have been forced to introduce if they had to face up directly to their agricultural shortcomings.

To a lesser extent, the same type of changes might have been necessitated in Soviet industry if there were no possibility of trade with the United States. Thus Harry Schwartz of the *New York Times* has argued that the Russians have been able to concentrate their best scientists and engineers on perfecting military technology (such as their SAM 6 and 7 ground-to-air missiles) because they knew they could satisfy their other industrial and consumer needs by the importation of American goods and technology.[3] In other words, the United States is supplying them with butter so they can make guns. Of course, such speculation is predicated on the false assumption that if it cannot buy in the United States, the Soviet Union will be unable to purchase what it needs elsewhere. Certainly in industry it probably could have bought most of what it wanted somewhere else. But in agriculture, since only the United States had granaries with extra supplies, the answer remains less certain. What would the Soviet Union have done if it had not been able to buy American grain in 1964 and 1972? Would it have abolished the collective farms, or would it instead have increased the pressures on the peasants even more? Scholars now have another "what if" question to puzzle over for the next several decades.

IMPROVED INTERNATIONAL RELATIONS?

Although the availability of American supplies may make it possible for the Soviet government to avoid pursuing certain liberalizing reforms, the hope exists that increased trade and commerce with the United States will enhance the possibility of an improved international political climate. It has been argued that the more dependent both countries become on one another, the less likely it is that there will be political and military clashes. Similar reasoning helped generate support for the Common Market and the close trading arrangements between those traditional enemies, France and Germany. To some extent it may have been the desire to maintain trade relations and political détente that led the Soviet Union to adopt a somewhat more moderate stance during the 1973 Middle East war than they might have adopted during the cold war. (Needless to say, other observers such as Senator Henry Jackson argue that the Soviet position was hardly moderate.)

Yet it would be self-deceiving to believe that closer economic relations will necessarily bring an automatic improvement in political relations between the United States and the Soviet Union. It is important to recognize that, on occasion, trade can also generate tension or at least do nothing to reduce it. This was true of Germany and Europe before World War II, Japan and the United States in the 1970s, and China and the Soviet Union in the 1950s and 1960s. As a matter of fact, the Soviet Union and China exported and imported more with each other than with anyone else in 1959. Yet in 1961 relations between the two countries had become very tense. By 1962 China had less trade with the Soviet Union than with anyone else in the socialist bloc except Rumania and Albania. By 1964 there were armed clashes between the Chinese and the Russians. The belief that trade leads to peace can sometimes be as much a product of fanciful hope as of actual experience. Nonetheless, on balance, the likelihood of peaceful international relations seems to be greater with a reasonable level of mutually beneficial foreign trade than without it.

INTERNAL REFORMS?

Another expectation is that with a higher standard of living and more material comforts that will come from more trade with the United States, Soviet internal political conditions will also improve. The presumption is that as the Soviet citizen becomes attached to his material possessions, his level of expectations will rise and he will become enamored of the softer life. As he sees an improvement not only in international relations but in his own standard of living, the Soviet citizen will question the need for the continuing state of readiness and vigilance which has characterized the Soviet Union since the revolution. This in turn will increase the demand for more political freedoms at home. The argument is that American-Soviet trade is an important element in making for a more enlightened, more tolerant, and more liberalized U.S.S.R. Similarly, tight political controls are supposedly incompatible with running a sophisticated industrial system. Presumably Soviet factory managers need freedom to make managerial decisions and will insist on similar privileges outside the factory walls.

But history has not always demonstrated that a high standard of living and more automobiles per capita inevitably bring with them political liberalization. If proof is needed, Hitler managed to run a fairly efficient industrial system in a climate of very strict political control.

It is also necessary to recognize that a turn to the West by the U.S.S.R. in foreign affairs or foreign trade has often been accompanied by increased reaction and even repression at home. Soviet leaders seem to fear that their population will view increased interaction with the democratic West as a sign that more democratic forms will also be tolerated within the Soviet Union. Reactions of this sort were common in Russia long before the revolution, but the communist leaders do not seem to have outgrown their concern that increased exposure to Western ideas, products, and individuals might undermine political control. As much as possible, therefore, Western technicians and tourists are kept isolated so they will have as little contaminating effect as possible on the average Russian.

But while increased American-Soviet trade may not make the Soviet Union a model of democracy, a strong case can be made for arguing that increased trade will bring some changes, and that whatever liberalization we can expect from the U.S.S.R. is more likely to come under the impact of détente than of the cold war. There may be controls and periodic crackdowns within the Soviet Union whenever the dams are opened up to Western techniques, but the inflow of ideas and goods nevertheless has some impact and provides some momentum for those who otherwise have had no hope of internal liberalization. Despite the dismay Americans might feel about the crackdown on Solzhenitsyn and Sakharov and other Soviet dissidents, the repression is nowhere near as draconic as in the days of Stalin. Nor for that matter were the Russian peasants left to starve during the poor harvests in 1964 and 1972 as they were in the 1930s and 1947 by Stalin. Thus, despite the numerous reservations one may have about increasing the technological capabilities of a police state, the chances of internal reform and the ameliorations of domestic conditions in the U.S.S.R. seem to be greater with détente and increased trade than they would be without it.

A CAUTIONARY NOTE

But while trade with the U.S.S.R. is to be favored (which means that Americans must be prepared to buy from as well as sell to the Russians), it is absolutely necessary that its proponents keep their eyes open and maintain a critical, sometimes skeptical tone. Since American-Soviet trade is so political, nonfinancial considerations and concessions often play as much of a role as the financial considerations. Those who refuse to recognize this are doing themselves as well as their country a disservice. The Russians seek and expect to engage in political as well as economic bargaining, just as a Middle Eastern merchant expects to haggle over prices. The Russians may appear to be offended by demands for political concessions, but whatever offense they feel is usually compensated for by the goods they hope to obtain in exchange. Thus those who insisted that the Russians would probably never agree to settle their Lend Lease debt failed to take into account how badly the Soviet Union wanted new credits and most favored nation treatment. Similarly, despite Soviet protestations, under pressure they suspended the exit tax on Jews, agreed to permit commercial arbitration in third countries, and conceded that freight rates on the American grain being shipped to the U.S.S.R. should be revised upward because of the devaluation of the dollar and the increase in international freight rates.

Insistence on concessions from the Soviet Union becomes all the more imperative in light of the haunting issues raised by dissidents like Andrei Sakharov, father of the Soviet hydrogen bomb. Whether or not one cares about political and intellectual developments inside the Soviet Union, one still must pause to ponder his arguments. Undoubtedly the Russians could easily find dissidents in the United States willing to plead with foreign countries to take a harder stand toward the United States. Yet how can anyone be certain that Sakharov is wrong when he urges that the United States should not provide large amounts of technical aid to the Soviet Union. To do so under the present circumstances, he argues, makes it possible for the Russians to ignore the basic political and economic questions they should be forced to deal with for the well-being of their own people. Instead, because it can depend on American and Western goods, the Soviet government can concentrate on accumulating political and military strength. If this trend should continue, "The world would become helpless before this uncontrollable bureaucratic machine." [4] Sakharov warned in particular about attempts to trade with the U.S.S.R., "to buy its gas and oil," while ignoring such other things as its treatment of dissidents and Jews.

Yet whether Sakharov is right or wrong, there is no doubt that some caution is called for when any American governmental policy is adopted which appears to be diametrically opposite what it was a few months ago. The innocent bystander can be forgiven his bewilderment at the recent turn of events and attitudes. Granted that we as a nation tend to go to extremes, particularly when we deal with communist countries, the present transition has been a remarkable spectacle. Officials ranging from the president of the country to the presidents of some of our largest banks and corporations, who only a few years ago were among the most outspoken opponents of the Soviet Union, now have become some of its most ardent friends. Indeed, there is a danger that a growing number of American businessmen may become so heavily committed to American-Soviet trade that they may lose their perspective. As they stand to make more money with détente and to lose sizable investments if trade is disrupted, groups like the U.S.-U.S.S.R. Trade and Economic Council may begin to argue more as hostages of the U.S.S.R. than as impartial adherents of mutual compromise by both the Soviet and American governments. Some senior corporation officials, such as those at IT&T and Rockwell International, have switched from enemy to friend literally in a single day. There have been actual instances in which they denounce the communist conspiracy and fuss about "national security" in the morning and then sign treaties and multimillion dollar contracts with the same Russians and Chinese in the afternoon.[5] Nor is this a reaction unique to Americans. The Soviet government reacts in the same way to the United States, particularly if failure to deal with the United States might generate a serious economic crisis at home. The poor wheat harvest was a more important consideration to them than the resumption of American bombing of North Vietnam. Yet it must never be forgotten that the minute the Russians feel they no longer need American goods or technology, their purchases from the United States may dry up as they did in the 1930s and the 1940s.

Indeed there is a possibility that the Soviet rejection of the Jackson amendment in the 1975 Trade Reform Act was motivated not only by Soviet resentment over "interference in Soviet domestic policies" but by the improved Soviet financial position arising from their export of petroleum and other raw materials. For that reason, American officials must be especially sensitive to the existing political and economic situation. They must know when to insist on how much. When they bid properly as they did in late 1974, they emerge as heros. When they underbid as was the case in 1972 or overbid as in early 1975, they emerge alternatively as dupes or cold warriors.

TO BUILD A SOLID BASE

Since American-Soviet trade is being built on a heretofore nonexistent, or at best shaky, foundation, it is necessary that as much as possible be done to build a solid and trustworthy base. Toward that end, both sides must seek to generate a pattern of positive experience and mutual compromise that will help to provide the cushion of good will that is so important in almost all our trade negotiations with other countries. If American-Soviet trade is to flourish, not just the United States, but the Soviet Union as well, will have to show signs of compromise. It is all right for the United States to agree to political and economic concessions sought by the Soviet Union, including some affecting issues that involve a complete reversal of policy and which would normally be regarded as internal policy matters, such as extending diplomatic immunity to trade officials. But the Soviet Union must be prepared to make similar concessions. In particular it is disillusioning to find that after President Nixon's Moscow visit in 1972, the Russians apparently made no effort to allow any continued liberalization of their system. If anything, incidents like the forcible expulsion of writers like Alexandr Solzhenitsyn suggest that controls and repression have intensified. The future for East-West trade will be problematic if the Russians expect all the give to come from the United States and reserve all the take for the Soviet side. In other words, East-West trade involves more than a specific company winning some special economic gain. What is good for General Motors, Armand Hammer, or Control Data may not necessarily be good for the United States as a whole. East-West trade is worth pursuing only as long as American economic and *political* interests also benefit in the process.

BUILD UP COMMERCIAL GOOD WILL

To help establish a pattern of business trust, as many transactions as possible should aim for a short-run payback. With a solid record of mutually profitable contracts to fall back on, the way will be paved for negotiation of more complicated arrangements. Fortunately, many of the agreements signed thus far are relatively straightforward and provide for short-run mutual benefits for all concerned. But there are many businessmen who appear to be premature in their eagerness to deal with the Russians and who have already committed themselves to unusually intricate and complicated deals in which, for instance, repayment will consist of the delivery of goods from the project which the Americans undertake to construct. Such deliveries often will not begin for four or five years after the American equipment is delivered, and they can stretch over a decade or more. Moreover, the collateral for such projects is generally unredeemable and inaccessible. The hazards for the American corporation mount rapidly in these situations. In the passion of the moment, many American corporations appear to have signed injudicious contracts and evidenced a lack of caution that may come back to haunt them. In normal business transactions between long-established allies and trading partners, there is usually a reservoir of good will that can be drawn upon to help resolve any serious disagreements that might arise from complicated relationships in the commercial sphere. There is no such reservoir to fall back upon in American-Soviet relations.

As much as there is in common between the needs and natures of the two countries, there is even more in divergence. Our methods, our attitudes, and our systems are quite different, and our trading experience with each other is relatively limited. Consequently it is unrealistic to expect that "common interests" and accumulative trading experience can be counted on to provide continuity and good will when attitudes and political considerations can change as abruptly as they often do in Soviet-American relations. This is especially true if the commercial agreements are unique to begin with. If anything, potentially contentious contracts or deals will weaken rather than strengthen détente. The more regular the character of the transactions between the two countries, the less likely it is that there will be recriminations, and the sooner normal and long-lasting relationships can be created. At the least there will have to be years of mutually satisfactory trade transactions and mutual give and take before such good will can be generated.

When one party begins to sense that it is consistently "quidding" more than it is "quoing," the future of improved economic and political relations is jeopardized and détente is hurt more than it is helped. When Party Secretary Brezhnev left the United States in 1973, he and President Nixon exchanged gifts. The Russian was given a rifle and a Lincoln Continental. The American ended up with a silver samovar and a tea set. This one-sided exchange, just like the wheat deal, seems to symbolize a good portion of American-Soviet trade so far. If the relationship is to continue and to flourish as it should, there will have to be not only equal enthusiasm, but equal concessions by both parties.

APPENDICES

APPENDIX

I

Restrictions on East-West Trade

EXPORT RESTRICTIONS

Export Control Act, 1949. Administered by the Office of Export Control in the Department of Commerce, this is the main law regulating U.S. trade with the communist bloc. The purpose of the law is to ensure that nothing of military or strategic significance is exported to the bloc. In 1962 the act was extended to prohibit goods of "economic" significance as well. Under the law, two kinds of export licenses are available:

1. A "general license" which covers a specific list of "nonstrategic" commodities which can be exported to specified destinations under specified conditions without the need for special permission each time. Sales to Yugoslavia, Poland, and Rumania are less intensively regulated than are similar sales to other countries in the bloc.

2. A "validated license" is required for the sale of all goods not covered by the "general license." Before the Department of Commerce will approve a "validated license," the exporter must submit Form FC-842. This describes the purchaser, the commod-

ity, and the final use of the commodity as certified by the ultimate consignee—not just the purchaser.

At one time the Department of Commerce had a "positive list" of about 1,000 items that were considered of a strategic nature and normally were not exportable to the bloc. As of July 1973 the list had been pared to 73 products. Even the sale of such goods to a friendly country requires a license to ensure that the products will not be reexported to a bloc country. At one time a total embargo existed on the sale of goods to Communist China, North Korea, North Vietnam, and Cuba.

The Mutual Defense Assistance Control Act (Battle Act), 1951. This law is designed to pressure other countries into observing the embargo on the sale of strategic goods to the bloc. Any country which permits the sale of certain goods to the bloc is to be denied U.S. military, economic, and financial assistance.

COCOM, 1950. A coordinating committee of NATO countries (excluding Iceland, but with Japan) maintains a list of strategic items which are banned in East-West trade. The list has been revised and reduced several times and has lost much of the impact it had during the Korean War.

Agricultural Trade Development and Assistance Act, 1954. Agricultural products sold under this act (Public Law 480) may not normally be sent to communist countries. The exceptions have been Yugoslavia and Poland.

Agricultural Appropriation Act, 1966. The export of subsidized food is prohibited to any country which supplies equipment and materials to North Vietnam.

Export Administration Act, 1969, as amended by the Equal Export Opportunity Act, 1972. Export controls are to be abolished on all goods which can be purchased from other countries in the West or Japan unless their sale would threaten American national security.

FINANCIAL RESTRICTIONS

Johnson Act, 1934. Private parties are prohibited from lending money for more than 180 days to any government which is in default on its obligations to the United States. However, government-controlled corporations, such as the Export-Import Bank, are exempted from such restrictions, provided the president decides such a loan is in the national interest and notifies Congress that the loan is to be provided. As of 1963, it also became legal to provide "supplier's credits" (i.e., on specific products) for medium-term periods of up to five years.

Foreign Aid Appropriation Act, 1964. Regulates the issuance of credit guarantees.

Berne Union, 1934. Until recently, most Western countries agreed not to extend government-guaranteed credit for more than five years to any country. It was also agreed that a 20 percent down payment would be required on all sales. Most members of the Union now provide more liberal terms.

IMPORT CONTROLS

Trade Agreement Extension Act, 1951. This law prohibited the importation of certain specific items (e.g., certain skins and furs) from the U.S.S.R. and Communist China.

"Most Favored Nation Treatment." In 1951 this privilege was withdrawn from all the communist countries. Several have since been reinstated. This means that bloc country products, except those from Poland and Yugoslavia, are subject to the tariff levels of the 1930s, which are often four times higher than currently prevailing rates.

Miscellaneous restrictions: 1) U.S. government funds must not be used to purchase school laboratory equipment made in communist countries unless such material is unavailable from other sources; 2) Until 1961 the purchase of Soviet crabmeat and bamboo pipestems from other communist countries was prohibited.

APPENDIX

II

U.S. Corporations Which Have Signed Contracts with the Soviet Union Since 1972

CORPORATIONS DEALING WITH THE SOVIET UNION

U.S. Enterprise	Field	Amount in Millions of Dollars
TRW Corporation	Petroleum production equipment—submergible pumping units	$ 20
Baxter Laboratories	Design and equipment for enzyme plant	20
Continental Can	Can-making plant	11
Combustion Engineering and Monsanto	Acetic acid plant	45

U.S. Corporations Which Have Signed Contracts Since 1972

U.S. Enterprise	Field	Amount in Millions of Dollars
Allis Chalmers	Iron ore pelletizing plant	36
J. F. Pritchard	Gas treatment plant	53
Alliance Tool and Die Corporation	Tableware factory	28
General Electric	Gas turbine compressors	250
Honeywell	Computers	65
Occidental Petroleum and Bechtel	Hotel and foreign trade center	80
Occidental Petroleum	Fertilizer exchange	8,000– 20,000
International Business Machines	Computers	10
International Telephone and Telegraph	Electronic message switching system	1
PepsiCo	Vodka for Pepsi and Pepsi factories	?
International Harvester	Turbine-powered gas compressors	26
Caterpillar	Tractors and pipelaying equipment	40
Chemical Construction Corporation	Ammonia plants	200
Dresser Industries	Compressors	27.5
CMI Corporation	Road-building and paving machinery	9.5

U.S. Enterprise	Field	Amount in Millions of Dollars
Swindell Dressler	Machinery for Kama River truck plant	42.6
C-E Cast Equipment	"	34.5
Holcroft	"	23
Ingersoll-Rand	"	20
National Engineering	"	15
La Salle Machine Tool	"	12
Cleveland Crane	"	10
Gleason Works	"	10
Carborundum	"	10
Landis Tool	"	9
Sutter Products	"	7
Borg Warner	Submersible electric pumps	6
Jones and Lamson	Machining friction drums	6
LaSalle Machine Tool	Piston manufacturing equipment	29
Gidding & Lewis	Transfer line for machine flywheels	7
Gould	Engine bearing plant	47
Intertex	Textile plant	23

CORPORATIONS WHICH HAVE SIGNED
TECHNOLOGY AGREEMENTS

Joy Manufacturing—with the Ministry of Heavy Power and Transport Machine Building—exchange of licenses and documentation in the manufacture of mining machinery—7/26/72.

The American Can Company—a three-year exchange agreement over container and packaging technology—12/21/72.

General Electric Company—the joint development of electric power generating technology—1/13/73.

Arthur Anderson Accounting—exchange agreement over services and managerial techniques—6/6/73.

Rank Xerox (British firm)—protocol agreement on Xerographic copying—6/6/73.

Brown and Root—managerial methods and organization for engineering and construction with special attention to the joint projects of gas and transmission. The agreement also calls for working arrangements in third countries—6/7/73.

IT&T—an exchange on telecommunications, electrical, and electrical machanical components and consumer products—6/15/73.

Bechtel Corporation—technology transfer in heavy industry including use of managerial techniques in construction and petrochemical and pipeline operations—7/3/73.

Stanford Research Institute—cooperation on discussions of business opportunities and managerial techniques—9/26/73.

General Dynamics—agreement on commercial ships and ship building, telecommunication, asbestos mining and processing, commercial and special purpose aircraft computers, microfilm and navigation and weather buoys, and liquefied natural gas ships—10/3/73.

Control Data—for ten years to share computer-related technology and communications and specialized application of computers—10/24/73.

The Monsanto Company—cooperation on the use of computers in the chemical industry—10/24/73.

Singer—data collection and communication, education and training devices, aerospace and marine electronic instrumentation, advanced sewing machines, textile machinery, climate control, and industrial controls and metering—11/12/73.

American Food Machinery Corporation—cooperation in food processing, petroleum equipment, material handling, construction equipment, and mining machinery—11/19/73.

The oilfield products division of Dresser Industries—to increase well logging efficiency for offshore and Arctic operations. Also to make Dresser-Clark model compressors in Kazan—11/21/73.

Armco—cooperation in the fields of metallurgy, chemistry, and oil field equipment for five years—12/9/73.

Kaiser Industries—a five-year agreement to cooperate in such areas as alumina and aluminum, ferrous metals, coal engineering, cement and gypsum production, and seaport construction—1/24/74.

Philip Morris—cooperation in the production of tobacco products, chemicals, and packing paper materials—3/24/74.

Industrial Nucleonics Corporation—automation in the pulp-paper, plastics rubber, and steel industries—5/15/74.

Sperry Rand—joint work with computer systems, farm equipment, office machine and consumer products, hydraulic and pneumatic systems, and marine navigation guidance and control systems—5/23/74.

American International Paper—joint work with the Ministry of Pulp and Paper Industry to increase production and processing of paper and pulp—6/4/74.

Boeing—cooperation in the field of civil aviation and possibly helicopter engineering—6/5/74.

Coca Cola—cooperation in the production of beverages, processing of tea products, development of enriched foods, protein-enriched drinks from milk waste, water purification and desalting, and growing vegetables and fruits in wasteland areas, swamps, and deserts—6/26/74.

Varian Associates—technical cooperation on high energy accelerators, vacuum instruments, and analytical and measuring equipment—7/17/74.

Bendix Corporation—five-year agreement on automobiles, aerospace, electronics, scientific instruments, automation, and machine tools—10/10/74.

Gulf Oil—exchange of information on petroleum, coal, and related industries—2/20/75.

Allis-Chalmers—metallurgy and hydraulic-turbine equipment exchange—3/18/75.

(With the exception of the American Can Company, which signed a three-year agreement, and Control Data, which signed a ten-year agreement, almost all these agreements were for five years, signed with the State Committee on Science and Technology.)

APPENDIX

III

Selected Soviet Joint Stock Companies Operating in Noncommunist Countries

1. BANKS

> Moscow Narodny Bank—London
> > Beirut
> > Singapore
> Banque Commerciale pour L'Europe du Nord—Paris
> Ost-West Handelsbank—Frankfurt
> Wozchod Handelsbank—Zurich
> Danube Bank—Vienna
> also a Soviet bank in Kabul
> Banque Unie Est-Quest S.A.—Luxemburg

2. OIL

> Nafta GB—England
> Nafta B—Belgium

3. AUTOMOTIVE EQUIPMENT

    Konela—Finland
    Konela-Norge-Bil—Norway
    Matreco-Bil A.B.—Sweden
    Scaldia-Volga—Belgium
    Actif-Avto—France
    United Machinery Organization (UMO)—England
    WAATEGO—Lagos Nigeria
    Belarus Equipment Ltd.—Canada
    CATECO—Cameroon

4. MACHINERY AND EQUIPMENT

    Ethso Trading Co. Ltd.—Ethiopia
    Marinexport—Morocco
    Stankofrance—France
    Stankoitaliana—Italy
    Coram South America—Argentina
    Neotype Techmashexport G.M.B.H.—Germany (partnership
        with Anton-Ohlert)

5. LABORATORY, OPTICAL, AND ELECTRONIC EQUIP-
    MENT

    East-West Joint Stock Company—Netherlands
    Slava Company—France
    Koniesto—Finland
    Technical and Optical Equipment—England

6. MISCELLANEOUS

    Timber
        Russe Bois Co. France (partnership of Exportles with
            Bernier and Nielson, Konow and Smith, and Compagnie
            Francaise de Cellulose)
        Russian Wood Agency—England (partnership of Exportles

with Churchill and Sim, LTD., Foy Morgan Ltd., and
Pharaoh Gane)

Chemicals

    Sogo Co.—France

    Ferschimes—Belgium

    Sobren Chemie Handel GmbH—Germany

Diamonds

    Almaz—Belgium

Computers

    Elgorg—Netherlands

    Finn Elorg—Finland

Food

    Plodimex Ausenhandels Gmbh—Germany

Retailing

    Belgo-Soviet Trading Corporation (Belso)—Belgium

Shipping

    United Orient Shipping and Agency Co.—Japan

Insurance

    Inostrakh—Iran

    Inostrakh—Rumania

    Black Sea and Baltic General Insurance Co.—England

    Black Sea and Baltic General Insurance Co.—Germany

    Garant Insurance Co.—Austria

WESTERN BANKS WITH OFFICES IN MOSCOW

Banca Commerciale Italiana—Italy

Barclay's International—United Kingdom

Chase Manhattan Bank—U.S.

Bank of America—U.S.

First National City Bank—U.S.

Credit Lyonnais—France

Deutsche Bank—Germany
Dresdner Bank—Germany
Banque de Paris et des Pays Bas—France
Societe Generale—France
Kansallis Osake Pankki—Finland
Svenska Handelsbanken—Sweden
National Westminster Bank—United Kingdom
Banque Nationale de Paris (BNP)—France

U.S. CORPORATIONS WITH OFFICES IN MOSCOW

Pullman Corporation
Occidental Petroleum
IBM
American Express
Pan American

ADDRESSES OF SOVIET ORGANIZATIONS
WHICH FACILITATE TRADE

Amtorg
355 Lexington Avenue
New York, N.Y. 10017
212 MU2-7404

Kama River Purchase Commission
GM Building
767 5th Avenue
New York, N.Y. 10022
212 593-2600

Embassy of the U.S.S.R.
1125 16th St. N.W.
Washington, D.C. 20009
202 NA8-7550

Trade Representative of the U.S.S.R.
1521 16th St. N.W.
Washington, D.C. 20009
202 232-5988   232-2917

Moscow Narodny Bank
24-32 King William St.
London, EC4P 4JS
Phone: 01-623-2066
Cable: Narodny London EC4
Telex 885 401

Soviet Ministry of Foreign Trade
32/34 Smolenskaia Sennaia Pl.
Moscow
Information Bureau 244 19 47
                  244 24 09

Soviet Chamber of Commerce
Ul. Kuibysheva, 6
Moscow
Phone: 221 08 11
       223 68 45   223 43 23
Telex 126

International Exhibitions Department
Soviet Chamber of Commerce
1a Sokolnichesky Val
Moscow, 107232
USSR

Phone: 268 71 51
      268 70 83
Telex 7185

The State Committee on Science and Technology
(Gos. Komiteta po Nauke i tekhnike)
Ul. Gor'kovo, 11
Phone: 229 11 92
      127 09 79

APPENDIX

IV

Institutions That May Be of Help to Anyone Engaging in American-Soviet Trade

U.S. FIRMS AND ORGANIZATIONS SPECIALIZING IN EAST-WEST TRADE

General

Tower International
Tower Building
Cleveland, Ohio 44113
216 241-0266

Satra
475 Park Avenue South
New York, N.Y. 10016
212 679-6098

International Affairs Associates
1739 Connecticut Ave., N.W.
Washington, D.C.
202 232-8877

Intertag
147 Bell Street
Chagrin Falls, Ohio 44022

Printer of Russian Material

Media Engineering
145 Portland Street
Cambridge, Mass. 02139
617 492-1800

Translation

Associated Translating Services
P.O. Box 7164
Pittsburgh, Penna. 15213
412 682-3287

Other

U.S.-U.S.S.R. Trade and Economic Council
280 Park Avenue
New York, N.Y. 10017
212 490-8500

Bureau of East-West Trade
Department of Commerce
Washington, D.C. 20230
202 967-3583

SOVIET FOREIGN TRADE ORGANIZATIONS
(IN MOSCOW)

Almaziuvelireksport (Diamond Jewelry Export)
Prosp. Kalinina 29
Phone: 291 34 05
Telex 125

Aviaeksport (Aviation Export)
Smolenskaia Sennaia Pl. 32/34 (all addresses at Ministry of
Foreign Trade, Smolenskaia Sennaia Pl. 32/34, unless otherwise
noted)
Phone: 244 26 86
Telex 257

Avtoeksport (Auto Export)
Volkhonka 14
Phone: 202 85 35
202 83 37
Telex 135

Avtopromimport (Auto industry import)
Piatnitskaia 50/2
Phone: 291 72 22
231 81 26
Telex 264

Berëzka Stores (Foreign Currency Shop Administration)
Frunzenskaia nab. 8
Phone: 246 30 49

Elektronorgtekhnika (Electronic Technical Trading Organization)
Phone: 251 39 46
Telex 7586

Energomasheksport (Electrical Machinery Export)
Mosfil'movskaia 35

Phone: 147 21 77
     143 29 17
Telex 255

Exportkhleb (Wheat Export and Import)
Phone: 244 47 01
Telex 145, 147

Eksportlen (Linen Exports)
Ul. Arkhitektora Vlasovia 33
Phone: 128 07 86
Telex 203, 204, 205

Eksportles (Timber Export)
Phone: 241 60 44
Telex 229

Intourist (Soviet Travel Agency)
Prosp. Marksa 1
Phone—director: 225 63 51
Telex 211, 212

Litsenizintorg (Foreign Licensing Organization)
Ul. Kakhovka 31
Phone: 122 02 54
Telex 246

Mashinoeksport (Machinery Exports)
Mosfil'movskaia 35
Phone: 147 15 42
Telex 207

Mashinoimport (Machinery Imports)
Phone: 244 20 48
     244 33 09
Telex 231

Mashpriborintorg (Machine Instrument Trading Organization)
Phone: 244 27 75
Telex 235, 236

Medeksport (Medical Export)
Ul. Kakhovka 31
Phone: 121 01 54
Telex 247

Metallurgimport (Metallurgical Import)
Phone: 241 82 75
244 17 14
Telex 7588

Mezhdunarodnaia Kniga (Foreign Book Trading Organization)
Phone: 244 10 22
Telex 160

Neftekhimpromeksport (Petroleum-Chemical [Petro-Chemical] Industry Export)
Ovchinnikovskaia nab. 18/1
Phone: 220 11 09

Novoeksport (New Products Export)
Ul. Bashilovskaia 19
Phone: 285 66 90
Telex 254

Prodintorg (Food Trading Organization)
Phone: 244 26 29
Telex 201

Promimporttorg (Industrial Import Office for Industrial Goods of the Ministry of Internal Trade of the Soviet Union)
Ul. Razina 26
Phone: 298 33 17
298 48 81
133 44 65

Prommasheksport (Industrial Machine Export)
Ovchinnikovskaia nab. 18/1
Phone: 220 15 05
220 16 00

Prommashimport (Industrial Machine Import)
Phone: 244 43 57
Telex 261

Promsyr'eimport (Industrial Raw Material Import)
Ul. Arkhitektora Vaslova 33
Phone: 128 07 75
Telex 151, 152

Rasnoeksport (Miscellaneous Export)
V. Krasnosel'skaia Ul. 15
Phone: 264 56 56
Telex 161

Raznoimport (Miscellaneous Import)
Phone: 244 37 61
Telex 153, 154

Soiuzkontsert (Soviet Union Concerts)
Neglinnaia 15
Phone: 221 82 39
223 82 97

Soiuzkhimeksport (Soviet Union Chemical Export)
Phone: 244 22 24
Telex 295, 296

Soiuzkoopvneshtorg (Soviet Union Cooperative Trading Organization—Department of Foreign Trade)
Phone: 223 79 30
225 09 14
Telex 127, 128

Soiuznefteekhsport (Soviet Union Petroleum Export)
Phone: 244 40 49
Telex 148, 149

Soiuzneftekhimzarubezhstroi (Soviet Union Petroleum—Chemical
Foreign Construction Organization)

Ul. Kirova 24
Phone: 294 58 09
          295 97 98

Soiuzplodoimport (Soviet Union Fruit Import)
Phone: 244 33 58
Telex 262

Soiuzpromeksport (Soviet Union Industrial Export)
Phone: 244 19 79
Telex 268

Soiuzpushnina (Soviet Fur Trading Organization)
Ul. Kuibysheva 6
Phone: 223 09 23
Telex 150

Soiuzvneshtrans (Soviet Union Foreign Transport)
Phone: 244 39 51
Telex 266, 291

Sovflot (Soviet Merchant Marine)
Ul. Zhdanova 1/4
Phone: 296 53 76
Telex 217

Sovfrakht (Soviet Stevadore Agency)
Phone: 244 36 68
Telex 168–172, 217

Stankoimport (Machine Tool Import)
Phone: 244 21 32
Telex 227

Sudoimport (Ship Imports)
Kaliaevskaia 5
Phone: 251 05 05
Telex 272

Tekhmasheksport (Technical Machine Export)
Mosfil'movskaia 35
Phone: 147 15 62
Telex 256

Tekhmashimport (Technical Machine Import)
Phone: 244 15 09
Telex 194

Tekhnoeksport (Technical Export)
Ovchinnikovskaia nab. 18/1
Phone: 220 14 48
Telex 1158

Tekhnopromeksport (Technical Industrial Export
[Foreign Aid Office])
Ovchinnikovskaia nab. 18/1
Phone: 220 15 23
       220 14 26

Tekhnopromimport (Technical Industrial Import)
Phone: 244 33 52
Telex 233

Tekhsnabeksport (Technical Supply Export)
Phone: 244 32 85
Telex 239

Tiazhpromeksport (Heavy Industrial Export)
Ovchinnikovskaia nab. 18/1
Phone: 220 16 10
       220 15 89
Telex 531

Traktoreksport (Tractor Export)
Kuznetskii Most 21/5
Phone: 244 32 37
Telex 273

Vneshposyltorg (Foreign Mail Order Service)
Phone: 241 89 39
241 89 23
Telex 250

Vneshtekhnika (Foreign Technical Sciences of the Committee on Science and Technology)
Ul. Gor'kogo, 11
Phone: 229 16 20

Vneshtorgreklama (Foreign Advertising Agency)
Kakhovka, 31
Phone—director: 121 04 34
foreign advertising: 121 41 80
film advertising: 193 71 61
Telex 265

Vostokintorg (Far East Trading Company)
Phone: 244 20 34
Telex 123

Zapchast'eksport (Spare Part Supply Export)
Vtoraia Skotoprogonnaia 35
Phone: 278 63 05
Telex 243

Notes

CHAPTER 2

1. The rate of exchange from 1961 to 1972 was $1.11 = 1 ruble. To provide for continuity, Soviet foreign trade officials recalculated their earlier trade statistics back to 1913 to reflect these new values. In 1972, after the American devaluation of the dollar, the Soviet exchange rate was revalued to $1.21 = 1 ruble. In February 1973 the Soviet government decreed the ruble equal to $1.34, and then to $1.46 in August. As the dollar strengthened, the Soviet rate was lowered to $1.34 again in November. We shall use the rate of $1.34 = 1 ruble for all of 1973.

2. Ministerstvo Vneshnei Torgovli SSSR (hereafter MVT SSSR), *Vneshniaia Torgovlia SSSR za 1918–1940gg* (Moscow: Vnestorgizdat, 1960), pp. 1063, 1066, 1071. (Hereafter statistical handbooks of the MVT SSSR will be referred to as *VT SSSR* and the appropriate year or years.)

3. Tsentral'noe Statisticheskoe Upravlenie (hereafter referred to as TsSU), *Narodnoe Khoziaistvo SSSR 1922–72* (Moscow: Statistika, 1972), p. 216. (Hereafter statistical handbooks of TsSU will be referred to as *Nar Khoz* and the appropriate year or years.) TsSU, *Sel'skoe Khoziaistvo SSSR* (Moscow: Gosstatizdat, 1960), p. 199; TsSU, *Strana Sovetov za 50 let* (Moscow: Statistika, 1967), p. 122.

4. Antony C. Sutton, *Western Technology and Soviet Economic Development, 1917 to 1930* (Stanford: Hoover Institution Publications, 1968), p. 320. (Hereafter referred to as Sutton, *1917–30*.)

5. Ibid., p. 142. Antony C. Sutton, *Western Technology and Soviet Economic Development, 1930 to 1945* (Stanford: Hoover Institution Press, 1971), p. 249. (Hereafter referred to as Sutton, *1930–45*.)

6. Sutton, *1930–45*, pp. 135, 249–250.

7. Joint Economic Committee, Congress of the United States, *Soviet Economic Prospects for the Seventies* (Washington, D.C.: U.S. Government Printing Office, 1973), p. 640. (Hereafter referred to as *JEC* 1973.) Sutton, *1930–45*, p. 137.

8. Sutton, *1930–45*, pp. 100, 185, 246–248, 343.

9. Ibid., p. 268.

10. Ibid., p. 40; Sutton, *1917–30*, p. 219.

11. Egon Neuberger, "Is the USSR Superior to the West as a Market for Primary Products?" *Review of Economics and Statistics*, August 1964, p. 287.

12. *VT SSSR 1918–1966*, p. 64.

13. For two varying views see Adam B. Ulam, *Expansion and Coexistence: The History of Soviet Foreign Policy 1917–67* (New York: Praeger, 1968) and Gunnar Adler-Karlsson, *Western Economic Warfare, 1949–1967; A Case Study in Foreign Economic Policy* (Stockholm: Almqvist & Wiksell, 1968).

14. Figures for Albania are not available for all years, but because Soviet trade with Albania was so small, the effect is barely noticeable.

15. Nicholas Spulber, *The Economics of Communist Eastern Europe* (Cambridge, Mass.: MIT Press, 1957), pp. 153–173.

16. Marshall I. Goldman, *Soviet Foreign Aid* (New York: Praeger, 1967), p. 8.

17. Frederic L. Pryor, *The Communist Foreign Trade System* (Cambridge, Mass.: MIT Press, 1963), pp. 136–137; Franklyn Holzman, "More on Soviet Bloc Trade Discrimination," *Soviet Studies,* July 1965, p. 44.

18. E. Nukhovich, "Ekonomicheskoe sotrudnichestvo SSSR s osvobodivshimisia stranami i burzhuaznye kritiki," *Voprosy Ekonomiki,* October 1966, pp. 83, 85, 86; N. Volkov, "Struktura vzaimnoi torgovli stran SEV," *Vneshniaia Torgovlia,* December 1966, pp. 10, 12.

19. Volkov, "Struktura vzaimnoi," pp. 10, 12; G. Prokhorov, "Mirovaia sistema sotsializma i osvobodivshiesia strany," *Voprosy Ekonomiki,* November 1965, pp. 84, 85; O. Bogomolov, "Khoziaistvennye reformy i ekonomicheskoe sotrudnichestvo sotsialisticheskikh stran," *Voprosy Ekonomiki,* February 1966, pp. 85, 86; M. Sladkovskii, "XXII s'ezd KPSS i problemy ekonomicheskogo sotrudnichestva sotsialisticheskikh stran," *Voprosy Ekonomiki,* April 1966, p. 96.

20. Samuel Pisar, *Coexistence and Commerce* (New York: McGraw-Hill, 1970), p. 35.

21. *Chemical Week,* September 3, 1960, p. 42; March 11, 1961, p. 3.

22. *Chemical Week,* March 21, 1964, p. 27.

23. *Pravda,* December 10, 1963, p. 1.

24. David W. Bronson, "Scientific and Engineering Manpower in the USSR and Employment in R and D," *JEC* 1973, pp. 580–581.

25. Organization for Economic Co-operation and Development, *Science Policy in the USSR* (Paris: OECD, 1969), p. 57.

26. *Pravda,* April 6, 1966, p. 7.

27. *Wall Street Journal,* October 30, 1972, p. 12.

28. *Wall Street Journal,* May 7, 1973, p. 6.

29. Joint Economic Committee, Congress of the United States, *Soviet Economic Outlook, Hearings,* July 17, 18, 19, 1973 (Washington, D.C.: U.S. Government Printing Office, 1973), p. 157. (Hereafter referred to as *JEC Hearings* 1973.)

CHAPTER 3

1. "Survey," *Fortune,* September 1945, pp. 233, 238.

2. Jozef Wilczynski, *The Economics and Politics of East-West Trade* (New York: Praeger, 1969), p. 286.

3. Ibid., p. 278; V. I. Morozov, *Sovet ekonomicheskoi vzaimopomoschi-soiuz ravnykh* (Moscow: I.M.O., 1964), p. 45.

4. Harold Berman, "Potential U.S. Trade with the Soviet Union," *Export Trade and Shipper,* July 9, 1956.

5. *Report to the President of the Special Committee on U.S. Trade Relations with East European Countries and the Soviet Union* (Washington, D.C.: Department of State, 1965), pp. 14–15; Franklyn D. Holzman, "East-West Trade and Investment Policy Issues: Past and Future," *JEC* 1973, p. 667. Holzman also make reference to Leon Herman, "Economic Content of Soviet Trade with the West," in *East-West Trade:* a Symposium, ed. P. Uren (Toronto: Canadian Institute of International Affairs, 1966), p. 34.

6. The history of trade legislation with the U.S.S.R. is quite complex. For the reader who is uninterested in the details, the simplest thing is to look at the abbreviated summary of the laws provided in Appendix I. For a fuller analysis, see Harold Berman and John R. Garson, "United States Export Controls—Past, Present and Future," *Columbia Law Review* 67, no. 5 (1967): 791.

7. Gunnar Adler-Karlsson says: "The first decisions to use an export embargo as a weapon in the cold war were made in the United States in the second half of 1947." "International Economic Power: The U.S.'s Strategic Embargo," *The International Review,* January 15, 1973, p. 35; see also his *Western Economic Warfare 1947–1967* (Stockholm: Almquist & Wiksall, 1968), pp. 22–25.

8. John P. Hardt and George D. Holliday, *U.S. Commercial Relations: The Interplay of Economics, Technology Transfer and Diplomacy,* Committee on Foreign Affairs, U.S. House of Representatives (Washington, D.C.: U.S. Government Printing Office, 1973), p. 48; Samuel Pisar, *Coexistence and Commerce* (New York: McGraw-Hill, 1970), p. 115; Committee on Foreign Relations, U.S. Senate, *A Background Study on East-West Trade* (Washington, D.C.: U.S. Government Printing Office, 1965), p. 38.

9. For a more complete discussion see Pisar, *Coexistence and Commerce,* p. 107, or Hardt and Holliday, *U.S. Commercial Relations,* p. 55.

10. Pisar, *Coexistence and Commerce,* p. 109.

11. *JEC Hearings* 1973, p. 107.

12. *New York Times,* March 7, 1973, p. 14; September 11, 1973, p. 14; July 6, 1974, p. 5; *Wall Street Journal,* January 24, 1974, p. 22; September 25, 1974, p. 24.

13. See Holzman, "East-West Trade," p. 671.

14. *Red Flag,* November 19, 1963; *Peking Review,* May 8, 1964, p. 7.

15. Peter P. Peterson, *U.S. Soviet Commercial Relationships in a New Era* (Washington, D.C.: Department of Commerce, 1972), p. 17.

16. White House, "Fact Sheet—Trade Agreement, Lend Lease Settlement, Reciprocal Credit Arrangements, Joint US-USSR Commercial Commission," mimeographed, October 18, 1972, pp. 5, 6.

17. MFN tariffs are explained in the "Import Restrictions" section of this chapter.

18. Holzman, "East-West Trade," p. 670; Max Beloff, *Foreign Policy of Soviet Russia, 1929–1936* (Oxford: Oxford University Press, 1947), p. 124.

19. *JEC Hearings* 1973, p. 107.

20. Anton F. Malish, Jr., *United States-East European Trade,* Staff Research Studies No. 4 (Washington, D.C.: United States Tariff Commission, 1972), p. 71.

21. White House, "Fact Sheet," p. 5.

22. Malish, *United States-East European Trade.*

23. Gregory Grossman points out that even though the Soviet Union enjoys MFN treatment in Canada, it has so far been unable to export significant quantities of goods. See "US-Soviet Trade and Economic Relations: Problems and Prospects," *Association for Comparative Economic Studies Bulletin,* Spring 1973, p. 6.

24. *Vneshniaia Torgovlia,* October 1961, p. 5.

25. As an historical note, in line with the Soviet promise of increased imports after the 1935 agreement (and maybe also because of Hitler's rise to power), Soviet imports from the U.S. rose by 62 percent in 1936, by 12 percent in 1937, and by 66 percent in 1938, but fell by about 25 percent in 1939.

26. Compare Mose L. Harvey, *East-West Trade and United States Policy* (New York: National Association of Manufacturers, 1966), and the interview with Burt Raynes, 1974 NAM president, in the *Daily Courier News,* Elgin, Illinois, February 13, 1974, p. 29.

27. John G. Schmitz, "How Mr. Nixon's Red Trade Helps the Communists," *The Review of the News,* August 30, 1972, p. 1.

28. Asked to participate in a 1965 questionnaire about attitudes toward East-West trade, an executive of one of the largest corporations in the United States responded by writing a special covering letter: "In view of the delicate nature of the subject and the prospect that almost any company position on East-West trade might be subject to wide-spread public misinterpretation, we request that our responses to your questionnaire, and the fact of our participation, remain confidential."

29. *Congressional Record,* July 26, 1965, p. 17612.

30. Committee on Foreign Relations of the U.S. Senate, *East-West Trade* (Washington, D.C.: U.S. Government Printing Office, 1964), pts. I, II, III; Marshall I. Goldman and Alice Conner, "Businessmen Appraise East-West Trade," *Harvard Business Review,* January-February 1966, p. 6; U.S. Senate Committee on Banking and Currency, *East-West Trade* (Washington, D.C.: U.S. Government Printing Office, June 1968).

CHAPTER 4

1. John T. Farrell, "Soviet Payments Problems in Trade with the West," *JEC* 1973, p. 691; *Allocation of Resources in the Soviet Union and China,* Hearings before the Subcommittee on Priorities and Economy in Government of the Joint Economic Committee, Congress of the United States (Washington, D.C.: U.S. Government Printing Office, April 12, 1974), p. 24.

2. *Wall Street Journal,* August 16, 1973, p. 12.

3. Statement of Hon. William E. Colby, Director of Central Intelligence, CIA, in *Allocation of Resources in the Soviet Union and China,* p. 24.

4. Austria, Belgium, England, Italy, Canada, Netherlands, U.S., West Germany, Finland, France, Sweden, Japan. *VT SSSR* 1972, p. 16.

5. *VT SSSR* 1972, p. 16.

6. Oleg Hoeffding, "Recent Structural Changes and Balance of Payments Adjustments in Soviet Foreign Trade," in *International Trade and Central Planning,* ed. Alan A. Brown and Egon Neuberger (Berkeley: University of California Press, 1968) p. 232.

7. *Izvestiia,* May 8, 1973, p. 4.

8. *Soviet News,* December 11, 1973, p. 524.

9. *New York Times,* November 4, 1973, p. 3.

10. *Foreign Trade,* June 1973, p. 14.

11. I. D. Kozlov and E. K. Shmakova, *Sotrudnichestvo Stran Chlenov CEC v Energetike* (Moscow: Nauka, 1973), pp. 5, 86.

12. Marshall I. Goldman, *Soviet Foreign Aid* (New York: Praeger, 1967), p. 110.

13. Adding to the confusion, a footnote in the Soviet foreign trade handbook states that the Soviet Union delivered to Japan an additional million tons of oil for 13.4 million rubles in 1972 and 15.8 million in 1973, that is not included in the regular statistics (*VT SSSR* 1973, p. 269). Why these figures are excluded and where the oil came from, no one explains. If the figures had referred to 1971 instead of 1972 and 1973, this difference might have helped to fill in some of the unaccounted for 2.3 million tons of oil purchased by the Soviet Union in 1971. (See Table 4–2.)

14. Personal communication from an importer of Soviet oil.

15. *Soviet News,* December 4, 1973, p. 508; December 11, 1973, p. 524.

16. *Moscow Narodny Bank*, September 13, 1972, p. 3; January 9, 1974, p. 3.

17. Personal correspondence with European oil dealers.

18. *Petroleum Press Service,* May 1973.

19. *Foreign Trade,* June 1973, p. 14.

20. *Moscow Narodny Bank,* July 25, 1973, p. 2; December 19, 1973, p. 3.

21. *Soviet News,* February 29, 1972, p. 68; *Foreign Trade,* May 1973, p. 9.

22. *Moscow Narodny Bank,* June 21, 1971, p. 5; February 28, 1973, p. 11; *Soviet News,* April 3, 1973, p. 153.

23. *Moscow Narodny Bank,* February 4, 1971, p. 2.

24. Ibid., January 14, 1971, p. 2; April 8, 1971, p. 3.

25. Ibid., January 14, 1971, p. 2.

26. *New York Times,* June 20, 1972, p. 53.

27. United Nations, *Statistical Yearbook 1971* (New York: United Nations, 1972), p. 184; British Petroleum, *British Petroleum Statistical Review* (London: British Petroleum, 1973), p. 16.

28. *Moscow Narodny Bank,* January 12, 1972., p. 5; March 14, 1973, p. 8; August 15, 1973, p. 10; January 16, 1974, p. 6; May 22, 1974, p. 3; June 19, 1974, p. 4; *Foreign Trade,* May 1973, p. 12.

29. *Wall Street Journal,* June 18, 1973, p. 20 (italics in original).

30. United Nations, *Statistical Yearbook, 1971,* 23rd ed. (New York: United Nations, 1972), p. 187.

31. *Pravda,* June 1, 1974, p. 5.

32. *Moscow Narodny Bank,* April 18, 1973, p. 11.

33. Robert Campbell, *The Economics of Soviet Oil and Gas* (Baltimore: Johns Hopkins Press, 1968), p. 208.

34. *New York Times,* March 16, 1973, p. 8; March 28, 1973, p. 17.

35. *Izvestiia,* March 20, 1973, p. 1.

36. *Moscow Narodny Bank,* June 28, 1973, p. 8.

37. Kiichi Saeki, "Toward Japanese Cooperation in Siberian Development," *Problems of Communism,* May-June 1972, pp. 7–8.

38. John Hardt, "West Siberia: The Quest for Energy," *Problems of Communism,* May-June 1973, p. 27.

39. *New York Times,* July 18, 1973, p. 46; *Moscow Narodny Bank,* July 18, 1973, p. 10; *Wall Street Journal,* July 26, 1973, p. 7.

40. Saeki, "Toward Japanese Cooperation," pp. 7–8.

41. Campbell, *Economics of Soviet Oil,* p. 210; Hardt, "West Siberia," p. 27.

CHAPTER 5

1. C. H. McMillan, "Factor Proportions and the Structure of Soviet Foreign Trade," *The Association for Comparative Economic Studies (ACES) Bulletin* 15, no. 1 (1973): 57.

2. *VT SSSR* 1918–1940.

3. Barry L. Kostinsky, *Description and Analysis of Soviet Foreign Trade Statistics,* Foreign Demographic Analysis Division, Bureau of Economic Analysis, Social and Economic Statistics Administration, U.S. Department of Commerce, Foreign Economic Reports, No. 5, 1974, p. 53.

4. U.S. Department of Commerce, Domestic and International Business Administration, Bureau of East-West Trade, *Export Administration* (Washington: U.S. Government Printing Office, Fourth Quarter 1973), pp. 63–64. (Hereafter referred to as Bureau of East-West Trade.)

5. *Moscow Narodny Bank,* February 7, 1973, p. 2.

6. *Moscow Narodny Bank,* March 6, 1974, pp. 2–4, for an example of regulations for mixed companies in Hungary.

7. Marshall I. Goldman, *Soviet Foreign Aid* (New York: Praeger, 1967), p. 55.

8. *Izvestiia,* August 17, 1971; *Foreign Trade,* November 1971, p. 6; January 73, p. 13; *Soviet News,* July 27, 1971, p. 222; August 17, 1971, p. 247.

9. *Foreign Trade,* May 1959, p. 16; *East-West Trade,* January 1969, p. 38; May 1972, p. 67.

10. *Foreign Trade,* February 1974, p. 40; *Moscow Narodny Bank,* March 13, 1974, p. 7.

11. V. I. Morozov, *Soviet Ekonomischeskoi Vzaimopomoshchi Soiuz ravnykh* (Moscow: I.M.O., 1964), p. 45; *Vneshniaia Torgovlia,* March, 1965, p. 4; *Ekonomicheskaia Gazeta,* April 17, 1965, p. 40.

12. *Foreign Trade,* February 1970, p. 19.

13. *Moscow Narodny Bank,* October 4, 1972, p. 14; July 11, 1973, p. 14.

14. *Moscow Narodny Bank,* August 15, 1973, p. 12; February 27, 1974, p. 11; June 19, 1974, p. 12.

15. *Vneshnia Torgovla, USSR,* 1967, Special Advertising Edition, p. 43.

16. *Nar Khoz* 1958, p. 242.

17. *Foreign Trade,* May 1972, p. 35.

18. *JEC* 1973, p. 303.

19. *Moscow Narodny Bank,* June 14, 1972, p. 5.

20. McMillan, "Factor Proportions," p. 76; Steven Rosefielde, "The Embodied Factor Content of Soviet International Trade: Problems of Theory, Measurement and Interpretation," *ACES Bulletin,* Summer-Fall 1973, p. 3; idem, *Empirical Aspects of Soviet Foreign Trade and Heckscher-Ohlin Theory,* Occasional Papers on Soviet Input-Output Analysis (Durham, N.C.: Duke University, 1973), p. 10.

21. C. H. McMillan, "Soviet Specialization and Trade in Manufacturers," *Soviet Studies,* April 1973, p. 522.

22. John T. Farrell, "Soviet Payments Problems in Trade with the West," *JEC* 1973, p. 702.

23. *JEC Hearings* 1973, pp. 153–154.

24. *JEC Hearings* 1973, pp. 27, 156.

25. *New York Times,* May 31, 1973, p. 59.

26. *Aviation Week and Space Technology,* August 13, 1973, p. 20.

27. Samuel Pisar, *Coexistence and Commerce* (New York: McGraw-Hill, 1970), pp. 182, 275.

CHAPTER 6

1. *Nar Khoz, SSSR* 1972, pp. 577, 697.

2. C. H. McMillan, "Factor Proportions and the Structure of Soviet Foreign Trade," *ACES Bulletin* 15, no. 1 (1973): 76.

3. White House, "Fact Sheet—Trade Agreement, Lend Lease Settlement, Reciprocal Credit Arrangement, Joint US-USSR Commercial Commission," mimeographed, October 18, 1972.

4. *JEC* 1973, p. 656.

5. Bureau of East-West Trade, Second Quarter, p. 17; Third Quarter, pp. 3, 30–31.

6. *Moscow Narodny Bank,* July 18, 1973, p. 1.

7. *Foreign Trade,* March 1973, p. 56.

8. Bureau of East-West Trade, inside front cover.

9. U.S. Senate Committee on Banking and Currency, *East-West Trade* (Washington, D.C.: U.S. Government Printing Office, June 1968), p. 91.

10. *New York Times,* September 1, 1973, p. 58; October 12, 1964, p. 74.

11. Personal interview with Albert Wentworth.

12. I am indebted to Edward Keenan for this information.

13. Sutton *1917–30,* p. 181.

14. Personal interview with Georges Potter of the Singer Company.

15. Harold J. Berman, "Business Before Pleasure," *The Nation,* May 14, 1973, p. 623.

16. Ibid.; Interview with David Rockefeller in *U.S. News and World Report,* August 13, 1973, p. 36.

17. *Ekonomicheskaia Gazeta,* no. 33, August 1973, p. 4.

18. *JEC Hearings* 1973, pp. 27–28, 156.

19. *The Role of the Export-Import Bank and Export Controls in U.S. International Economic Policy,* Hearings before the Subcommittee on International Finance of the Committee on Banking, Housing, and Urban Affairs, United States Senate, April 2, 5, 10, 23, 25, and 26; and May 2, 1974 (Washington, D.C.: U.S. Government Printing Office, 1974), p. 68; *Business Week,* July 13, 1974, p. 64.

20. James R. Basche, Jr., *East-West Trade, The Lessons from Experience* (New York: The Conference Board, 1971), p. 18.

21. White House, "Fact Sheet," p. 4.

22. Senate Committee on Banking and Currency, *East-West Trade,* April 1969, p. 48; *Wall Street Journal,* April 12, 1967, p. 14; September 26, 1968, p. 19; Jozef Wilczynski, *The Economics and Politics of East-West Trade* (New York: Praeger, 1969), p. 182.

23. White House, "Fact Sheet," p. 4.

24. Personal interview with Ed Bayer of Holcroft.

CHAPTER 7

1. Committee on Government Operations, United States Senate, *Russian Grain Transactions* (Washington, D.C.: U.S. Government Printing Office, July 20, 23, 24, 1973), p. 218 (hereafter referred to as Committee on Government Operations); idem, *Russian Grain Transactions* (Washington, D.C.: U.S. Government Printing Office, July 29, 1974) (hereafter referred to as Committee on Government Operations 1974); *Moscow Narodny Bank,* November 8, 1972, p. 4; Radio Liberty Dispatch, Keith Bush, *Soviet Grain Output, Deliveries and Imports,* October 16, 1972, p. 4.

2. Comptroller General of the United States, *Exporters' Profits on Sales of U.S. Wheat to Russia,* (B-176943) Department of Agriculture (Washington, D.C.: United States General Accounting Office, February 12, 1974), p. 14. (Hereafter referred to as GAO 1).

3. *Wall Street Journal,* November 8, 1971, p. 9.

4. Comptroller General of the United States, *Report to the Congress, Russian Wheat Sales and Weaknesses Export Subsidy Program* (Washington, D.C.: United States General Accounting Office, July 9, 1973), p. 18. (Hereafter referred to as GAO 2).

5. GAO 2, p. 19.

6. GAO 2, p. 20.

7. *New York Times,* April 13, 1972, p. 11.

8. GAO 2, p. 2.

9. *Wall Street Journal,* April 20, 1973, p. 11.

10. Committee on Agriculture, House of Representatives, *Sale of Wheat to Russia,* Serial No. 92-KK (Washington, D.C.: U.S. Government Printing Office, 1972), p. 277 (hereafter referred to as Committee on Agriculture); Committee on Government Operations, p. 218.

11. GAO 1, pp. 14–15.

12. GAO 2, p. 80; Committee on Government Operations, p. 104.

13. Committee on Agriculture, p. 279.

14. *Wall Street Journal,* July 10, 1972, p. 4; Committee on Government Operations, p. 232.

15. Committee on Agriculture, p. 278.

16. Continental Grain acknowledges that it registered much of its grain late and received the $.47 subsidy. Yet for some unexplained reason, apparently it did not move into the domestic market to cover as much as 30 percent of its wheat sales to the Soviet Union until August 31, by which time market prices had already skyrocketed. Committee on Government Operations, p. 66.

17. Committee on Agriculture, p. 282; Committee on Government Operations, p. 23.

18. *New York Times,* December 5, 1972, p. 1; Committee on Government Operations, p. 120.

19. Committee on Agriculture, pp. 284–285.

20. GAO 2, p. 51.

21. GAO 2, pp. 15, 51.

22. Committee on Government Operations, p. 223; GAO 1, p. 16.

23. Committee on Government Operations, pp. 20, 243.

24. GAO 2, p. 81.

25. GAO 2, p. 16.

26. Committee on Agriculture, pp. 16, 75.

27. Committee on Government Operations, pp. 73–76.

28. Committee on Agriculture, pp. 16, 75; Committee on Government Operations, p. 184.

29. *Wall Street Journal,* August 14, 1973, p. 5; Committee on Government Operations, p. 213.

30. Committee on Agriculture, p. 11.

31. Committee on Government Operations, p. 142.

32. Committee on Agriculture, p. 8.

33. Committee on Government Operations, p. 33.

34. *New York Times,* November 3, 1972, p. 53.

35. GAO 1, pp. 10–11.

36. GAO 2, p. 82.

37. Committee on Government Operations, p. 157.

38. *JEC Hearings* 1973, p. 106.

39. Reportedly the State Department and the Department of Agriculture were both consulted earlier by the Soviet government about the possibility of buying grain. The State Department advised the Russians to stay out of the market. Secretary Butz, however, advised entering the market slowly. The Russians followed his advice. When President Ford ordered the deal canceled, the Russians were shocked, embarrassed, and angered. As far as they could tell, they had acted exactly as they had been advised to. As angered as they were, however, the U.S.S.R. itself canceled parts of its order and broke its contract. The Russians acted this way when they found that world prices had fallen below what they had originally contracted to pay and that they could buy the grain cheaper in the open market.

40. *New York Times,* January 29, 1974, p. 1.

CHAPTER 8

1. *Aviation Week and Space Technology,* December 18, 1972, p. 30.

2. Much of what follows is based on personal interviews with Raytheon executives.

3. *Aviation Week and Space Technology,* August 16, 1973, p. 14.

4. *Astronautics and Aeronautics,* October 1973, p. 45.

5. *Astronautics and Aeronautics,* September 1973, p. 71; *Aviation Week and Space Technology,* August 6, 1973, p. 14.

6. *Aviation Week and Space Technology,* August 6, 1973, p. 15.

7. Ibid., p. 14.

8. In the long run, even the Soviet Union could lose. Whether it is the American or the Soviet government which is doing the buying, an effort to induce price cutting among the suppliers of something like ATC equipment can be dangerous. The manufacturer may be forced to cut back on his design. Since plans and specifications for an ATC system cannot be spelled out to the last "gnat's eyebrow," this means there is likely to be less room for contingencies if the manufacturer is forced to cut too many corners. As one Raytheon official put it, "In ATC, the very best is still not perfect. If foreign govern-

ments install ATC systems which have been arbitrarily cut back because of price considerations, this could result in problems with the system's operation or its failure with the resulting loss of life."

CHAPTER 9

1. Armand Hammer, "American Entrepreneur—First Foreign Concessionaire in the Soviet Union," *East-West Trade,* March/April 1970, p. 14.

2. Sutton, *1917–30,* pp. 237, 268.

3. *New York Times,* April 15, 1973, p. 17; May 20, 1973, sec. 3, p. 1.

4. Herbert Meyer, "What It's Like to do Business with the Russians," *Fortune,* May 1972.

5. Personal interview with Donald J. Morfee.

6. Meyer, "What It's Like to do Business with the Russians."

7. Personal interview with Samuel Casey, Jr.

8. *New York Times,* May 26, 1973, p. 39.

9. *Izvestiia,* July 7, 1973, p. 2.

CHAPTER 10

1. *New York Post,* January 31, 1974, p. 40.

2. Raymond Vernon, "Apparatchiks and Entrepreneurs: U.S.-Soviet Economic Relations," *Foreign Affairs,* January 1974, p. 260.

3. *New York Times,* October 30, 1973, p. 43.

4. Ibid., August 22, 1973, p. 3.

5. Ibid., June 26, 1973, p. 63: *Wall Street Journal,* July 6, 1973, p. 11.

Index